Praise for
Building a Digital Analytics Organization

"The allure of Big Data is immense. There is SO MUCH DATA! Yet, data collection does nothing by itself. It actually does financial harm left in the wrong hands. Fix that, and you win. Let Judah show you how to build an organization where Big Data's primary imperative is to drive Big Action."

—**Avinash Kaushik**, author of *Web Analytics 2.0* and *Web Analytics: An Hour a Day*

"Without a digital analytics organization, you aren't optimizing your business, your site, or your app. Reading this book can help you. I just hope you adapt before one of your competitors does."

—**Bryan Eisenberg**, author of *Call to Action*, *Waiting for Your Cat to Bark*, and *Always Be Testing*, Keynote Speaker, Cofounder of the Digital Analytics Association, and Publisher of UseTheData.

"Since founding Gomez 15 years ago, I've had the privilege of working with many pioneers in the field of web site and e-commerce excellence. I am impressed with the managerial principles and analytical techniques Judah has developed and presented in this book. A must read for the 21st century analyst and executive who wants to learn how to create value and deliver excellence with digital analytics."

—**Julio Gomez**, Founder of Gomez, Inc., General Manager at Attivio

"Before 'Big Data' and 'Data Science' became buzz words, Judah was extracting actionable insights from immense data sets and revolutionizing the field of business analytics. Unfortunately, the digital version of his nerdy brain is still too big for a download, so reading and internalizing this book is the second best option for anyone interested in improving their business via an intelligent approach to data and analytics."

—**Yaakov Kimelfeld**, Ph.D., Chief Research Officer of Compete

"Among the most valuable things you'll find in Judah's book is his experience. *Building a Digital Analytics Organization* is packed with real-life guidance and wisdom from his years of work as a practitioner and manager in the analytics field. From defining measurement needs, to analyzing data, to comparing analytics tools, Judah has done just about everything. We can all put his experience to use as a guide as we build out our own analytics organizations."

—**Justin Cutroni**, author of *Google Analytics*, Analytics Evangelist at Google.

Building a Digital Analytics Organization:

Create Value by Integrating Analytical Processes, Technology, and People into Business Operations

Judah Phillips

Vice President, Publisher: Tim Moore
Associate Publisher and Director of Marketing: Amy Neidlinger
Executive Editor: Jeanne Levine
Operations Specialist: Jodi Kemper
Marketing Manager: Lisa Loftus
Cover Designer: Alan Clements
Managing Editor: Kristy Hart
Senior Project Editor: Jovana Shirley
Project Editor: Elaine Wiley
Copy Editor: Apostrophe Editing Services
Proofreader: Anne Goebel
Senior Indexer: Cheryl Lenser
Senior Compositor: Gloria Schurick
Manufacturing Buyer: Dan Uhrig

© 2014 by Judah Phillips
Publishing as Pearson
Upper Saddle River, New Jersey 07458

Pearson offers excellent discounts on this book when ordered in quantity for
bulk purchases or special sales. For more information, please contact
U.S. Corporate and Government Sales, 1-800-382-3419,
corpsales@pearsontechgroup.com. For sales outside the U.S., please contact
International Sales at international@pearsoned.com.

Printed in the United States of America

First Printing July 2013

ISBN-10: 0-13-337278-2
ISBN-13: 978-0-13-337278-6

Pearson Education LTD.
Pearson Education Australia PTY, Limited.
Pearson Education Singapore, Pte. Ltd.
Pearson Education Asia, Ltd.
Pearson Education Canada, Ltd.
Pearson Educación de Mexico, S.A. de C.V.
Pearson Education—Japan
Pearson Education Malaysia, Pte. Ltd.

Library of Congress Control Number: 2013939001

To the loves of my life, Elizabeth and Lilah;
Steven and Elyse for always believing in me;
and to every analytics professional who has ever
wondered what they got themselves into.

Table of Contents

Foreword

The disciplines for managing information and information technology have grown up over more than half a century. Computing and programming had been largely academic activities in the early days, but these disciplines transformed the field into a true profession. When corporations first applied "data processing" approaches to financial and other forms of internal information, they introduced formal processes and structures to a previously unstructured field. Operators in computer centers often wore white coats to signify their professional and scientific focus. The high level of formality may have been misplaced, but it allowed information management for structured, internal information to eventually be mastered and to flourish as a field.

Over the past decade, an entirely new era in information management has emerged. It's the product of the Internet—digital data coming from the Web, email, online content, mobile devices, millions of apps, and increasingly the "Internet of things." Like the earliest computing efforts, the management of digital data began as a casual, "hobbyist" activity. Companies often had a part-time "Web guy" to design, install, and maintain a website. There was very little measurement of digital activity, and loose management in other respects as well. Some large and respected companies had frequent website outages and sometimes even allowed their domain name registrations to lapse.

This book, however, is clear evidence that the management of digital data is growing up. A key function of the management of any resource is analytics—establishing metrics, reporting on them, and prediction and optimization of key variables. There has been talk of Web or digital analytics for a number of years, but until recently it was not a serious effort for most firms. Web analytics consisted largely of counting unique visitors or page views, and was again often undertaken by part-time staff.

A rigorous, professional approach to digital analytics requires the types of management approaches that are laid out in this book. You need more than part-time people. You need careful thinking about what your metrics and Key Performance Indicators (KPIs) are. You need to move beyond reporting into prediction, optimization, and rigorous testing. Judah Phillips has been an advocate of these serious disciplines for a long time, but now the world is ready to adopt them—and the book comes along just in time.

There are plenty of books on Web analytics, but I think this one is distinctive in a number of ways. One is that it is broader than Web analytics, treating the areas of social media, mobile, behavioral targeting, and other sources of digital data. Most companies would be well advised to take a more expansive view of digital analytics than just clickstreams on the Web.

Second, this book brings into the digital analytics space a sophistication in both data management and data analysis that is not often found in Web analytics sources. On the management side, it addresses topics like how to staff a digital analytics function, how to think about data governance in this environment, and the relationship between the digital analytics group and others in the organization who are working on other types of analytics. Something like data governance may not appeal to hobbyists, but it's essential for a mature corporate information environment.

On the data analysis front, I am very happy to see that Phillips brings in some of the best classical thinking on data analysis. I have always thought that John Tukey's ideas on "exploratory data analysis" (EDA) were a great way to get close to your data and understand its basic parameters, but you seldom see the idea in recent writing on analytics of any type. So I was very happy to see a section on EDA in this book; it's a great technique for exploration of digital data.

Someday, I suspect, we will have analytics organizations that can address all types of data—the digital types covered in this book, and other data about customers, finances, and operations that are normally addressed in business analytics functions. This book is a great step toward that integration, because—unlike many Web analytics books—it doesn't assume that digital analytics are the only type, and it encourages many of the same principles and approaches used by the business analytics movement. Encouraging readers to go beyond reporting into predictive analytics and testing is exactly what I have done in my own writing, for example. So it is nice to read that a similar convergence is taking place from the digital analytics side of the house.

So read this excellent book from a man who knows whereof he speaks. He has done this sort of work as a consultant and as a head of digital analytics in mostly online firms (Monster.com and Karmaloop), and mostly offline firms (Nokia and Reed Elsevier). If you put the ideas in the book into action within your organization, you will be well ahead of most others, and your leading-edge work will undoubtedly propel your career to stratospheric heights. Someday you may even wear a white coat as a "Doctor of Digital Analytics"!

Thomas H. Davenport
Professor at Harvard Business School and Babson College
Cofounder of the International Institute for Analytics

Acknowledgments

I realized a couple years ago that most people I met had no idea what I did for work—even when I told them my job title. Of those who did understand what I was doing, it was because they likely worked in the Internet industry. But few people I met had any experience doing my job, which was running a digital analytics organization. At one time, I think I was one of only a handful of analytics practitioners who worked for a brand and managed people who did digital analysis and combined it with traditional analytics. Certainly, there were analytics teams in brands and in agencies and consultancies, but there were few practitioners who had the opportunity to manage centralized business analytics teams in globally distributed companies with accountability for technology, the people, the process, and overall analytical deliverables. Actually, only several years ago, I could count on one hand the number of people who had both built from scratch or inherited analytics teams that concentrated solely on understanding digital behavior and using the data to drive both strategic and tactical decision making. Few had run analytics in both private and publicly traded companies reporting to senior executives (that is, C-level executives) where the data could not risk being "wrong" because the markets could act on it—and the stakeholders (and shareholders) had high expectations. I realized in these complex and often highly matrixed environments that there was a right way and a wrong way to build a digital analytics organization. The right way and the wrong way was nuanced, but it was similar whether the company was building an analytics team from the ground-up or if the company already had "baggage" from previous attempts at analytics.

When I began building analytics teams in brands, little precedent existed from people who had done similar work before, so my peers and I figured out how to do the job and how to succeed in the work. My philosophy when orchestrating analytical activities and building teams was that the work needed to be focused on helping the business either reduce costs or increase profitable revenue. That way, if analytics could help impact the top or bottom line, the team would be secure in its role and employment. It sometimes worked that way, and other times, externalities, such as the Great Recession, got in the way.

Along the course of my career in analytics, I've self-developed a practitioner's perspective on how to execute analytics in organizations. Many people over the years asked me, "When are you going to write a book?" and, encouraged by a few people in 2012, I decided to write this one. What you have in your hands is the result. This book provides a useful handbook for analysts, managers, and executives at all levels in all industries to learn the organizational aspects of digital analytics, to understand and appreciate the process of analytics, the necessity of analytics teams, and the importance of applying rigorous analytical techniques and methods to accurate digital data. You can gain additional knowledge and an appreciation for reporting, KPIs, data governance, and how market research, qualitative data, and other types of competitive and business intelligence data and technology enhance analytics and analytical decision making. I hope that you find value in the content of the book and use my perspectives to help contextualize and inform your own decision making at your companies—as I have leveraged the perspectives of others in my career.

Writing a book is never an easy task. It takes not only considerable time and effort, but it also requires saying something that has to be unique, real, and true. For a business book, what is written also must be relevant, helpful, and useful to people employed in the profession. This book is all those things and more. And it was only possible for me to author because of the knowledge and perspectives I've gained during the course of my career from working, collaborating, and befriending among the smartest and most talented people working with the Internet and analytics today, including but not limited to the following people:

Jesse Harriott, Thomas Davenport, J.P. Isson, Ben Green, Frank Faubert, Nate Treloar, Enno Becker, Julio Gomez, Akin Arikan, Jonathan Mendez, Raj Aggarwal, Joel Rubinson, Justin Cutroni, Jonathan Corbin, Rand Schulman, Eric T. Peterson, Steven J. Mills, David Mahoney, Sean Keaveny, Chris Boyle, Jim Sterne, Gary Angel, Bob Page, Bryan Eisenberg, Andreas Cohen, Jeffrey Eisenberg, June Dershewitz, Joe Stanhope, Jeff Quinn, Ellen Julian, Nikolay Gradinarov, Kounandi Couliably, Kurt Gray, Abby Mehta, Lauren Moores, Rand Schulman, Bill Gassman, Matt Cutler, David Cancel, Andrew and Luchy Edwards, Keith Lehman, Thomas Boselivac, Stan Ingertson, Brian Suthoff, Mark Gryska, Brian Induni, Seth Romanow, Alex Yoder, Frank Faubert, Gary Angel, Aaron Bird, Josh James, Alex Yoder, Casey Carey, Jascha Kaykas-Wolff, Scott Ernst, Yaakov Kimelfeldt, Andy Fisher, David Churbuck, Brett House, Brooks Bell, Matt Finlay, Ian Houston, Avinash Kaushik, Yaakov Kimelfeld, Larry Freed, Eric Hansen, Kim Ann King, Ali Benham, Josh Chasin, Yuchun Lee, Kevin Cavanaugh, Ken and Ross Fadner and the Mediapost.com/OMMA team, the members of the Analytics Research Organization (ARO), the people who support Digital Analytics Thursdays (DAT), eTail, I-COM, eMetrics, the Digital Analytics Association and the Boston Local Chapter, and finally, Jeanne Glasser-Levine and Tim Moore and their staff and colleagues at Pearson.

About the Author

Judah Phillips specializes in helping people create economic value using data, analytics, and research. He works with leading global companies whose executive and management teams are building, adapting, or reengineering their approach to digital analysis in order to increase profitable revenue, reduce cost, and boost profitability. Phillips has managed global business and digital analytics teams including Sun Microsystems (now Oracle), Reed Elsevier, Monster Worldwide, Nokia, and Karmaloop.

Phillips founded and globalized Digital Analytics Thursdays (DAT) and launched the Analytics Research Organization (ARO). He serves or has served on the advisory boards to several companies, including YieldBot, Localytics, and Webtrends. Phillips speaks at technology and Internet industry events and guest lectures at top universities and business schools worldwide. He lives in Boston and holds an MBA and MS.

1

Using Digital Analytics to Create Business Value

Today's business organizations must apply analytics to create new and incremental value. A significant and important source of analytical data in 2013 is digital experiences—from websites to social networks to mobile applications and more. Thus, it is critical in today's economy for businesses to develop and enhance their understanding of how digital data is collected and analyzed to either or both generate new or incremental profitable revenue or reduce cost.

Although digital analytics can significantly maximize profits in today's competitive global markets regardless of sector or industry, creating and staffing a fully functional digital analytics organization is a complex and multifaceted initiative. Building a digital analytics organization requires rethinking and reengineering the people, processes, and technology used for creating analysis. After all, many companies believe digital analytics is about tools and technology (and data collection, like "tagging"). That belief is not accurate. While the technology and tools that support analysis are critical and necessary, they are insufficient by themselves in creating business value. Simply adding a standard basic JavaScript page tag for a free Web analytics tool to your digital experiences and providing access to reports does not create data-driven decision making or easily yield insights. Some companies believe that to be "data-driven," they simply need to provide self-service access to business intelligence (BI) tools that provide department-specific reports and dashboards—or the basic, vanilla reporting in free or paid analytics tools.

Both these approaches are helpful to some degree and certainly move the firm toward building a digital analytics organization that considers analyses as part of the decision-making process—both strategic and tactic. After all, providing the business with the tools that collect and report data is, as previously mentioned, definitely critical and absolutely necessary. But tools and reporting are only part of digital analytics operations. Technical work and tool activities, whether used by themselves or together, are entirely insufficient for creating sustained business value through the application of digital data in business context. In other words, all the technology, servers, tagging, and tools can help you count and measure all sorts of digital metrics and dimensions, but do not by themselves (or even with the default installation) provide for any inherent actionability or impact directly delivering business value. The value from analytics is created by humans—alongside machines, tools, and technologies—analyzing data to provide insights and answers to business questions and within established and sustained business processes.

Digital analytics teams enable fact-based decision making and measure the performance and profitability of digital business channels. Data from the digital channel enhances offline data—and the combination of both (called *data integration*) can yield new insights and opportunities. If your company isn't forming a team of analysts to address its digital data—whether you have big data or not—then it's operating at a competitive disadvantage. A lack of data analysis leads to missing enormous business opportunities. A well-resourced, funded, process-oriented digital analytics team backed up by cross-functional teams from IT to marketing to finance can help your business in many ways—from determining ways to reduce costs, improve efficiency, generate new and incremental revenue, improve customer satisfaction, and boost the profitability and impact of the digital business channel. To understand what is involved with digital analytics from the beginning to the end to the beginning of the next project, see Chapter 2, "Analytics Value Chain and the P's of Digital Analytics." Before discussing these concepts, let's dig deeper into what composes digital analytics, the digital analytics organization, and how establishing and evolving deep competency in digital analysis now can bring immediate and future value to the corporation.

Big Data and Data Science Requires Digital Analytics

The need for a digital analytics organization is greater than ever before—for the amount of data available to apply toward solving a business challenge is more numerous and multivariate than at any time in human history. IBM estimates that humanity creates 2.4 quintillion bytes (quintillion is one billion billion) of data every day (see Figure 1.1)—so much that *90 percent* of the data in the world today has been created in the last two years alone. Obviously, much of this new data is being created by digital systems or systems linked to the Internet. Because the multitude of digital data is growing exponentially every day, a digital analytics organization is absolutely necessary to generate insights, recommendations, optimizations, predictions, and profits from this data. Whether big data, data science, omnichannel data, media mix modeling, attribution, audience intelligence, customer profiling, or predictive analytics from the applied analysis of digital data, it is essential to create a team accountable and responsible for digital data analysis. This analysis can be used for decision making, business planning, performance measurement, Key Performance Indicator (KPI) reporting, merchandising, prediction, automation, targeting, and optimization. As you read this book, you can learn how to lay solid foundations for building a successful digital analytics organization to make sense of and value from digital data analysis.

24,000,000,000,000,000,000 bytes per day

Figure 1.1 Humanity creates 2.4 quintillion bytes of data every day. That's the number above: 24 billion billion bytes per day.

The volume of the data being created right now and that will be created in the future is, of course, staggering even beyond IBM's estimates. International Data Corporation (IDC) projects that the digital universe will double in size through 2020 and reach 40 ZB (zetabytes), which means 5,247 GB for every person on Earth in 2020. The behavioral data—call it the *digital behavioral universe* currently being and going to be created from the clickstream and the digital footprints of every person across Earth interacting, participating, and behaving with this data—means that exponentially more behavioral data will be created on top of the predicted 40 ZB digital universe in 2020 (see Figure 1.2). Data collected about the human behavior, transactions, and metadata may be many multiples of the size of the site content. In other words, if the average size of a web page in 2013 is approximately 1.4 MB, then the behavioral and transactional data and metadata collected about visitors during their visits could be many hundred megabytes or more—especially when considering data integration from both internal and external data sources, such as advertising, audience, and Customer Relationship Management (CRM) data. The future of analytics will be enabled by innovation on top of all this big data created digitally from websites, mobile sites, social media, advertising, and any other Internet-enabled experience—from interactive TV and billboards to set-top boxes to video game consoles to Internet-enabled appliances to the mobile ecosystem and world of apps.

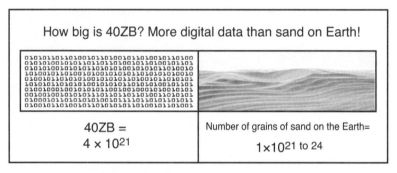

How big is 40ZB? More digital data than sand on Earth!

40ZB = 4 × 10²¹

Number of grains of sand on the Earth= 1×10²¹ to 24

Figure 1.2 It is estimated that by 2020, there could be four times more digital data than all the grains of sand on Earth.

Source: IDC and Wolfram Alpha

According to the Pew Research Center's Internet & American Life Project, during 2012 in the United States (US), more than:

- 59 percent of people used a search engine to find information and send email.
- 48 percent used a social network such as Facebook, LinkedIn, or Google Plus.
- 45 percent got news online, whereas 45 percent went online just for fun and to pass the time.
- 35 percent looked for information such as checking a hobby or interest.

Actually, the United Nations claims that more people on Earth have access to mobile phones than restrooms. Six billion of the world's 7 billion people have access to mobile phones. Only 4.5 billion people have access to working restrooms. Meanwhile, 2.5 billion people don't have proper sanitation. *Big data* created from mobile devices is more common than the global infrastructure used for human sanitation.

The volume of digital analytics data being collected about online behavior is already being tapped and mined in 2013 (see Figure 1.3); however, the promise of digital analytics remains still largely unrealized and not demystified. EMC estimates that the majority of new data is largely untagged, file-based, and unstructured data, which means little is known about it. Only 3 percent of the data being created today is useful for analyses, whereas only .05 percent of that data is actually being analyzed. Thus, 99.95 percent of useful data available today for analysis is not being analyzed (see Figure 1.4). By 2020, IDC estimates a 67 percent increase in data available for analysis.

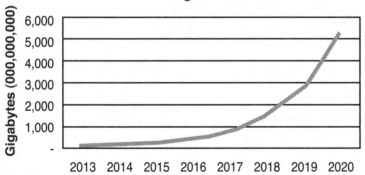

Estimated Gigabytes of Data per Person in the Digital Universe

Figure 1.3 Growth in digital data per person.

Source: IDC

Without a digital analytics organization firmly in place, a business will not be able to take advantage of the opportunity in digital data analysis that has resulted from all this data now and the huge surge of audience, media, and consumer data in the future. A business, of course, can only create competitive advantage with data if they can hire talented people who have digital analytics skills. Right now, a huge gap also exists in talented people to analyze and create insights from the data, which is an obstacle to staffing digital analytics teams. As a result of all the big data in the public and private sector, McKinsey estimates that 1,500,000 more "data-savvy" managers (who can understand and use analysis) and 140,000–190,000 new roles for analytical talent are needed to support the growth in big data in the future. The digital analyst and the digital analytics team needed to make sense of all this new data rarely exists and certainly not in sufficient quantities to create value from current and future big data. Actually, the industry faces an acute shortage and huge gap of the talent and technology needed to tag and analyze digital data even though analytical jobs are top-paying, high wage jobs.

It can take months to find a talented digital analyst and even longer to find managers and other analytical business leaders. This fact is precisely why this book can help you and your business determine how to manage and succeed with digital analytics while minding the gap in analytics talent. The need for building your own digital analytics organization is totally real, because you certainly can't easily or quickly hire even a single analyst and rarely a talented manager and never an entire team of analysts in one shot. This book tells you what you need to know right now to get started building your own digital analytics organization and/or what you can do to take your existing digital analytics organization to the next level.

This business book is as much about building a digital analytics team as it is about building a digital analytics organization. The team exists within the organization, and the organization exists within the business. Thus, this book is about much more than digital analytics. This business book is a truly one-of-a-kind text, derived from real-world, practitioner experience that is about understanding what is truly necessary to create, manage, win, and succeed with digital analytics, while focusing on analytical ideas, methods, and frameworks for generating sustainable business and shareholder value.

Defining Digital Analytics

But what is digital analytics? *Digital analytics* is the current phrase for describing a set of business and technical activities that define, create, collect, verify, or transform digital data into reporting, research, analysis, optimizations, predictions, automations, and insights that create business value.

The activity of digital analysis, at the highest and best application, helps companies increase revenue or reduce cost. The activities performed in digital analytics require coordinating processes, people, and technology internally within a company and externally from partners and vendors to produce analysis that answers business questions, makes recommendations based on mathematically and statistically rigorous methods, and informs successful business activities across many functions from sales to marketing to management.

Digital analytics can help a business in many ways. The two goals for the highest and best usage of analytics are to create value by 1) generating profitable revenue, and 2) reducing cost. The McKinsey Global Institute (MGI) claims that a 60 percent increase in retailers' operating margins are possible with big data, whereas just location-based big data has the potential to create a $600 billion market annually. The opportunity to generate commerce in an ethical and productive way is possible with digital data, but how does a person, a business, and a global enterprise get there? The answers are in this book with comments on the activities critical and necessary to analyze data, from the technical and process work (requirements/questions, data collection, definition, extraction, transformation, verification, and tool configuration) to the analytical methods to apply to data in order to analyze, report, and dashboard it. By bringing together data from different systems to create cohesive and relevant analysis, you can understand how digital data and analytics can be used to answer business questions and provide a foundation for fact-based decisions.

This book explains how to build and manage digital analytics teams to tell "data stories" based on answering "business questions" asked to the analytics team by stakeholders. The analytical insights in these answers can provide recommendations and data-oriented guidance to management that helps make their company money. Digital analysts, the people on the digital analytics team, are able to navigate effectively the upstream technical and downstream social and organization processes inherent in executing a data-driven communication function via processes that unify teams across technology and the business. If that last sentence is hard to deconstruct or if it makes perfect sense, read on because this book covers the following topics:

- The fundamental building blocks to understanding and creating processes for digital analytics, called the *Analytics Value Chain*. The Analytics Value Chain is a new concept I created for describing the process and work necessary for tactical and strategic success with digital analytics. The Analytics Value Chain starts with understanding business requirements and questions, to defining and collecting data, to verifying, reporting, and communicating analytics to the next steps of optimizing, predicting, and automating from digital data using data sciences. The goal of the value chain is, of course, the creation of economic value from digital analytics.

- The P's of digital analytics: people, pre-engagement, planning, platform, process, production, pronouncement, prediction, and profit

- Business considerations when justifying investment in the analytics team, and how to propose an investment consideration for funding the creation or enhancement of a digital analytics team and its operations

- Creating tactical and strategic goals for the analytics team and the responsibilities of the team

- Buying or building analytics tools and what it takes to succeed with tool deployment and maintenance, including discussions about social media and mobile analytics tools

- The importance of storytelling with analytics and using Exploratory Data Analytics (EDA) to understand digital analytics data

- Applied analytics techniques, as a go-to reference for the types and shapes of data, including a business-focused review of basic statistics such as the mean, median, standard deviation, and variance and other more advanced statistical concepts

- A review of data visualization techniques, such as plotting data, histograms, and other charts and visualizations

- Analysis of digital data for a businessperson: data correlation, and linear and logistic regression

- Good ideas and best practices when experimenting with data, sampling data, and building data models

- How digital analytics fits into other analytics, research fields, and qualitative disciplines such as competitive intelligence, market research, and Voice of Customer (VoC) data

- Data governance and the role of defining, collecting, testing, verifying, and managing changes to data, analysis, and reporting and how the Data Governance team plays a critical role

- How to set up a digital optimization program; a review of optimization using digital data with A/B (champion/challenger) and multivariate testing, while reviewing the statistical and mathematical models behind optimization and optimization engines, such as Taguchi and Choice modeling

- An overview of common and popular KPIs used by consultants, brands, and practitioners—and a review of useful ways to get started creating and extending your KPIs

- The importance of reporting and analysis and the difference between them, including RASTA dashboarding (Relevant, Accurately actionable answering, Simply structured and specific, Timely, Annotated, and commented) and LIVES reporting (Linked, Interactive, Visually-driven, Echeloned, and Strategic)

- The use of digital data for the many types of targeting—from geographic to cookie to behavioral and more

- A discussion of omnichannel data and the convergence and integration of data from multiple channels for understanding the customer, media, audiences, and for creating addressable advertising solutions using digital data

- The future of analytics from interacting with data in customer experiences to using sense and respond technologies for customer interacting and alerting to perceptual analytics

- The Analytical Economy and the importance of consumer and customer privacy and ethics within all facets of digital analytics now and into the future

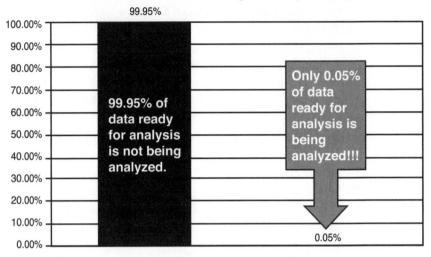

Figure 1.4 The opportunity to create value exists in the 99.95 percent of data available for analysis that is not being analyzed.

2

Analytics Value Chain and the P's of Digital Analytics

If you have taken a graduate-level business marketing course, you have likely read Philip Kotler's well-regarded treatise on marketing titled *Marketing Management*. This essential text teaches the modern marketing student about the four P's of marketing: price, place, promotion, and product. A professor of mine at Northeastern University in Boston, while teaching a lecture on services marketing, expanded Kotler's four P's by adding three new P's related to the delivery of services. The new P's were people, process, and physical evidence. Thus, the class concluded that there were really seven P's to marketing. The thesis was that after a marketing team determined the product, its price, the channels, and location in which to promote it, if a service needed to be delivered (for example, an appliance installation or car repair), people applied the process and had the proof in the form of physical evidence. It makes sense: You drop off your car to get repaired to a person who adheres to the garage's process. You leave with a repaired car—that shiny new bumper or maybe just the invoice for your records—as your physical evidence. In the spirit of Kotler's four P's and the additional three P's, the similar model makes sense for digital analytics.

Following are the P's to digital analytics, and these P's operate within a macro-analytics process called the Analytical Value Chain. This optimal process of the Analytical Value Chain involves nine analytics P's as follows:

- **People** on the team, their skill sets, and the unique experiences and perspective they all bring to the analysis of digital data.

- **Pre-engagement:** All analytical efforts require speaking with the people who are the "customers" (whether internal or external) to verify the proposed analysis is feasible and possible, given available and potential data collected and systems necessary for data analysis.

- **Planning:** All analytical efforts require a given level of planning in the project management sense to give them structure, milestones, and timelines.

- **Platform:** The technology or set of technologies used to collect, analyze, and communicate analysis.

- **Process:** All analytics efforts function within processes that may or may not already exist to support analytics. The importance of process and solid operations management of analytics is important to success.

- **Production** of analysis involves people who have pre-engaged with stakeholders to plan an analysis within the corporate process.

- **Pronouncement:** All analytics efforts require the analyst to not only report and analyze the data, but also to socialize and communicate the analysis to answer the business question asked.

- **Prediction:** The most advanced analytics efforts involve the usage of predictive analytics as part of digital optimization. Prediction includes applications of data science on big data.

- **Profit:** All analytical activities should be ultimately tied to how the data (and thus the transaction or behavior you are analyzing) contributes to profit. Although not all analysis ultimately references profit as a metric, analytical outcomes that reduce cost and increase revenue are all valid to helping profitability.

The Analytics Value Chain discussed later in this chapter takes the alliterative P's of digital analytics and places them into a tactical framework that explains the work activities that occur both linearly and recursively to support the creation of analytical business value. What follows in the subheadings of this chapter is an explanation of the Analytics P's in a strategic context based on the types of work, ways of working, and some of the tactics the team might perform when doing digital analytics across these P's.

Explaining the P's of Digital Analytics

The P's of digital analytics are discussed in more detail in the following sections. Think about how the concepts expressed by the P's are applied or how they could be applied to your team.

People, People, People

The first analytics P is **People**. The mantra of the analytics manager could be "people, people, people" just as the adage in real estate is "location, location, location." This book is written in the context of a "digital analytics organization," which by the definition of "organization" requires more than one person. People—from the analysts to stakeholders to supporting teams—are, by far, the most important part of any digital analytics organization. While tools and technology are critical, the people use tools and apply technology. Thus, the best analytics team invests considerably in the acquisition, growth, and retention of people. For more information about how people fit into analytics, see Chapter 3, "Building an Analytics Organization."

Pre-engaging the Customer and Stakeholder

The next P is **Pre-engagement**. Pre-engaging your customers and stakeholders on their business requirements for analytics is one of the most important activities the digital analytics team can complete diligently. Remember,

> *Success of your analytics team, process, and initiatives are directly related to the perception of how well the analytics deliverable meets the expectations of stakeholders.*

Implicit in the P of pre-engagement is, well, the concept of "pre." That means you talk to people first before you start doing anything analytical. And this means anything. Certainly you may already know on Day 1 what needs to be done, and you may even be right, but until you can compel your stakeholders to see your analytics vision, it is nothing but a vision. And a hallucinogenic vision it may be—until you make people see your goal.

Pre-engagement is a social activity that involves understanding the needs, motivations, and catalysts for the analytics work. Inherent in socialization is empathy, which is putting yourself in others' shoes to understand where they are coming from. After all, the finance people who are more quantitative have different needs, treatment, and handling than the user experience (UX) team who may be more aesthetic and visually driven when understanding data. Finance people are more accustomed to examining and analyzing data in tables whereas UX people may respond more favorably to charts and graphs. Thus, when considering how to pre-engage with your stakeholders, you need to consider what is necessary from their perspective, from "standing in their shoes," based on their goals.

When time allows, you should create a pre-engagement plan for use by the analytics team to understand the stakeholders who request work from the analytics team, and, ultimately, whose positive perception of the team will be critical to success. By allowing the team to deconstruct and understand its business stakeholders and their requirements from already known information and activities, the plan helps the team understand the human and social side of analysis. The pre-engagement plan has the following structure:

- **Audience:** Identify the named stakeholder and stakeholding group.
- **Activities:** List the business activities of this named stakeholder or stakeholding group.
- **Business questions:** Define the general theme of the business questions asked by this stakeholder.
- **Preferred type of deliverable:** Identify the preferred deliverable format.
- **Preferred communication method:** Identify the preferred communication method.
- **Frequency of contact:** List the frequency and periods when the analysis should be delivered.
- **Known biases:** Identify any issues, concerns, complaints, or overall feedback this stakeholder has had about analytics and the analytics team.

- **Current analytics work:** List any analytics work currently underway or delivered to this stakeholder during the last six months.

The Pre-engagement Plan, when completed, could take the format for each stakeholder and stakeholding group, as shown in Table 2.1.

Table 2.1 A Basic Pre-engagement Plan for the Marketing Team

Audience	Marketing Team
Activities	The marketing team coordinates research about the customer and manages inbound and outbound direct response and awareness campaigns.
Business Questions	What is the performance of paid search, display, and email campaigns on a month-to-month basis? Compare and analyze campaigns based on conversion rate and profitability.
Preferred Type of Deliverable	Use PowerPoint, not Excel.
Preferred Communication Method	Have in-person meetings.
Frequency of Contact	Have a formal two-hour meeting monthly and ad hoc as needed.
Known Biases	Distrust data that shows email is *not* the best performing campaign.
Current Analytics Work	Have two outstanding tickets: ABC-123 and ABC-124. Receives a monthly analytical deliverable.

After having a pre-engagement plan for all stakeholders, your team is in a position to engage with them. Although in-person meetings are recommended for pre-engagement, the global nature of business does not make this possible. As a result, following are the common models for interacting with stakeholders, each with its own nuances and risks:

- **In person, one to one:** A team member meets with the business stakeholder in a formal environment, such as a conference room or office, or informally, over lunch or coffee. Do not underestimate the importance of informal meetings with stakeholders when doing analytics.

- **In person, many to one:** A group of team members meet with the business stakeholder in a formal environment.

- **In person, group to group:** Multiple members of both the analytics team and stakeholding teams meet together in a group in a formal environment.

- **Video conference N to N:** Individuals and groups meet and collaborate in a virtual online or mobile environment.

- **Phone conference N to N:** Individuals and groups meet over the phone in a conference call.

- **Email communication:** Requirements, questions, and answers are passed along in email directly via email attachments.

- **Formal process artifacts: Agile or Waterfall:** Software development models such as Agile or Waterfall require certain modalities, ways of working, and process-related artifacts that can be applied to analysis and working with business stakeholders.

Each of these interaction models presents the opportunity to pre-engage. But what does the analytics team do in a pre-engagement model? The following questions and discussion topics are useful for covering:

- **What are the business goals?** Stakeholders should identify clear, realistic business goals that create business value.

- **What are you going to do with the data?** Stakeholders need to tell the analytics team what they are going to do with the data. This need is multifold. First, the team should know context to help data selection and also to ensure that data is not misused or used in ways for which the data was never intended.

- **What type of data do you think you need?** In organizations in which there is a lot of data of multiple types, it would be foolish to think the digital analytics team will know immediately the type of data required for an analysis. However, in many cases, digital analytics teams are so good that they *do* know the details of big data. Regardless, in all cases it helps to have the stakeholders tell the team, as best they can, what data and data sources to use or examine for the analysis.

- **How and when do you want the analysis delivered?** Expectations on delivery format and the timing/periodicity of any reporting or analysis should be determined in advance.

These facts help you understand the resources and technology needed behind the level of effort.

- **How will you judge successful delivery from the team?** Among the most important questions you can ask is how the stakeholder defines success. Each stakeholder will have a different idea. Some stakeholders measure success by simply getting accurate data or timely reporting, whereas other stakeholders need more or less hand holding, and others may prefer more data tables, charts, and graphs versus written analysis and vice versa.

Although these questions may seem basic, they are also core to understanding the analytical work you and your team are being asked to do. These questions require explicit answers and clarify the intent of the stakeholder and the deliverables from the team. The last question is among the most important. When you, the business owner, express what success to you is directly, the clarity is helpful for creating your analytical plan.

From the results of your pre-engagement, you can then understand the following concepts:

- **Level of effort:** How much work is required in terms of hours, human power, hours of coordination, and project management as a project and as comparable to other projects.

- **Feasibility:** Simply put, feasibility is your subjective and objective judgment that the work requested can actually be delivered. *Feasibility* is the opposite of "being nice" in that you must figure out if you can or can't regardless of the outcome. Of course, how you communicate feasibility analysis when the work is not possible in order to reject the work influences the perception of the analytics teams' capabilities.

- **Technology required:** The internal and external data collection, reporting, and analysis systems required to be implemented, used, touched, or involved to execute the work.

- **Resources required:** An estimate of the number of people, whether full time or part time, necessary to execute the work put into the context of available resources both internal and external to the company, such as consulting or vendor professional services.

- **Teams required:** Most analytics projects touch other teams and require them to not only do work on the behalf of the analytics team. Thus, it is important to identify to those teams a specific time and process for when the work needs to be done. Because other teams have their own work that is not digital analytics, the teams required to do the work must be identified and ultimately aligned before the work begins (or shortly thereafter). Without cross-functional alignment and adequate support from necessary teams, many analytics initiatives will be challenged to succeed.

- **Time required:** Because work needs to be delivered when relevant to the business, you must set correct expectations with stakeholders on when work can be delivered. Make sure you don't overcommit to work or timelines that result in enormous pressure for your team and the teams that support analytics.

At this point, by following the suggested pre-engagement plan, you have learned the following:

- Who the stakeholders are and what they need; why; in what business context; when; how; and with what existing biases from past work

- The project's business goals, audience, type of data (which points to analytical methods), and criteria against which success is measured

- A full scoping of the feasibility of the request, including the level of effort across people, process, technology, and time

By considering all these numerous facets of the stakeholder, the analytics work requested, and the process, people, and technology needed to deliver on-time, then you will be positioned for not only the perception of success by stakeholders, but also with an approach for planning and sustaining analytics projects over time and for initiating and controlling new work.

Planning for the Analytics Project

The second analytics "P" is for *Planning*. The concept of requirements planning means going through a process to understand what needs to be done, why it needs to be done, how it should be done, who needs to do it, when to do it, and where it needs to be delivered. When creating a requirements plan, you must base the plan on the pre-engagement plan that you or your team created with business stakeholders.

The pre-engagement plan identifies the business questions you need to answer: the preferred format for delivery, the frequency for delivery, and what the business stakeholders judge for success (see the previous section). In this context, the plan needs to communicate to the stakeholder, to the team, to your management, to project management, and perhaps even to program management and other business groups within your corporation what the analytics team is going to do in a written deliverable that communicates the project requirements, the resources required, and the format and frequency for communicating analysis.

An analytics plan typically has the following sections:

- **Intended audience:** Ask yourself who is the person that will read and review the written analysis? What does this person need from the analysis? What is the best way for people to determine the answers to their questions from this analysis? What is the stakeholders' preferred format for delivery of this analysis? What are the analytical questions to answer? As part of your pre-engagement plan, you identified the business questions that the stakeholder wants the analysis to answer. In your analytical requirements plan, you then list the formal written questions you intend to answer with the data. These questions may be identical to the questions provided by the stakeholder in your pre-engagement, or you might work with the stakeholder to create new questions based on your understanding of available data.

- **Teams required:** The teams, both within and outside the company, should be identified in advance to set expectations on the level of human effort, team coordination, and project management required. By listing the teams in the plan, and involving them in the socialization of the plan, you reduce the chance that you won't have adequate resources or support to execute the work. In addition, if there are gaps in the resources needed or the availability of the teams, this section can communicate the gaps and proposed solutions for overcoming the gaps.

- **Data required:** Based on your pre-engagement, understanding of the business questions, and the work involved executing the analysis, you must identify preliminarily the types of data you expect to use to fulfill the analysis and the data sources that contain these data. Although you may have some idea of the data required, you need to speak with stakeholders, supporting teams, and other analysts to reconcile, qualify, and possibly expand on the data and data sources considered for the work.

- **Technology required:** The technology necessary to use when creating the analysis must be included in the analytical plan. Because technology can come from both internal and external sources, you must identify the systems, the data sources, the functional teams, and the types of skills you need for most teams to execute the plan. Make a realistic estimate of the impact to the systems and technology teams that will be touched by your analytical project. By framing a realistic understanding of the work you ask other teams (including technology) to do against their existing set of committed projects and "roadmap," you can communicate expectations in the analytical plan. For example, if you know there's a business intelligence (BI) initiative underway being planned by the IT department in their project roadmap, it makes sense to consider your analytics project in the context of the larger program and overall IT roadmap.

- **Format for deliverables:** Although a business stakeholder may prefer a certain format for a deliverable, you cannot always provide the deliverable in that format. You must clarify with stakeholders and align with them on the type of format for the analysis. The most common formats for analytical deliverables include PowerPoint, Excel, and various other methods for communicating analysis, such as Word—even use of various reporting and analysis tools from multiple software vendors—from the large BI vendors to smaller niche vendors specializing in data visualization. Your goal here is to put the analysis in the best possible format of the deliverable for your stakeholder, which will vary by stakeholder. Some people are more quantitative whereas others need more help understanding data and numbers that support an analysis. The best format for analysis is what the stakeholder prefers, not necessarily what the analytics team prefers.

- **Frequency of deliverables:** In analytics, one of the hardest things to identify is when to deliver something, because often downstream/upstream service providers exist on which the analytics team is dependent. When creating analytics deliverables, you must identify the frequency of deliverables regardless of this fact—the fact that your work can be bottlenecked or driven off-track and schedule by teams you don't control and who may not be aligned with the work of the analytics team. The goal of the analytics team is to provide deliverables at the frequency needed by the business; when that's not possible, then the goal must be to most effectively manage expectations as to why and how analytics can help solve that problem going forward (if not now) and what is required to do so. Thus, the analytics leadership must overcome obstacles presented by other teams when attempting to schedule or execute analytics work.

- **Presentation outline:** The analytics plan must include a presentation outline, which communicates the basic structure for the deliverable. In PowerPoint, this could be a high-level mapping of the types of slides and a view of the potential content area. In Excel, this could be a report structure with named column headings and rows. Regardless of how you choose to present the information, the goal of the plan is to identify, communicate, and align with the business stakeholders so that the presentation style is effective for presenting and communicating the meaning behind the analysis.

- **Review and follow-up:** Include in any analytics plan the process for reviewing and following up with stakeholders after presenting the initial analysis. In most cases, analysis needs to be followed up with stakeholders because stakeholders' requirements, needs, wants, and goals change from the moment they asked the initial business question to the moment you present the analysis, and then to the next moment when they are actually using the analysis. It is a best practice after delivering analysis to stakeholders to remain connected and follow up a couple days, a week, and a month after the analysis to make sure you continue to stay in step and aligned with the ever-changing and evolving business needs of stakeholders.

Consideration and alignment across the business communicated in an analytical plan can help you succeed. One of the ways to communicate an analytical plan across the business is through a regularly scheduled set of meetings (perhaps weekly) to review proposed plans with stakeholders. Regardless of how you choose to communicate your analytical plan, certain methods work better than others. The following aspects of communicating an analytical plan can help the business understand and synthesize the work you suggest doing to drive the business:

- **Regularly scheduled planning meetings:** By establishing a regular schedule for meetings to discuss proposed analysis and the business impact of such analysis, alignment and communication can occur across functional business units. The right cadence for an analytical planning meeting or set of meetings can vary by the culture of the corporation. The best frequency can also vary by the maturity of the organization, as well as the way digital experiences are created. More Agile approaches to working require less formality and meetings, and more alignment with ongoing business activities. Whereas more Waterfall-based approaches to the creation of digital experiences require more regularity and planning sessions, especially on an annual basis well in advance of the turn of the year. Larger companies whose resources are already potentially overwhelmed with meetings benefit from less frequency. Startups, of course, where the rapidity of new product innovation is necessary, need more meetings.

- **Formal agenda:** What may seem obvious, having a formal agenda for an analytics planning review meeting, is something that's easier said than done. An agenda can prevent a group of people getting bogged down discussing one topic, digressing, or not covering the overall goal of the meeting. Agendas help to maintain focus and alignment. Set a formal agenda that is written out, published, and sent to all meeting invitees in advance of the meeting so they know the topics proposed and can prepare. This agenda should be reviewed at the beginning of the meeting in case it needs to be modified to suit the current business need. Each section of the agenda should be associated with a responsible person, and in the best cases, where resources allow, written minutes noting important topics and decisions should be kept. It may help to rotate the responsibility for keeping meeting minutes from one person to another as the meeting schedule moves throughout the year.

- **An expectation of the decisions to be made:** If pre-engagement has already occurred and the people invited to the analytical planning review meeting have already reviewed the analytical plan, the question may be asked why the meeting needs to occur. After all, people are busy, and one of the modalities for communicating with the analytics team can be using email. Thus, it is important in face-to-face meetings where there is an expectation of attendance to identify what business decisions need to be made. For the analytical planning review session, the projects are reviewed at a high level, presented to the stakeholders, discussed among the analytical team and stakeholders, and accepted or rejected by the teams. In addition, priorities may be assessed, reorganized, and identified for the first time in the analytical planning review meeting. All of this will lead to decisions on what to do next and the identification of future analytics work.

- **Next steps with dates:** Now assume that your analytical planning meeting is already regularly scheduled with a formal agenda, and the business as well as the analytics team knows what decisions need to be made; then, you are in better shape than many of your competitors. The outcome of a successful meeting is a set of next steps that are mapped to dates in time. The exercise of prioritizing analytical plans needs input that may occur outside of the analytical meeting; however, you should still identify some level of a timeline to the analytical plans approved for execution by the team. The development methodology and the way digital experiences are engineered at your company will drive timelines. In more Agile environments, work could be executed possibly every two weeks, whereas in Waterfall environments, it may take months or years for work to be executed to known dates. And even then, putting dates on analytics work can be more of an art than a science. Keep in mind that unless you and your team control all aspects of analytics, you will need to ensure that the next steps and dates you propose are agreed upon by other teams required to help analytics.

- **Follow-up review email:** The follow-up communication from the analytics team formally lists what was discussed, what was agreed upon, and what will be done in the next steps with dates, if possible, to all stakeholders. After an analytical planning review session where decisions are made and work is decided— and in the best case associated with dates—the analytics team must follow up with all stakeholders at the meeting to propel and catalyze the next steps. Given that analytical projects formally reviewed in planning sessions tend to be larger in scope than day-to-day ad hoc projects, it might make sense for the leader of the analytics team to follow up with stakeholders. In other cases in which teams are large or highly matrixed, it may be common for the analytical leader to take a more hands-off approach to following up with the analytics leadership, only following up with their peers or other business leaders, delegating the work of following up with line-of-business stakeholders to other team members.

This P for Planning is certainly a crucial activity. By carrying the learning from pre-engagement into the planning process, you can formally communicate analytical projects in a simple way. Concentrate on what's important to your stakeholders and place your analytical plan around an understanding of the technology's resources and work required to help lay the foundations for success in all your analytics projects.

Platform for Defining, Collecting, Storing, Reporting, Analyzing, and Optimizing

Another P in digital analytics is the **Platform**. The set of underlying technologies and software products that support the collection, processing, reporting, and analysis of digital data can be considered the platform. The number of technologies that you can use to do digital analysis can vary by a number of factors: from the type of data, analysis, and analytical goals, to even simpler concepts like budget and a skill set. In some cases, the digital analytics team may use one tool, such as Google Analytics, whereas other teams might have created their own customized solutions from vendor tools or from home-grown coding. Other teams use both internal data from a number of systems and external data provided by more than one vendor. In the latter case, it may be that many teams across the company contribute both technology and resources to the creation and maintenance of the analytics tool set. In all cases, a digital analytics team requires an analytics platform on which to build the technical foundations and infrastructure necessary to win with analytics. Again, the exact technology or set of technologies is highly dependent on business requirements. For more information about analytics platforms and analytics tools, see Chapter 4, "What Are Analytics Tools?"

Processes for Repeatable and Sustainable Analytics

The next P in analytics is **Process**. The concept of process creation is necessary to understand when building a digital analytics organization. When doing analytics, multiple business processes across multiple business functions and teams must work together to enable success with analytics. The analytics team always works within the larger set of corporate processes whether those are technological, financial, and/or organizational. Thus, it becomes extremely important for the analytics team to work effectively with pre-existing teams and within existing business processes. Sometimes the analytics team must modify existing processes to support analytics. Other times the analytics team must create a set of entirely new cross-functional business processes that, when sustained, allow for analytics to be executed successfully in alignment with other teams like IT, engineering, release management, product, marketing, sales, and more.

Corporate culture always wins in analytics. What that means is that the analytics team can't expect to create an entirely new set of processes and drop them on the business without considering the culture. That heavy-handed tactic just won't work. Instead, the analytics team needs to take a more sensitive approach to understanding existing processes and fitting analytics work into them where possible. When analytics doesn't fit into existing processes or doesn't create its own processes, the analytics team cannot deliver expected value. A corporation must support the evolution and creation of analytical processes to win with analytics. Senior management may need to provide authority to the analytics team when creating new processes or changing existing ones.

Whether you are tasked with creating new processes, evolving existing processes, or optimizing a set of new processes created in the last couple years by somebody else, the following list of activities can be helpful to consider when developing and defining analytics processes:

- **Socialize the need for process and gain alignment across the business.** Whereas the need for process may seem basic for an analytical professional, not everyone in the business sees the world the way you see the world. Actually, processes create transparency, transparency creates accountability, and accountability means being responsible for the successful execution of work. Thus, when an analytics team creates processes that require other teams to do work, it's logical to expect that those teams may not want to do that work in the way the analytics team wants them to do it. Socializing the need for process means communicating and aligning with the leaders of the teams and team members. Discuss and gain alignment on how clearly defined processes both upstream and downstream can also help those other teams do their jobs quicker and better. When necessary and appropriate, involve senior management to remove obstacles, politics, and other challenges when creating or modifying analytics processes.

- **Identify the teams that are required to support the analytics value chain.** Because the analytics team cannot do the entirety of their work alone, other teams are, of course, required. When creating processes that touch the analytics team and involve other teams, those teams must be mapped out and understood. Teams likely impacted by analytics processes include IT, engineering, systems operations, BI, finance, marketing, external vendors, management stakeholders, and more.

- **Use action-based verbs and phrases to describe the list of processes that need to be created.** Action verbs ending in the letters "ing" begin action phrases. Using action phrases with action verbs is an easy way to identify the type of processes the analytics team needs to create. For example, deploying a marketing campaign; tagging a new website; selecting a new vendor; integrating the new data source; and communicating analysis to the business. As you can see, all these examples use action verbs to start the process. This simple technique gets people thinking about what the activity is that needs to be done and what teams need to support it.

- **List the set of action-oriented phrases and verbs that describe the process(es) in one list and consolidate into topics.** After you have created the set of action phrases to describe the different analytics processes you need to create, refine, or optimize, the next step is to create and consolidate the full list of processes. It may be necessary in this list to remove redundancies. The end result should be a set of processes that represent the internal analytics team activities as well as the external linkages and intersections between upstream and downstream supporting and dependent groups for analytics.

- **Map the consolidated processes to responsible teams.**
  When your team has a consolidated set of analytics processes,
  you must have your team map the processes to the supporting functional teams and other stakeholders on which the processes depend. Identify the teams that support the analytics
  processes—and make sure they know they do and are aligned.
  Don't surprise other teams with analytics work. The number of
  teams responsible for each process depends. It's entirely possible that for internal activities the only team necessary is the
  analytics team. In other cases in which the process crosses multiple groups, every group touched by the process must be listed.

- **Assess whether the process suggested is new, existing, or
  a refinement of an existing process.** Unless you work in a
  startup and have the luxury of defining entirely new processes,
  it is likely that you've entered a situation that has some baggage
  associated with it, from bad data, to bad processes, to bad technology, to bad staff. In such cases, the analytics team ends up
  working to optimize and refine existing processes. Don't be too
  quick to judge, but be swift to take corrective action when you
  know processes need to be created or changed.

- **Create the steps in the process(es).** The hardest part of creating any analytics process is identifying the steps in the process. This activity is generally something that needs to be done
  across the teams. Other teams will need to agree with the work
  you propose they do. A responsible person should be assigned
  to completing the elaboration on the details of the steps for
  each process. The steps should also be action-oriented and
  associated with the responsible teams. Each step in the process should have an associated estimate of the level of effort in
  terms of hours and overall time to execute the step. Be careful
  to review multiple times the steps in the analytics processes you
  create. Run them by the functional groups that support the processes—and do your best to gain support and alignment. Don't
  develop them in the dark—seek feedback from whoever will
  give it you.

- **Start with what is achievable and build off that success.**
  After successful processes have been established, the analytics
  team should promote an advocate for the efficiencies created
  by those processes across the business, especially with senior
  management. It may make sense to delegate an analytics team
  member to document, review, and act as the focal point for
  extending and refining processes.

Processes reduce cycle time and increase the speed at which analysis and business decisions can be delivered. As a result, successful processes reduce cost and thus increase bottom-line profits. An analytics team that operates according to a set of sustainable processes that have been agreed upon across functional units in a business will be a successful analytics team.

Production: Producing Analysis and Executing on the Plan

The next P in analytics is **Production**. After pre-engaging and planning for analysis, the analytical team must produce it. This analytics work and project execution is where "the rubber hits the road." The analyst may perform one, many, or all the following activities when producing analysis:

- **Write the data collection requirements.** Digital analytics data often does not exist and must be created. Some years ago, there were only a couple ways to collect digital data: log files and page tags. Other methods did exist, but they were not widespread among the common set of available vendor technologies. Nowadays, common methods for digital data collection include Application Programming Interfaces (API's) that get and set data within both internally hosted and externally hosted analytical data collection systems as well as lower-level programmatic methods for collecting data such as Java, Objective–C and Python.

  As a result of the proliferation of different types of data collection methods, analysts are expected to know how to not only collect existing types of digital data, but also accommodate for innovation around data collection and be able to learn quickly how to use new data collection methods. Data collection requirements often take the form of written specifications that communicate the types of relationships (often name/value) that need to be created between the digital interface and human behavior. For example, a mobile application may have many click events, and some of those click events do the same thing, but many of those events are unique or are useful to segment using unique values. Thus, the data collection specification would specify which click events to track and the names of those events, For example, when someone clicks Search within a mobile application, the keyword associated with the search can be collected, counted, and reported to understand segmented search behavior. You may want to call some searches "first search in visit" and other searches "second search" and so on.

- **Work with various teams to ensure accurate data collection and to verify data accuracy.** Regardless of whether a digital analytics team wants to, the team often becomes the steward, governor, and identifier of truth and accuracy in data to teams throughout the company. This fact is especially relevant when new data is created or existing data is modified as release cycles progress or new products are released. The analytics team is often asked to verify new data and changes to data from internal sources, which the team may or may not know about, and even from external sources whether publicly available or privately procured.

  The digital analytics team may be expected to access the data in various repositories across the business and compare it to the data in the digital analytics systems, even if other systems are outside of the digital analytics team's control. Although much of this comparative work to verify accuracy and data matching across systems is done in spreadsheets and manually, it is also possible to automate these types of common and repeatable data audits. One of the benefits of having a centralized analytics team is that it controls what is considered "the truth." As the controller of the truth, the central analytics team is empowered to reconcile the differences between data sources and identify the single source of truth. Without centralization of analytics, it is difficult for an analyst or even the entire analytics team to prove that X data is better than Y data or that the analytics team's data is more accurate to business definitions than other data. Like it or not, the digital analytics team must ensure data accuracy, and that may be one of the most frustrating as well as one of the most rewarding aspects of an analyst's job.

- **Verify the data collected meets expectations for utility.** Time is often spent producing analysis in the earliest phases after data is collected by verifying that it is suitable for use for your particular purposes. People often expect that verified, accurate data will meet their business needs; however, that's not always a guarantee. Because a time delay occurs between when data is specified for data collection and the implementation of data collection, the business may change in ways that can't be anticipated days, weeks, or even months in advance. The result is accurate data for a business question in the past, which may not be sufficient to answer new business questions. As a result, data previously specified and agreed upon may not have utility for the particular business purpose. The business wants a different version of that data, so the analytics team needs to verify the data against new requirements. In the worst case, the work done previously is no longer useful and thus was wasted. Now, this sounds less than ideal. And it is. But it happens all the time unless you watch out for it.

- **Audit data across multiple systems or within the same system.** In complex, data-rich environments, the digital analytics team may come across data sources, reports, dashboards, and other analysis that overlaps and may be redundant with currently produced or planned analysis. In other cases, analysis may be produced across the company that is historical or new and may have applicability to the analytics team's current projects and goals. Although this situation may not sound ideal, it actually has benefits. The primary benefit is that it is easier and quicker to audit data sources, in most cases, than to specify, implement, verify, and report new data collection. The secondary benefit is that the analytics team learns about the existing business by examining, understanding, comprehending, and auditing other teams' data. When auditing data, it is important for the analytics team to not assume the roles and responsibilities of other teams. Data audits often involve the analytics team delegating support work as appropriate to other teams.

- **Create and modify reports.** Tools used to create reports most commonly include spreadsheets and BI tools that have a reporting interface. During the pre-engagement and analytical planning phases, the analyst identified what the reporting should look like. In that sense, the stakeholder, with the analyst's help, has likely been provided and approved a mockup of the columns and rows within the report—or the location and placement of key performance indicators (KPIs) and other metrics within a dashboard. In other cases, the business stakeholder expects the digital analytics team to build the reporting as it thinks it should be to best represent the data. In cases in which business requirements for reporting or the structure of reports are not known, the digital analytics team can expect a series of multiple back-and-forth's with business stakeholders. Do your best to always elicit from stakeholders what they think the reporting and dashboarding should look like.

- **Use the techniques outlined in Chapter 5, "Methods and Techniques for Digital Analysis," to produce business analysis.** Create various types of analytical deliverables, such as dashboards, PowerPoints, and other communication forms to distribute analysis. I often say that reports are not analysis. Analysis is something an analyst does before reporting; although I admit in all cases this is not necessarily true. Although it is all too easy to call a report an "analysis," the best analyses communicate complexity in simple ways with narration and written words expressing concepts and conclusions about the data. For example, a box and whisker plot can easily show the distribution of data. A histogram can show the differences between counts and totals. A regression analysis can, to a certain significance level, identify the impact of independent variables on the dependent variables. Time series analyses show fluctuations in metrics that can be associated with changes in business activities. An analyst's job is to make sense of the data using analytically valid and rigorous approaches that yield insights. Then those insights need to be communicated in words and sentences that explain the numbers, not just in numbers but also accompanied by words and visualizations.

- **Respond to questions about the existing analysis related to what's being worked on and set clear expectations on when work will be completed.** After pre-engaging a stakeholder, presenting an approved plan for analysis, and beginning to create an analysis, you can expect to be contacted by stakeholders. Stakeholders will check in and want to know when you'll be done with an analysis. They may want to learn how you're producing a particular analysis. The analytics team must make itself available to answer these questions. In order to respond to stakeholders, set appropriate expectations and guidelines for regular communication and project check-ins. Also have a process set up so that the analytics team goes to stakeholders or at least is available to stakeholders for a given period of time. One idea is for the analytics team to host open office hours either in person or virtually where stakeholders can ask the analytics team whatever they want. Publish a schedule for analytical deliverables.

Pronouncing the Analysis: "Stochastic" but You Just Say "Random"

The next P in analytics is **Pronounce**. Pronouncing may sound a little odd, but what is meant is simply normal and typical human communication. Pronouncing is communicating in a way appropriate for your business stakeholder. In the subheading for this section, the attempt at making a joke is as much humor as it is a lesson. In analytics, it takes time to realize that nobody cares about the detailed statistical, mathematical, and analytical techniques and methods you've used to create an analysis. Your stakeholders care about business issues not the mathematics or clever tagging. Say "random" instead of "stochastic" when it makes sense for the audience. Other times you will want to use considerably more academic terminology for expressing the complex concepts.

Although the team and even you may be impressed by the perfect application of a particular model to solve a business problem—for example, a logistic regression applied to a marketing mix model—it is more likely than not that your audience hasn't actually thought about regression analysis since college, if even at all. As a result, pronouncing the analysis means speaking and writing in terms that business people can understand. Actually, your analysis should be communicated in the way a 12-year-old or your grandmother could understand. While I jest to some degree, the best analysis is easily comprehendible by a wide range of people by being as simple as necessary for the topic.

Suffice to say, your conclusion at this point in the chapter should be that the best analysis is communicated in the simplest way. Now that does not necessarily mean dumbing down anything. That's not what I mean by making your analysis suitable for understanding by 12-year-olds. The point of analysis is to communicate clearly using data to answer a business question. Said another way, analysis enables and contributes to strategic and tactical decision making and inputs in the decision-making process. For analysis to accomplish these goals, it must be comprehensible to the audience with as little complexity as possible but as much as is necessary. You need to express analysis in vocabulary that business people will understand—and the appropriate vocabulary will vary by the audience. Again, as put in the section heading, don't use fancy words, like "stochastic," to communicate simple concepts, like "random."

Here are some tips of pronouncing and communicating an analysis:

- **Set up formal analytics review meetings.** One of the simplest ways to communicate an analysis is to schedule a set of formal analytic review meetings. These meetings can be set up in a cadence based on a software release cycle, Agile sprints or iterations, various development workflows, and other ways of working. The regularity of such meetings can vary based on need and the availability of analyses.

- **Don't rush the analytical communication.** By the time the digital analytics team has prepared an analysis, it is likely that the stakeholder has waited several weeks or months, so there is no need to rush the communication beyond the normal expected sense of urgency. Actually, it is essential to be deliberate when communicating your analysis. Take the time to reflect on the pre-engagement documentation and the analytics plan. Make sure that you're preparing to communicate an analytical deliverable that meets expectations already set, answers business questions, and fulfills business goals.

- **Intend to understand.** To frame an effective communication back to stakeholders, make sure you have the intention to understand their needs and not just pontificate about the data and what you think it says. By intending to understand your audience, your communications can likely hit the mark even if the message derived from your analysis is surprising.

- **Be open-minded when answering questions.** Although you may have spent months gathering requirements, writing specifications, working with various teams to collect data, and verifying, reporting, and analyzing the data, you may be biased due to the familiarity of subject matter. Thus, when dealing with stakeholders, make sure that you remain open-minded when listening to their questions and concerns. Do not get defensive if stakeholders disagree with your analysis or comment on or criticize your work. Instead, as mentioned previously, focus on understanding and remaining open-minded and doing your best to deliver analysis in a non-political way that helps the business make progress.

- **Determine the next steps and schedule when the next meeting is appropriate.** When communicating analysis, you'll eventually reach the point of diminishing returns. This conclusion may occur when there is an otherwise complete and total mutual understanding. The discussion about the analysis may yield more questions of more immediate concern than the analysis itself, and next steps will be planned. In all cases, you should plan a follow-up session to the meeting or via email or the corporation's preferred communication method within two weeks after the analysis is first presented.

Predicting the Future by Reading the Tea Leaves in Your Cup of Data

Another P in analytics is **Prediction**. The concept of predictive analytics has almost entered the mainstream in more common ways than the related term, data science. Prediction is a type of data science. As I was sitting on my couch the other evening, I heard a commercial on television talking about using predictive analytics to make robots work efficiently. I even think there was a reference to big data and data science in this ad. How exciting! Because it made me think about how digital analytics is one of the major sources of data now being used for predictive modeling.

The goal of prediction with data is not that dissimilar to a gypsy reading your palm or the tea leaves in your teacup. Predictive analytics is just way more scientific and based on mathematical principles than reading tea leaves and much more accurate, too. Whether 1,000 years ago, or using the most sophisticated data clients available, the idea that humans can predict the future or at least what may happen in the future has always been perceived to be beneficial to humanity. The age of information and technology combined with the massive infrastructure available for computing and working with gigantic sets of data, as well as the availability and evolution of mathematics and business statistics, has created an environment in which prediction is not only possible, but done quite frequently.

Today's predictive analytics are used throughout many different industries, such as the insurance, automotive, and financial industries. Predictive models are used in insurance to identify risky customers and prospects. In the automotive industry, predictive models are used to understand future inventory trends. The financial industry uses predictive models to estimate the movement of various equities on the global market. Massive amounts of money are traded based on statistical models, many of them predictive models.

The most mature analytics teams maintain a predictive modeling capability. It's common for analysts to understand the general themes behind predictive modeling. It is less common to find people who actually know how to apply a given predictive model to an actual business problem. As a result, these people who can build predictive models and apply data sciences can command high salaries. One of the best ways for a digital analytics team to grow in a skill set is to develop predictive analytics and predictive modeling skills.

You can use digital analytics predictive modeling in a number of ways:

- **Customer segmentation modeling:** Today's modern companies use various customer attributes to segment their customers. Segmentation can be based on any number of factors such as campaigns, geography, time, value, demographics, psychographics, behaviors, transactions, and so on.

- **Predicting customer lifetime value:** Calculating the lifetime value of a customer is important for brands. The prediction of customer lifetime value can take multiple forms and generally is about determining the future value of existing customers or the future value of potential customers.

- **Identifying inventory items to merchandise:** Predictive analytics can be applied to merchandising by using the various attributes within inventory-level data and by using data collected about the way inventory moves both in the store and online. This information can also be based on various customer behaviors in order to determine the best possible inventory to merchandise at the optimal time to the right customer segment in the best location.

- **Determining when to best display an online advertisement to a given audience:** Premiums and higher value can be achieved in online advertising using predictive analytics. Models can suggest and automate when certain ad inventory is most appropriate for effectively targeting an advertisement to a customer. Predictive analytics can help with this challenge.

Controlled experimentation, multivariate tests, and data analysis techniques such as regression can be applied to online advertising data.

- **Predicting the profitability of a marketing campaign:** Marketing campaigns can be analyzed and the cost of those campaigns can be associated with proxy values for behaviors on a site to calculate profitability. Additional data collected from third parties, event-level data, and customer, behavioral, and transactional data collected from digital experiences can be modeled using predictive analytics to predict the potential performance of a marketing campaign.

Profiting from Today's Data

The final P in analytics is *Profit*. All analytical activities should be tied as directly as possible to how the analysis (and thus the data, transaction, event, or behavior you are analyzing) contributes to helping create value, generate revenue, reduce cost, and enhance profitability. As easy as this seems, it's a much harder task to pull off in real life. Digital analytics often is associated with marketing instead of finance, and as a result, the digital analytics team may not have access to the necessary financial data to apply financial calculations. In some companies, data such as revenue isn't shared publicly, and the incremental cost of various business initiatives can be hard to determine—and political when they are determined. Regardless of the difficulty and complexity in identifying the correct financial data to use in your digital analysis, it is always possible to do—even if arguable proxy values are the only option.

Several ways exist to show the profit from the digital analytics team:

- **Track the results of recommendations by estimating the impact of the resulting activities that occurred because of the analysis.** The best analysis provides the business with a set of recommendations that help inform stakeholders and guide decision making. Although the digital analytics team can't ensure that stakeholders take any recommendations, the team can follow up to find out the impact of any recommendations followed. Business stakeholders may be interviewed to estimate the financial impact of the analytics team work on their initiatives. All these inputs can be recorded across multiple projects and used to estimate and prove the business value of analytics.

• **Work with financial teams to understand the cost of various business activities and also the revenue from digital behaviors.** The finance team has a wealth of knowledge about the money that flows into and out of your business. It understands in intricate detail the profit and loss associated with each functional group in your company. For groups such as marketing, the finance team often keeps track of the various "cost per" metrics and other derivative advertising and marketing metrics. You can also identify the various behaviors that create revenue on a website or within a digital experience. By combining the cost per metrics identified by the finance team and the proxy values for behaviors, you can begin to estimate profitability. This calculation can be tied directly to analytics activities, and the decisions made from analytical recommendations, optimizations, predictions, and automations.

• **Tie common digital analytics metrics like conversion rate to revenue and profit.** Digital analytics teams understand the incremental impact of fluctuations in conversion rates. The best teams can estimate the impact of revenue and profitability of the shifting conversion rate by tens or hundreds of a percentage. For example, for every one-tenth increase in site conversion, revenue goes up by $200,000 a week and average order value goes up by $17.00.

• **Determine the value of a visit to an advertiser, and use that value to show an impact from optimization activities.** A simple way to calculate value within a digital experience is to simply divide the total revenue or total profit from the digital experience(s) by the total number of unique people that have used it (them). For example, if your business made $1,000,000 from 100,000 visits, then each visit had an approximate value of $10. If analytics activities help to generate visits, then the change in visits over some time period (such as year over year) can be modeled using a $10 value and applied to create an estimated contribution of value from analytics activities. Obviously, this approach as presented here is raw and rough and can be refined to identify visit value by visitor segment and other segmentations. By tracking value-based metrics for audiences over time and associating changes in them with business activities, such as marketing programs, digital behavior can be understood in financial terms.

- **Ask stakeholders to estimate the benefit of having analytical data, reporting, and analysis provided by the analytics team at their disposal.** A potentially risky way to identify the profitability of analytics activities is by asking stakeholders to do it for you. The risk, of course, is that stakeholders may estimate negative profitability from analytics. Or a previously unknown issue may be brought to light. In the best case, stakeholders can provide a dollar-value estimate of the business value of analytics, which you can then take to your manager or use to justify the existence of an analytics team.

- **Calculate the efficiencies gained by deploying analytics solutions that automate previously manual work.** When deploying new analytics technology or teams, it may result in other resources being used in different ways. People can be deployed to new teams and projects, even moved to entirely new roles as a result of analytics automation. Because employees are often the most expensive asset a business has, there are often already tracked financial measures about the revenue impact of each employee. These can be proxied to create estimates of the impact of the analytics team were resources to change.

The Analytics Value Chain: Process for Tactical and Strategic Success

The **Analytics Value Chain** is a six-phase framework that explains the generalized process for "doing digital analytics." As such, the value chain encapsulates the generalized analytics process. The execution of each phase in the value chain completes necessary work for creating value with analytics. The goal of the value chain is to provide people who want to understand digital analytics and improve their teams with a simple way to illustrate the various activities that the analytics team performs when it's "doing analytics."

Often people think analysts have all the data needed to answer business questions immediately at their disposal in easy-to-access, specific formats, that are already analyzed and ready to give to the business stakeholder. Although that may be true in some cases where the data exists, is ready, and has already been analyzed and placed into a report when it is requested, the more likely case is that some level of preparation is necessary to make the data ready for the businessperson. In other words, the data in digital analytics doesn't just exist because there's a website or social or mobile experience. It takes a lot of complex work to create and verify accurate digital data. It also takes different types of expertise to prepare and analyze it in a business context for business stakeholders. The following Analytics Value Chain explains the analytics process in a linear way for easy comprehension by the businessperson. As analysts know, the nature of analytics work and team activities can begin with any one of these phases and cycle back (recurse) as opposed to one phase always following after another. The linear step-by-step value chain as presented below, however, makes sense as a forward-progressing framework for comprehending how to do digital analytics. Just remember that analytics work can start in any of these phases, and the type of work the analytics team does in each of these phases will vary based on the company. The larger the company, then the more people and teams will be involved in the various phases, while in smaller companies fewer people and technologies can be needed to execute the value chain.

The Analytics Value Chain has six phases:

- **Understanding what to analyze:** Work with business stakeholders to identify and collect business questions and requirements. Examine previous analysis and learn about already collected data. Ask "If you had the data and analysis in your hands right now, what business decision would you make?"
- **Collecting, verifying, and governing data:** Ensure the relevant and accurate data is defined, collected, verified, governed, and provided accurately for timely and relevant analysis.
- **Reporting and dashboarding:** Format, present, and visualize data in reporting and dashboarding formats that are relevant, actionable, accurate, and which answer specific questions in a timely, concise, and nonbiased way. Apply data visualization, information mapping, narrative techniques, and optimal design principles to reports and dashboards.

- **Analyzing data, and communicating and socializing:** Analyze data using mathematically and statistically rigorous and valid techniques and methods. Present recommendations focused on outcomes and the creation of business value. Focus on communicating accurate answers to business questions asked by stakeholders. Concentrate on helping business stakeholders use analysis to make decisions. Create and sustain business relationships focused on providing analytical excellence.

- **Optimizing, predicting, and automating:** Use controlled experimentation and testing, A/B (champion/challenger) and multivariate technologies and methods, to optimize and improve the user experience, features, flows, conversion, advertising and merchandising, and other elements of digital experiences. Applying data machine learning techniques and algorithms to predict future events and customer and audience behaviors. Use analytical data and inputs to automate business processes.

- **Demonstrating economic value:** Ensure all analytical work is focused on answering business questions and solving business challenges and issues. Track analytically driven and inspired recommendations, optimizations, predictions, and automations as business outcomes of analytical work that can be tied to financial business metrics, such as cost, revenue, margin, profit, and earnings.

Make sure you understand the value chain because it forms the foundation for knowing how to build a digital organization that can manage for profit with digital analytics.

Understanding What to Analyze

The first step in the Analytics Value Chain is to figure out what exactly you are being asked to analyze, which should always be phrased in the form of a business question with a relevant business challenge, issue, or problem tied to it. Please see the discussion at the end of this chapter for a suggested framework for prioritizing analytics requests within a work request process. The following questions are not business questions, though they are asked frequently to digital analytics teams by business people: "How many unique visitors do we have?" or "How did X campaign do this week compared to last week?" These questions may seem important to the requestor and may be easy to answer—or they may take an inordinate amount of time—but they aren't actually business questions. These questions can evolve, with the analyst's help, into a single business question such as, "What was the impact on revenue and audience reach from the modifications we made to our inbound marketing campaigns—and what should we do next?" A business question must tie to a business issue or business concern in a way that goes beyond asking simply how the numbers changed—and ideally in a way that makes money or saves money.

Business Questions

The first question to ask is, "Why does this digital experience exist?" or "Why does this site exist?" These questions get to the heart of why your business operates on the Web. The answer could be "to sell products" or to "link audience to advertisers" or to "market our services and generate leads" and so on. By deconstructing and getting deeper into the reasons why the digital experience exists, you can start to determine the data and analytical approaches that can help—as well as get a sense of possible analytical deliverables. It is absolutely necessary for the analytics team to meet with stakeholders and discuss, agree, socialize and communicate, and gain corporate buy-in for the business questions to answer with digital analytics. If you don't plan to answer business questions, then you are planning to fail and will never be very successful with digital analytics. Begin by asking simple questions about goals and then help the businesspeople evolve those often-simplistic questions into erudite business questions that when answered will help fulfill business objectives and make more money. Make sure that you get sign-offs for business questions you analyze from the stakeholders who asked them, so that you have traceability into the origins of your analytics projects and remain aligned with the business.

Data Definitions

Data needs to be defined. Definitions need to be business-focused, operationally capable, technically accurate, and consensus-agreed. As such, the best digital data definitions have three forms:

1) business definitions, 2) operational definitions, and 3) technical definitions. You may have a Data Governance team responsible for data definitions. If not, the analytics team needs to define, socialize, practice, and enforce data definitions. You should create and gain sign-off on a "data definitions" document. A master data definition document that lists the definitions for all business data can be maintained. Since definitions need to be written for technical, operations, and business audiences, ensure that the analytics team aligns definitions with other teams whose input is required or who work with the data. It may be necessary for other teams to help define or totally define data or certain parts of the data definitions. For example, it makes sense for the technology teams, like IT and engineering, to create technical data definitions. Thus, the analytics team should ensure that they delegate the creation of data definitions when necessary. For example, the business teams must approve business definitions and as such should certainly be consulted when the definitions are created. See Chapter 6, "Defining, Planning, Collecting, and Governing Data in Digital Analytics."

Collecting, Verifying, and Governing Data (Before Analysis)

After identifying business questions and defining data, the next steps are to collect the data and verify that it is accurate and usable. While the notion of data collection is simple to comprehend, it can be nuanced and complicated to collect new data—and it can also be complex to bring together existing data from multiple sources. While many vendors offer an assortment of options for data collection, from JavaScript to API calls—the options for data verification and governance are more limited. It is not uncommon to manually audit data, spot-check it, or have multi-step review processes to ensure analytical data maintains an acceptable level of accuracy. For a detailed discussion of this topic, see Chapter 6.

Data Collection Specification

After you identify why you need data, the data you need, and the definitions for the data, you want to define the digital data that should be collected in a written document titled the "data collection specification." Data collection specifications can have many names. They may be called "the tagging spec" or the "data collection requirements" and so on. At a generalized level, a data collection specification is a hardcopy or softcopy document that identifies what digital data needs to be collected, when the data should be collected, under what conditions/constraints, and often how (that is, the technical method) the data should be collected. This artifact is part of the software and Internet development process and is as important as other common documents and artifacts, like the Functional Requirements Document (FRD), the Technical Requirements Documents (TRD), and even the Product Definitions Document (PDD). The specification is written by the analytics team to collect the data necessary to answer business questions. Data collection, of course, refers to code that needs to be placed into the digital experience (often JavaScript or API calls or direct server-to-server connections and so on)—and the sets of name-value pairs (either one-to-one or one-to-many relationships) that create the digital data to analyze. You might also create and define metadata about digital data using a number of formats, markups, and encodings. This critical step of creating documentation about data collection is crucial for digital analytics. While the format for a data collection specification can vary by team, the document generally includes the name of the behavior/action/event being tracked, the trigger for the behavior/action/event, the specific data collection call that needs to be made to the tool, and associated metadata marked-up in the format expected for the technology.

Data Collection Implementation

By working cross-functionally with IT, marketing, and product (and possibly other groups), you may at some point gain support of your tactical and operational needs to fulfill business requirements. In other words, you will need to work with other teams to ensure that your data collection specification is understood and prioritized into an implementation schedule. Depending on the priority given to analytical implementation by your IT and development, the implementation can take varying degrees of time. It may be necessary to make change requests into existing work, or the analytical implementation may be part of a roadmap or sprint. Regardless, the engineering or IT teams will then execute the technical work necessary to implement the code for collecting the digital data—on the agreed-upon schedule. Technical work when implementing digital data collection can and likely will be challenging and problematic because functionality, features, and flows always take precedent over analytics data collection. As a result, data collection can fall victim to being last-minute work or neglected in priority by development teams, or the implementation of data collection may be such an afterthought of engineering teams that it is "hotfixed" on the site. Actually, one of the most challenging activities for any digital analytics team is ensuring that the "tags" and other digital analytics data collection methods are implemented accurately and are maintained on the site across releases as the UX (and thus flows and features) change. Technologies like TMS (Tag Management Systems) can help reduce the challenges and speed implementation time of digital data collection by requiring less dependence on IT when changing or customizing digital data collection.

Data Collection Testing (QA)

After the "tags" or "calls" or "whatever new method" is supposedly successfully implemented on the site or in the digital experience, the analytics team (in most cases) is expected to test it—and then sign off for all the accountability or another's team's work. In other words, the analytics team is often expected to test the code for data collection implemented by developers, or at least test the output sent to the analytics tool by developer code. Be aware. In many cases, a Quality Assurance (QA) team might help with this work, or the engineering teams might focus on accuracy, but don't count on it or expect support for testing analytics data collection. Due to a lack of support from other teams for testing and validation, data collection for digital analytics is currently a challenge (and often a nightmare) where many analytics managers get blamed for things that they did not foresee coming. Be careful. Don't get heat for not knowing that a random developer stripped off a tag that collects KPI data. Make sure to test data collection when released and periodically as the site evolves and changes. The best companies who are most successful with analytics adequately staff resources and allot time to test and perform QA and test all analytics data collection. The worse companies fail to resource digital analytics testing—and tag testing. In the case where the analytics team is getting little to no support for tag testing, then the analytics team leadership should escalate the concern and build a business case to fund an investment to staff analytics testing and QA resources. In the worst case, it may be necessary for some companies to assess their QA team's leadership to determine why the analytics team gets no support for the QA team. I firmly believe that QA executives who don't support testing of tags and digital data collection are deficient in fulfilling their technical responsibilities to not only the analytics team, but also to the business.

Reporting and Dashboarding

When data have been collected, integrated, and verified, the analytics team will want to start exploring the data to begin observational analysis and to get a feel for the values, patterns, and trends in it. The team will want to segment the data in multi-dimensional ways, filter it, and drill-down into it. One of the main artifacts for beginning analytical activities are reports. From cross-tabulations and pivot tables to more simple data tables, the step of reporting is a crucial step that also needs verification. It is entirely possible that data can be accurate in the database, but for one reason or another, not in a report. Perhaps a manual error or a formula error ensued. In order to prevent inaccurate data in reporting, the reports need to be reviewed and validated before being made public or sent to stakeholders. Make sure not to confuse reporting with analysis. Reporting comes after analysis (ideally). For more information about reporting and dashboarding, see Chapter 7, "Reporting Data and Using Key Performance Indicators."

Report Creation

After the data has been proven accurate (and has been verified for integrity), someone on the reporting team (or analytics team) needs to create the reports that communicate the data in a structured and designed way. Reports, of course, are not analysis. Reports contain data and associated visualizations that can be analyzed and applied within analyses. In the best case, your analytics team must have access to the tools, databases, and data needed to build the reports you promised when you agreed to answer the business questions. The reports must be presented with written analysis that accompanies the data and visualizations in order to help people understand what the data is communicating. Chapter 7 contains a detailed discussion on reporting and best practices for building reports and dashboards.

Report Testing

The reports are accurate, but how accurate are they when they become scheduled, automated, sliced, diced, and drilled-down? What happens to reporting when it is not audited or managed through change? It becomes inaccurate and useless. Although the aggregates may look good, the detailed data may not meet the expected standards of accuracy, so the analytics team always needs to test, test, and retest until the reports are accurate. Otherwise, you shoot yourself in the foot and could potentially release data or systems that fail at the detailed level and then compromise all the other hard work you and your team did. Test and retest the reports and any data hanging off them. Then you should periodically audit the accuracy of reports. The periodicity for a report audit will vary, but could be monthly, quarterly, or after every release or system change.

Analyzing Data and Communicating and Socializing Analysis

The ultimate deliverable of any analytics team is analysis. Analysis is defined on Wikipedia as "the process of breaking a complex topic or substance into smaller parts to gain a better understanding of it. The technique has been applied in the study of mathematics and logic since before Aristotle (384–322 B.C.), though analysis as a formal concept is a relatively recent development." The word is a transcription of the ancient Greek ἀνάλυσις (*analusis*, "a breaking up," from *ana-* "up, throughout," and *lysis*, "a loosening"). Analysis is what an analytics team gets paid to do. While there are many other activities necessary to support the creation of an analysis, the preceding steps in the Analytical Value Chain only get you to the point where you can do your analytical job. The work analyzing data is what you get paid for, not tagging or the esoterics of digital data collection. For a detailed discussion of analytical concepts, methods, and techniques, see Chapter 5, "Methods and Techniques for Digital Analysis."

The next step in the Analytics Value Chain is to discuss and communicate the results of the analysis to the stakeholders who requested the work. Communicating data and analysis is an activity that occurs between humans and as such is filled with, often unstated, emotion. In many ways, the analytics team is providing transparency into the success (or not) of people's work, which ties into people's notions of self-worth and identity. As such, the analytics team must be sensitive to the personalities and nuances of the people in the business and their organizational behavior. The way you communicate analysis and your sensitivity and emotional intelligence makes or breaks your message. In many ways, when you are communicating analysis, the data matters less than what you are saying about the data. Be emotionally sensitive when socializing data and—regardless of what the data says—it is more likely that your message will be heard, understood, and believed. Just remember that no matter what, if you communicate analysis that changes people's commonly held beliefs or shows poor performance or bad work, then your analysis will be challenged no matter what you do.

Analysis and Report Communication

After you prepare and verify the reporting as completely accurate, it needs to be delivered. Be wary of scheduling reports and just sending them. Actually, avoid as much as possible scheduled automation for reports. Certainly you need to automate the scheduled delivery of reporting, but only in rare instances. It is better to provide self-service environments that require a business justification for data than to just send out data automatically because people are asking. The analytics team's time is short, the team has a lot to do, and the team never wants the same person to keep asking the same question every week. Thus, it is entirely possible for 80 percent of common reporting requests to set up self-service environments that provide a standard set of top-level reports. These reports should contain all commonly requested information. That way, the team can concentrate on the 20 percent of reporting that needs extra work and customization and on analyzing the clean data in the accurate reports. In the same sense, it is entirely possible to create a self-service environment for placing analysis (beyond reporting). Many larger companies make use of technologies like Socialcast, Sharepoint, a Wiki, or a blog to communicate key analysis to stakeholders. Regardless of how you select to communicate reporting and socializing analysis, if you haven't set up some level of self-service, you aren't doing your job very well and are likely wasting inordinate amounts of time preparing reports that in the worst case no one really looks at. It is only appropriate, of course, to send out any reporting and analysis after it is verified for accuracy initially. Make sure to spot-check regularly and periodically audit your self-service reporting to ensure it remains fresh, relevant, and accurate.

Analytical Communication and Socialization

Almost as key as the analysis is how the data, analysis, and research are presented to the stakeholders who have proposed and asked the business questions at the beginning of the Analytics Value Chain. Presenting data is dependent on science, but like all social communication, it is a human process that is artful. Sometimes, in the communication of data, how you say what you say is more important than the numbers, data, trends, and so on within the analysis. As an analytical professional, what you say, how you say it, who you say it to (first), and the manner by which you articulate (and your body language) may be more important to the successful delivery of analysis than the data itself. Make sure that you have some level of understanding of the politics and both business and social relationships when communicating and socializing data. As a human-to-human activity, the process of communication is where the analyst encodes his message using data, charts, graphs, words, a spreadsheet, or presentation (either virtually or in person) and expects the stakeholder to decode the information and agree with the analysis. Since digital analysis is complex and uses new concepts, it may be more difficult for people to decode what the analyst is trying to communicate; thus, it makes sense to have a strategy for analytics team communications. Several strategies that I have used and seen work in the past include the following:

- **Assigning a Navigator to one or more specific teams.** The idea of a Navigator is an analyst who is in charge of aligning closely and working collaboratively with one or more than one different team(s). For example, you may have one Navigator for marketing and another for product. This person would then be responsible for gathering analytical requirements and work, but not necessarily for doing the work. Instead, a Navigator may delegate work to other team members (if they don't do it themselves) and ensure the needs of the teams with which they are navigating are being met overall by the analytics team.

- **Delegating a specific analyst to communicate to a given set of stakeholders.** One common method is assigning a specific analyst to work with a specific businessperson. Given the small size of most analytics teams, the one-to-one approach should only be applied judiciously and to more senior stakeholders. The analyst is basically in charge of delivering, and in many cases actually doing, the analytical work requested by the stakeholder.

- **Producing regularly scheduled reporting and analytical deliverables.** A common way for the analytics team to remain in the critical path and part of the ongoing conversation and workstreams is to create a set of regularly occurring deliverables that meet the needs of stakeholders. From line-of-business reporting to KPI dashboards for executives, the options for producing regular reporting and analysis are only constrained by your requirements, budgets, and resources.

- **Hosting open "office hours" and regular training sessions.** One or more analysts make themselves available every week at the same time, or on request, to provide training and help to stakeholders who want to attend.

- **Using social technology to promote analysts to work together.** Blogs, Wikis, and collaboration technology like Socialcast or Yammer can help companies communicate analysis to the rest of the corporation and provide a mechanism for gathering feedback and new projects.

Optimizing and Predicting

Mature and high-functioning analytics teams that can execute the Analytics Value Chain are ready to move to optimization, prediction, and automation, which are discussed in more detail in Chapter 8, "Optimization and Testing with Digital Analytics: Test, Don't Guess." Optimization, at its most basic, is the outcome of decisions made to improve a digital experience. The most common optimization in which the digital analytics team may participate is landing page optimization and conversion optimization. Other types of optimization include customer optimization, product optimization, and more. Testing hypotheses and controlled experimentation is necessary when optimizing a digital experience. Specialized software products for optimization like A/B testing and multivariate testing are available from many vendors.

Optimization may include predicting what may happen from past data, but frequently the data science of using data to predict a future state in order to improve the potential outcome of that state is a separate discipline named *Predictive Analytics*. As a type of data science, Predictive Analytics uses machine learning and statistical data mining methods, techniques, and algorithms in order to model data and apply analytical techniques like regression. The goal of Predictive Analytics is to apply existing data and the independent variables in it to predict a dependent variable or identify some potential future business condition. For example, predictive analytics can be used to identify what type of conversion, revenue, or profitability could occur if a customer behaved in a certain way, or based on current behavioral patterns, if certain customer segments are likely to convert or churn. Both optimization and predictive modeling can create opportunities for automation with digital data, from dynamic personalization to advanced recommendation engines to sense-and-detect technologies that automate interactions with digital interfaces.

Optimization

After the data has been collected, verified, analyzed, communicated, and accepted as truthful and valid for answering the business questions, the key is to take "action" by "optimization." Buzzwords, yes, but they make sense. *Optimization* involves answering the inevitable "What about this?" and "What about that?" questions that arise from stakeholders consuming your analysis.

What else and if questions need subsequent work efforts and cycles to establish answers—and such work can be requested by stakeholders via the formal analytics work request process. Be careful not to let stakeholders shift the analytical work initially requested to turn into an optimization process. Ultimately, analytics should lead to optimization, but optimization itself is distinct work. Analytical optimization is not easy and requires a full buy-in across the cross-functional business to execute on the Analytical Value Chain. Optimization may be as simple as testing features, functions, or flows over time to figure out which provides the best business performance. More complex and expensive optimization programs use entire teams that create "recipes" and various combinations of content, creative, offers, and text, which are deployed into digital experience using multivariate testing software. This type of software then tells the analytics team the best combination of the elements of UX that provide the best increase in business performance for a given goal. For example, multivariate software can recommend the optimal combination of site colors, graphics, creative text, and so on that provides the highest conversion to a specific customer segment. You may often hear "optimization" discussed about increasing the conversion rate of landing pages linked by marketing campaigns.

Prediction

Prediction is often discussed in the same context as optimization, which is demystified previously and in Chapter 8. Prediction is different than optimization. Optimization is more of an existential concept and set of related technologies and science, whereas prediction is the application of statistical methods for data mining and machine learning, often using software programs, to identify what might happen next or the next best course of action to take. Optimization can make use of predictive modeling, algorithms, and related data science. Predictive analysts, often called Data Scientists, create the algorithms and models for automating the prediction of future business events. As I mentioned, it is entirely possible that an optimization tool or analytics program might use predictive analytics in some way, but it is important to understand that prediction and optimization are different and unique but may co-occur in the delivery of analytical business value. Predictive analytics makes use of controlled experiments and data science in order to predict, optimize, estimate, and forecast future performance.

Automation

The outcomes and learning from testing and optimization programs and from data sciences, like Predictive Analytics, can create opportunities where digital data can be used to automate a digital experience. Even digital data about previous behaviors, expressed preferences and propensities, and other digital expressions of interest can provide digital data for *automation*. A simple example of automation is when a person self-identifies a preference for a specific topic and, upon the next visit, the person has dynamically customized content experience. Another example is where specific transactions, such as deposits in an online banking app and viewing an investment product, may cause a promotional offer to be automatically sent over email. In instances where digital data is recognized as necessary to automate business processes, the analytics team will help define, collect, verify, and confirm the preparation of digital data to power the automation to meet business requirements. Automation is one of the rare cases in digital analytics where it is absolutely helpful, and often critical, to have real-time, or near real-time data, as opposed to timely data.

Demonstrating Economic Value

Corporations and businesses exist to create shareholder value in the form of profit and retained earnings. Successful companies create substantial economic value by producing and selling products and services for consumers. As such, the highest and best use of analytics teams is tying back the digital behavior, events, and transactions to financial metrics, such as cost reduction, increased efficiency, new and incremental revenue, and boosted or enhanced profitability.

Tying to Revenue, Costs, and Profit

Any MBA or businessperson will agree that when an analytics program can tie itself to profit, then the future is so bright the whole team should wear shades. More seriously, to prove the analytics team value ties the team's actions to revenue, profit, or reduced cost, demonstrate the impact of your team on top-line revenues or bottom-line profit and retained earnings. The derivative metric, Conversion Rate, is one such metric that helps you tie human behavior to monetary performance. Other data can also be proxied for monetary value. For example, what is the revenue generated by a marketing campaign and what was the cost of the campaign in order to calculate profitability of digital marketing? Every action, event, transaction, and behavior on a website can be tied to a financial measure (or a score) and can be associated in real-value or proxied on approximate value to tie digital analytics into financial data. What's the value of an on-site search? What's the value of new user registration? What's the value of the newsletter signup? By benchmarking how the site's behavior and metrics translate into dollars, the analytics team can track the impact of their recommendations, optimizations, predictions, and automations on the top- and bottom-lines of the income statement—and, thus, hopefully prove that the business is not only competing, but succeeding and profiting with digital analysis.

The Analytics Value Chain presented encapsulates the complexity of executing on digital analytics cross-functionally from beginning to end in a way that can be applied and customized to your business as you execute work within your established processes.

The Analytics Work Request Process

The question still remains at the top of the digital analyst's mind, "How do I ensure that I do the right work for the right people?" An analytics team's time is limited and valuable, and can't be spent on reporting or analyzing data that doesn't have strong business justification behind it. In many cases, people in the business do not realize the work necessary to produce a report or analysis, so they ask the analytics team for reports that are just simply a waste of time to produce primarily because the data can't be actioned or the person requesting it can't do anything with it. These requests are called "Just Want to Look at It" requests. (I call these requests JWaLIT requests.) In order to reduce JWaLIT and ensure the analytics team concentrates only on the most high-value work, the team must create a process for collecting, reviewing, accepting/rejecting, approving, prioritizing, and scheduling analytics work.

The Analytics Work Request process is helpful for receiving, reviewing, allocating, initiating, executing, and closing reporting requests. It must be created within the company and fit into existing processes. As such, you may want to consider using an existing ticketing system already deployed by IT, engineering, customer service, the help desk, or maybe you want to create something proprietary or buy suitable software off the shelf. Regardless of how you choose to capture and close analytics work, just make sure you have one system to track your reporting requests from the initial analytics request to the confirmation from the person/team that requested the analysis is satisfied with the deliverable and finally to the follow-up meeting between the analyst and stakeholder.

After a ticketing system is available, all people requesting reports should fill out a form, preferably online. An online system enables the virtual workflow to be tracked. The form should request the following information—and clearly state that if the analytics team does not get the information required, the request will not be reviewed until the information required is submitted. Analytical requests also need a service-level agreement (SLA) so that the analytics team can review and respond to the reporting request within 48 hours. (Preferably sooner; however, within 24 hours is always appreciated by stakeholders.) Keep in mind that what your analytics team needs to start doing work may be different than what is presented below. Also note that there are exceptions to the work request process, and not all requests will end up in it despite best efforts:

- **Is revenue at risk?** If revenue is at risk, then the analysis will be done! Profitable revenue is the chi, the life force of any business. And analytics that supports revenue generation is the highest kind of analysis. But you must prove it. Just because you work for a group that produces revenue doesn't mean your request going unfulfilled puts revenue at risk. Tell the team exactly where the risk is—don't generalize.

- **Who's asking?** Is it your boss asking, her boss, his boss' boss? Then the work gets done. We're not talking HiPPO (Highest Paid Person's Opinion) here. We're just talking MoPPO (Most Powerful Person in the Organization). Keep your boss happy.

- **How difficult is the request?** Just because something is "too hard" doesn't mean it won't get done, but as an analytics professional, you need to set delivery expectations when requests are so difficult that they will take time. Perhaps the schema needs to be modified, changed, or just simply remodeled to get that data; maybe you need to rewrite the tags, reconfigure the tool, build a bunch of new reports, and figure out the data delivery tool. Maybe five other groups need to work collaboratively in coordination with all their other projects just to get the data to a point where it can be reported. Manage the expectations of the requester.

- **Can it be self-serviced?** Just because requesters don't know how to use the tool nor RTFM (Read The Fine Manual), it's too slow, don't know where the report is, can't understand the report, don't get Web analytics, don't know how to write SQL, or don't know where to look, doesn't mean the Web analytics team is going to do for you what your job requires you to do. The analytics team should teach self-servicing as a best practice because wasting time easy fishing in shallow waters means you may miss the big analytics catch in the deep data pool! Teach your stakeholders that the analytics team is not a mathematically inclined "pizza delivery service" that delivers reports with all sorts of special toppings as requested. Instead, work with stakeholders so they understand that the analytics team provides a value-added analysis service, for those who want it, and not just reports (in 30 minutes with special toppings requested).

- **When is the analysis needed?** Of course, a time frame helps you to prioritize. Make sure the stakeholders identify when they want the analysis delivered, and ensure that the timelines make sense to the analysts and any supporting teams required to help deliver the work. The requesters of analytics' work will always want the weight of the world at microsecond N during the equinox by the end of the day tomorrow. They're probably out of luck unless revenue is at risk or they are the bosses. A week? Well, maybe, but the weight of the world requires querying the

Atlas database and queries don't run like Mercury ran races in ancient times. With all classical kidding aside, the analyst needs to set expectations based on a number of interplaying factors about when the work can be delivered. Don't overcommit or commit to unreasonable timelines. Analysts need to stand their ground and take the necessary time to do the job while still working with a high level of urgency.

- **Why is the analysis needed?** Unless the C-level executive suite is asking, you must seek to understand "why" the analysis is needed. Are people simply curious about the number of X that goes to Y from Z, or about the time spent on page Z of your microsite? Or do they need to make a real business decision to advance the core mission of your company? By communicating to the analytics team the importance of the request's "why," analysts can use that information to prioritize against other work, and stakeholders can use that information to express priority for quicker service. Analysts that know why they are delivering can more effectively seek out data to collect or analyze—and can also more properly frame the final analytics deliverable.

- **What data do you think you need?** Oftentimes, especially in large corporations, the stakeholder may already have a good idea of what data they need from past experience. Thus, it is helpful to ask if they know what data they need. Perhaps another team or employee used to produce the analysis they want, or maybe the data exists but no one has built reporting. By asking this question, you may find out that the request takes less work and time than you originally thought. Don't just assume the data does or does not exist; even if the stakeholder says one thing or another, check around with your team and other teams.

- **What happens when you don't get the data?** Asking this question helps you assess the priority level and business impact—since most stakeholders think their requests are the most urgent. In many cases they are incorrect, but in other cases the work request may be of the utmost urgency for the analytics team to prioritize. The analytics team will reject or accept requests based on this answer in order to manage and deliver a workload. In cases when the analytics team determines that executing requested work will have limited impact on the business, the work can be rejected or pushed to a later date when resources are more available. On the counterpoint, this question also helps to identify critical work—and also provides insight into the business activities that occur after the analysis and who else might see the analysis.

As an analytics professional, use these questions to

- Help you prioritize your work.
- Figure out what's important.
- Determine how to communicate and manage expectations.
- Deliver what's necessary to drive the business as soon as possible.
- Not get caught wasting valuable time constantly servicing low-value or poorly requests.

Now that you have reached the end of this chapter, you're familiar with some fundamental concepts within analytics and when "doing analytics." The P's of analytics provide an easy mnemonic device for understanding what is required to succeed with digital analytics and digital analytics organizations. The Analytics Value Chain, on the other hand, explains the work activities that can be performed to generate value with analytics. The conceptual framework of the Analytics Value Chain encapsulates the different work that can be performed when managing or working on a digital analytics team. Finally, you have learned how to capture, articulate, and begin to understand how to prioritize the types of analytics work requested by stakeholders. Keep these foundational constructs in mind as you continue to read this book and learn more about building a digital analytics organization.

3

Building an Analytics Organization

The single most important element for succeeding with digital analytics is the analytics team. People, one of the P's of analytics, are the primary drivers of the perception of success (or not) of the analytics team. In fact, beyond technology, beyond process, beyond data science, beyond big data, beyond optimization and prediction, it is the analytics team that does the hard analytical work. The people on the analytics team offer the essential human interface to stakeholders for analytics projects. The team provides the manual processing through which requests for analytics are assessed for feasibility, prioritized, tracked, delivered, followed-up, and closed. More important, the people on the team provide the front-office support and act forward-facing as the representation of the team. Thus, you must employ people who have the right combination of technical, business, and social skills to deliver effective and insightful analysis to business people.

What is the right combination of technical, business, and social skills? The answer is certainly subjective based on the unique needs of each business. Due to the mainstreaming and growth of the importance in analytics in today's business world, I often hear the words "data scientist" and "growth hacker," and long lists of advanced statistical skills, expertise with newer technologies (such as Hadoop or Cassandra), or fluency with Business Intelligence (BI) software packages. Although it is undoubtedly important for the team to have the necessary level of skills and capability to collect, process, and manage the technicality of analytics, these skills are not always necessary; however, relevant technical skills are useful to hire when building an analytics team. After all, even the most esoteric technical and mathematical skills can be taught to intelligent (and willing) people who want to learn. That said, it is necessary, of course, to have the appropriate level of technical skills and/or support from the right technology teams, but remember, analytics is not database operations. Take for example, the dearth of data scientists who understand digital data. It is not unheard of to hire data scientists who have statistical skills developed in other fields, and then teach them the digital concepts to execute data science on digital data.

This chapter provides a framework for building or rebuilding an analytics team so that it can focus on creating business value, which must be the ultimate outcome of successful analysis regardless of the underlying technologies or analytical methods that are used. This chapter has been structured to provide the following:

- The types of skills helpful for analysts to possess
- The different types of work and organizational structures commonly seen on analytics teams
- A discussion about formulating a business justification for an investment consideration to create an analytics team and fund investment in analytics technology and tools—and a framework for presenting it to business stakeholders
- How to prove and present the proof that the analytics team is creating business value—and thus, justify the existence of the team
- The organization strategy and structure commonly seen for analytics teams as well as a discussion of the roles and responsibilities for analytics team members and how to create them
- Ways to enhance your career by getting involved in the analytics industry and community
- A set of steps and tips for building your digital analytics organization

At the eMetrics Business Optimization conference in 2009, I communicated my perspective on the general personality traits of a successful digital analyst. These attributes may not necessarily be found in professional activities or determined by reading a resume, but rather, these helpful life skills may be present in the best candidates from personal development outside the world of work (and, of course, within the world of work). Useful skills to find in people to staff the digital analytics team are as follows:

- **Numeracy:** Understanding how to work with numbers by applying mathematics and statistics. The analytics team must have the ability to think numerically and use quantitative skills.

- **Sufficiently Technical:** Knowing—in the required level of detail for the job—how to use the systems and technologies in which digital data is collected, stored, reported, and analyzed is necessary, and can often be grown from within the team if expertise already exists to mentor and coach.

- **Business-focused:** Centering analysis on business value by using data to reduce cost or increase revenue. The best analysts understand linking digital analytics to improving business planning, performance, and profit.

- **Data Visualizers:** Using tools that create charts and graphs to tell visual stories about important data and relationships between data. Beyond tool usage, the best analysts have the innate capability to think visually about abstract and concrete concepts.

- **Pattern Recognizers:** People who can see patterns in data and visualizations. Similar to the ability to think visually, analysts need to be able to see patterns in not only visualizations but also in data tables and related quantitative (and qualitative data).

- **Multi-dimensional:** Knowing how to think across multiple concepts and ideas that may or may not be related directly or indirectly. The ability to examine and drill down into data, reporting, visualizations, and analysis in many facets: internal and external data, social and political, strategic versus tactical, histograms versus scatterplots, profit versus loss, revenue versus cost, linear versus quadratic, and so on.

- **Curious:** Expressing a desire to learn new subjects, concepts, topics, and constructs. Analysis requires people who are curious and want to dig deeply into subjects both that they already understand and that are new and require learning.

- **Inquisitive:** Digging deeply into details of what one already knows and is learning. Following curiosity is the ability to inquire about the inner workings and underlying detail of data and research. The best analysts are naturally inquisitive and have personalities that want to explore, understand, reconcile, and make recommendations and decisions based on their learnings and knowledge.

- **Thoughtful:** Because analytics involves working with ambiguity and, many times, less than optimal data, the best analysts are thoughtful in their approach to problem solving. In addition, human communication demands a thoughtful approach when presenting data. Thus, a level-headed emotional intelligence that can socialize and convince people via empathy and alignment is important in analytical talent.

- **Strong-willed:** Analytics can be a challenging field to work in for many reasons: From having poor data, unclear requirements, insufficient systems, a lack of resources, and so on, the best analysts maintain a strong will to do the work required. The best analysts are persistent with their work, projects, analysis, and recommendations and are unwavering in their beliefs when they know they are correct, but also can see the same issue through the eyes of another with a differing opinion. The best analysts build consensus based on accurate information—potentially despite pressures to do otherwise.

A world-class, successful analytics team does not just form from stardust, magic spells, and the best intentions of technology or businesspeople. It takes years for analytics professionals to grow experientially and mature professionally within the right organizations to enrich their skill sets to inspire and deliver true analytical team greatness. Like managing any team, the theories of team psychology, personal and intrapersonal motivation, inspiration, and leadership are all relevant when managing digital analytics teams.

Thomas Davenport, in his book *Analytics at Work*, defines the following structures for analytics teams:

- **Centralized:** All analytical groups report into a common leader and function, like finance.

- **Consultative:** All analysts are part of one organization and "hired" out with appropriate cross-company and departmental chargebacks.

- **Functional:** The analysts are located within each functional group, like marketing and IT, where the analysts concentrate on the data in that function.

- **Hub and spoke:** Analysts are in each functional group but loosely unified, in some matrixed way to a larger conceptual team, often called an *Analytics Center of Excellence.*

- **Decentralized:** Analysts exist all over the company with little logic, control, or centralization of resources, accountability, data, reporting, analysis, or leadership.

You may be wondering, "What does a digital analytics team do?" Beyond the concepts in Chapter 2, "Analytics Value Chain and the P's of Digital Analytics," in my experience, a digital analytics team does the following:

- **Gather, collect, measure, report, and analyze data based on business questions and business requirements, coordinating with necessary teams to execute programs and projects.** The goal of the analytics team is, as mentioned, to analyze data and tell the business-relevant data stories that create value by either generating profitable revenue or reducing costs. Many methods, from key performance indicator (KPI) dashboarding to daily analytics meetings and so on, exist for improving, enhancing, and optimizing the profitability of your business with digital data by using it to improve conversion rates, refine and innovate product offerings, improve customer experience, and enable an accurate foundation based on real data for fact-based decisions. The analytics team often assesses feasibility, captures, prioritizes, and/or otherwise approves requirements communicated by the business and other corporate stakeholders—and may also support other teams when the analytics team is not directly creating or involved in the data and analysis (in such structures as decentralized analytics organizations).

- **Provide a cross-enterprise viewpoint into customer and user behavior across all the business globally.** A global analytics team, when effectively resourced, can help understand the macro and micro patterns that exist in rough data to smooth it to recognize common behavioral patterns that measure metrics across different business units. Analysis, such as customer attrition for the sales team or lifetime value for the marketing team, to profitability analysis for the executive team and so on, can be provided from digital analysis and the people on the analytics team.

- **Provide data to drive fact-based strategic and tactical decision making about the business.** The adage is, "You can't manage what you don't measure." (And, of course, that the chief marketing officer [CMO] knows half of the marketing budget is being wasted, but not which half.) If a company does not have a dedicated analytics team, it is likely not managing its data as effectively as possible—and thus its business isn't using analytics to assist and guide decision making and planning for maximizing revenue, profitability, and shareholder value.

• **Centralize analytics reporting (as required and as possible) for consistency and accuracy and provide a self-service environment.** If everyone's job were to work with the data and create meaningful reports and cogent business analyses, analytics teams would not need to exist. But undoubtedly where there are many "cooks" in the "data kitchen," there will be many "stews." And one thing an analytics professional never wants is too many people stewing around the multiple sets of data (which are most often contradictory). In fact, having multiple data sources that report similarly or identically named metrics, but are defined differently, can be common to find when building an analytics organization. In environments where data proliferation can cause redundancy, poorly defined data, and confusion, the centralized management of analytics is helpful. Thus, an analytics team's primary role, whether the team is centralized or not, should be to control the data, reporting, analytics, and research from phase zero to the final analytical deliverable. Undoubtedly, a business requires some level of self-service on managed and optimized data sources. Actually, some people outside the analytics team may even need access to the raw data and the ability to query it, too. Those cases and requests should be occurring rarely and with strong business justification followed up by a data governance process to authorize and enable data access permissions for a limited period of time.

Only an empowered analytics team that sits centrally within the organization, unbiased and removed as much as possible from corporate politics, will ultimately succeed.

Note

Although many managers may argue that centralization is not necessary, I would respectfully disagree based on the many years I have led analytics. One of my former managers and now a good friend used to joke with me that although certain aspects of analytics may exist across other teams, the CEO wants "a throat to choke" because I was accountable for all the behavioral data in a publicly traded company, and as my manager, so was he. Centralization provides that throat to choke, but also empowers the team by providing a full body to action and use the data.

- **Participate in the process to creating standard data definitions that are consistent with customer business data requirements.** Process, as discussed in Chapter 2, is crucial to successful analytical execution. Thus, it is also crucial that the analytics leadership and often key members of the team be "at the table" when decisions are made about data, data requirements, data definitions, data governance, data investigations, data maintenance, data correction and remediation, and so on. That way, the analytics team can be sure to participate in the creation or evolution of processes that support analytical delivery.

- **Coordinate with technology on backend infrastructure, reporting tools, and delivery platforms.** While the more simple analytics teams may have a limited set or even just one analytics tool, it is more common for the analytics teams to have multiple sources of data and tools that may collect and report redundant or very similar data. In some technology-rich and complex infrastructural environments, it is common to have hundreds or thousands of servers for analytics running in a data center—and even data existing in cloud environments, too. As the business owner of analytics, you need to understand how the technical environment impacts the business inside and out—in enough detail to be able to make decisions about the technology to use and the impact of using particular technology. That said, you don't need to understand every single technical detail and nuance. That is a waste of your business time. Leave the details to the technology and IT partners and hold them strongly accountable for delivering against a service-level agreement (SLA) that at least meets and exceeds the Software as a Service (SaaS) vendor's SLA (who may be drooling to replace your IT team's analytics responsibilities). Make sure that you have influence and, if possible, final say in the technology and tools used by the analytics team.

- **Facilitate faster, more informed decisions through consultative and analytical support of functional business partners.** An analytics team must be *consultative* and *social*. Remember the importance of communicating and socializing data in the Analytics Value Chain we reviewed in Chapter 2. If your analytics team simply sits in their cubes or is isolated from the business, is nested deeply in IT, and bases their work on Functional Requirements Documentation or some other Project Management Professional (PMP) artifact, then your analytics team is probably completely ineffective and is likely considered overhead (or soon will be). A team of "report monkeys" who don't get out and "teach the research" and collaborate, lock in step with business stakeholders is not really an analytics team at all. It's a glorified pool of computer typists who prepare reports—or worse, a team of database people who just make sure the tables have data but are uncertain about how the data are used or applied in the business. Analytics is a front office business function, which has a critical and necessary backend infrastructure for creating and reporting data. Analytics teams work with the business and help make money; whereas, technical teams (who may call themselves "analytics" but do not analyze) that manage infrastructure are not really analysts, but technologists who maintain the operations of servers, data collection, databases, tools, and reports.

- **Drive measurement and accountability through goal setting/KPIs and performance reviews.** If you "manage what you can measure," after (or before, preferably) you do work, you are already able to set benchmarks based on historical performance and goals to which to target performance. Your analytics team can help the business understand past performance to set benchmarks and future goals. Then, in your KPI reporting, you can use the past performance, benchmarks, and goals to analyze current performance and predict future performance. Analytics data, reporting, consulting, and research can then help the business understand if activities meet the goal— and if not, or if so, what else can be done to do even better.

- **Help internal customers navigate data and analysis reporting.** An analytics team, in the best case, is like the Delta Force. They can parachute into a business problem like cold-calculating mercenaries and identify with precision and validity the data, analytics, and research necessary to solve the business challenge. In this regard, the internal analytics team should act as consultants helping key members of the business (and the business in general) gain fluency, competency, and confidence in learning how to apply the data to their jobs to "compete (and win) with analytics."

- **Deepen customer relationships.** Customer Relationship Management (CRM) analytics applied directly to internal customer demographic, firmagraphic, and other sales data, both pre- and post-sales, is an emerging field in which analytics is being used to create, build, strengthen, maintain, and retain customers. A type of digital analysis named *social analytics* exists, which refers to using social media data collected from the various social sites and networks globally with internal CRM data and integrating it with behavioral data from digital experiences to create business value.

- **Create additional or new profitable revenue streams through data and analysis.** The best of the best outcome of a successful analytics team is making money for the business—and thus keeping shareholders, management, and employees satisfied. Many companies have opportunities for monetizing their data assets, but fail to take action. Data about customers and customer segments can be sold to other businesses. For example, a career website may sell skill set and labor rate information entered by users to companies that use it to plan labor investment activities. A fashion retailer may identify early adopting trends in global styles.

- **Reduce cost.** Data can be used to control waste, improve efficiency, optimize products, and many other ways specific to the nuances of the geography, sector, industry, company, corporate culture, and team. Analytical data can be used to target the best geographies in which to market offline events—or better targeted online advertising.

Digital analytics is often put into a marketing context or considered as part of a marketing function. You can use the data to identify the highest performing marketing and advertising campaigns and optimize the poorer performing ones. Analytics assists in identifying and helping to nurture leads. Analytics informs marketers of audience attributes and behavior so that the best and most appropriate messages can be targeted to them. Analytics must be used to optimize search. Although all these statements are true, several other business functions can benefit from having access to digital analysis:

- **Product development:** Data is crucial to the successful development and ongoing extension of the feature set for online products. Data-driven decision making helps inform product managers of how to enhance a product to meet core users' needs. From tracking and testing elements of user experience for measuring and optimizing conversion, the data captured and reported by analytics can help product developers quickly determine and extend what works and eliminate what doesn't work in the features and flows they design.

- **Sales:** Arming the sales staff with data that identifies the attributes of an audience and its demographics, psychographics, and firmagraphics provides the underpinning for sales presentations, for identifying potential customers and the reach and frequency of audiences, and for demonstrating success of a site compared to competitors. Sales teams armed with these data can take advantage of them and sell more strategically and with more information to guide the sales process.

- **Finance:** Specific actions taken by customers or users of a site generate value that can be quantified in hard currency—from product purchases to advertising revenue to real or proxy values for certain actions, such as registrations or clickthroughs. The bean counters can analyze trends and deviations in this data to realize, estimate, and predict business cycles and their material effect on corporate finance.

- **Customer service:** Data about trends and absolute numbers in customer attrition or account cancellations, surges in new registrations, increases in the purchases of certain products, and the volume of customer transactions can help inform staffing levels in customer service and pinpoint areas of concerns for customer service specialists.

- **Engineering and research and development (R&D):** Although marketers don't care much for the technical data available in analytics tools, such as Java-Script support, Flash, Flex, Silverlight, browser types, screen resolution, and more, these types of data are useful to technologists who are hard at work developing upcoming releases. Technically related digital data can also be used to help the creative teams design digital experiences and marketing teams better understand them.

• **User experience:** Designers should look at the (often-maligned) browser overlay and heat mapping visualizations, click tracking reports, and form completion and abandonment reports to understand how their designs can (or cannot) work to fulfill goals.

Other business functions can benefit from digital data as well. Business planners may look at data representing seasonal traffic trends and purchasing cycles. Strategists may use the data to generate recommendations for extending the business at its edges. Business line managers can segment data related to the performance of certain products or customers.

Justifying Investment in the Analytics Team

With the popularity of big data and data science, many companies are staffing analytics teams. Actually, it is no longer uncommon to see analytics teams at large companies that have 10 and even 20 people responsible for phases of the Analytical Value Chain—and perhaps even all phases whether directly, indirectly, or matrixed. However, it is much more common to see small analytics teams of 1 to 5 people. While I have seen teams of 50 people, such investment is uncommon and usually crosses both technology and business functions and resources.

Still, a number of reasons exist why companies do not fund investment in analytics teams. Following are some of the common reasons:

• No investment is available.

• Cost is prohibitive.

• The analytics team hasn't proven the investment is justified.

• A lack of understanding exists why the investment is necessary.

• Organizational limitations and process deficiencies exist.

As you progress through this chapter, we discuss each of these scenarios.

No Available Investment

The most common reason I've heard cited for not investing in an analytics team is that there is no investment money available. Often this excuse is met with a befuddlement in many companies because it may seem investment is going on all around you, in teams that help your team, compete with your team, and are unrelated to your team. It may be confusing and frustrating to accept a "no" answer to funding a new headcount in the analytics team, but there is undoubtedly a reason behind the answer you have been given.

Most often analytics teams do not get investment because they have not sufficiently planned ahead to justify the role. What happens is that the analytics team does work that gets noticed, or attempts to insert itself into business process and deliver value, which it does. Then the company starts to ask the analytics team to do a lot of work. Suddenly the team is inundated with analytics requests. Although the Analytics Value Chain (discussed in Chapter 2) may exist, the number of requests may overwhelm existing staff, leading to stress and demotivation. The team begins to complain to the analytics manager that they don't have enough resources, so the analytics manager then makes a request to hire a new analyst. And voila, rejected! No budget.

The issue with the common situation presented is, of course, to estimate in advance by *at least two quarters* the analytics staffing investment you need. Although two fiscal quarters may sound too slow, 26 weeks is sufficient time for business cycles to determine whether the expensive investment in headcount is necessary. In some cases, you need to plan for every fiscal year in advance. Thus, at best you must predict analytical team investment needs 6 months to 2 years out. And the request for headcount should be submitted at least 6 months before you need it.

Cost Is Prohibitive

Experienced analytics professionals who have sufficient business and technical skills are rare. Professionals who have achieved the upper echelons of analytical management in medium-to-large size corporations know that as of 2013, their skills are in high demand and command premium when compared to not only other analytics professionals with similar seniority (that is, years' experience) but often to other professionals in different fields who have more seniority.

The Digital Analytics Association and IQ Workforce produced the following data showing salary levels at various levels across the United States. The data shows salaries range from $60,000 USD for entry-level analysts to more than $200,000 for analytics leaders. Salaries in more expensive areas to live (such as New York City) did not necessarily maintain parity with less expensive cities such as Atlanta. In other words, you would have more discretionary income working as a digital analytics professional in the South than in the northern United States—all things being equal. Meanwhile salaries are about the same. This actionable data helps counter the idea that cost is prohibitive for justifying analytics investments, because if salaries are at a premium, then there is a scarcity of resources. Thus, if your company can't afford the cost of experienced professionals, the following paths can be taken:

- Train existing internal resources.
- Hire external consultants.
- Use interns.
- Co-share or chargeback the cost across business units.

The challenge, of course, with overcoming prohibitive cost is that you might end up creating experienced analytical professionals who can in their next job earn a significantly higher salary than their current salary, so they find a new job.

Lacking Proof of Business Value to Fund Analytics

Funding investment in a business function means the business must realize some form of value for the function to continue to exist and to pay back the investment—especially where hiring staff (a corporation's most expensive asset) is concerned. The same rule applies to analytics teams. The best analytics teams can show how the outcome of their analysis, insights, and recommendations can create business value. The challenge, of course, is tracking and estimating the business value. Following is a business example.

At one point in my career, I was responsible for managing analytics on a site focused on conversion. The goal of the site was to sell products. To move the audience through the site, an advanced customer profiling personalization and targeting engine was created that allocated all visitors (whether new or repeat) to a particular customer type. Based on that customer type, the visitors were then presented a series of merchandising modules with a relevant offer that was thought to match the intent of the customers, thus compelling them to click on the module and the eventual path to purchase and conversion.

It all sounded excellent in the product specifications; however, the data and my team's analysis showed the targeting of the various merchandising modules was not perfected, and actually, seasonality impacted the purchasing process. The analytics team recommended overhauling the content, offer, placement, and timing of the modules to better reflect customer behavior. As a result, the new merchandising mix was assessed after several weeks against previous performance and a known baseline. The result showed that that new modules were outperforming the previous modules in some cases by 500 percent, which translated into an increase of more than $200,000 in attributable incremental revenue per week, which otherwise may have been missed.

It is exactly these types of analytical "wins" that can be traced directly back to the business value that should be logged whenever they happen. This log can then be consulted to provide direct evidence that the analytics team creates value and how much value. It is so important to keep detailed logs of analytics value to not only justify expanding the team, but also to justify the existence of the analytical function if it is ever challenged.

Lack of Understanding of Why an Investment Is Necessary

An analytics manager may run into senior management who simply do not understand why an investment in analytics is necessary. The analytics industry often jokes about the concept of the HiPPO (the highest paid person's opinion), and although the term is insulting to management and promotes a negative lens through which to look at leadership, I have often thought "This is the HiPPO's excuse" when running up against senior management who doesn't "get it." "Getting it" is an analytics industry term that refers to an overwhelming cognition and recognition of competing and winning with analytics.

The analytics manager's goal to overcome a lack of understanding—to put it in digital analytics terms—is to make the HiPPO or the "slightly-paid-more-than you" manager "get it." The explanation behind the last two sections dealing with cost and proof can go a long way in helping a manager understand why investment is necessary. But be warned; you can always lead the proverbial horse to water but you cannot make him drink. Here are some of the main reasons why your colleagues in the decision process for funding analytics may not "get it":

• **No time.** Executives and people at all levels already have a lot to do.

• **I already look at the reports!** Confusion between reporting and analysis is frequent.

• **I already know the business.** Overconfidence in "gut," innate, or learned ability to manage without data is not uncommon.

• **The data has been wrong, so I have no confidence.** Poor prior experiences with data and reporting as well as with analytics teams may impact future consideration.

• **We have all the data we need but we aren't analyzing it.** Given the volume of, often extraneous, data collected by digital analytics systems, there may be a belief that the size of the data is indicative of quality. In addition, missed past opportunities may weigh on the mind.

• **The team is large enough, but the data isn't being produced.** Big data requires resources and infrastructure to handle it, and appropriate investments need to be made.

As you can see in the preceding themes, senior management doesn't see value in the analytics function. Whereas each of these "reasons" is different, the motif is the same. The analytics team isn't delivering the perception of value to senior management. This issue does not mean that the analytics team is not creating value, which may be the case, but it is often a function of the analytics team not effectively communicating the value. Changing perception of the analytics team such that the value is understood can be accomplished by the following:

- Create an analytics team meeting across functions and hosted virtually on a continuous and periodic basis.
- Provide "open office hours," and invite the internal customers of the analytics team to ask questions.
- Ask senior management to meet with the analytics team to introduce roles and responsibilities as well as projects and the value created by each team member and the team as a whole.
- Institute a data governance strategy. For more discussion about data governance, see Chapter 6, "Defining, Planning, Collecting, and Governing Data in Digital Analytics."
- Determine how the analytics team spends its time executing work from start to finish.
- Establish a newsletter that identifies key projects delivered within a specific time period, such as monthly or quarterly.

The preceding solutions involve additional work communicating and socializing with the people who ultimately decide whether the analytics team is useful and contributing to the business. Make sure not to simply expect people to understand what the analytics team does annually, quarterly, and daily. Remember you aren't doing the job if all you do is work with systems, data, and reports all day. You must teach people to understand and thus respect the Analytics Value Chain and the analytics process in Chapter 2.

Overcoming Resistance to Investment Due to Organizational and Process Deficiencies

Corporations are filled with people who have perceptions and opinions on business events, such as legacy products, new products and innovations, and the day-to-day course of business. Organizations, as a result, are inherently political, and the politics around analytics are a special case. Consider the centralized analytics team that is responsible for the entire Analytics Value Chain discussed in Chapter 2. The data, analytics, reporting, and predictive models created by the analytics team are powerful business tools. Analytics identifies performance and enables performance to be compared historically to a baseline. Data creates transparency and exposes both accurate and fallacious beliefs and successful and failed business actions. As a result, people get intimidated by data—often because they don't understand it—and people dislike when data shows a reality alternative from their perception of reality.

I always give the advice to my team that people like data as long as it supports their commonly held beliefs and shows their performance in a positive light. Otherwise people will claim, for one reason or another, that the data is wrong.

Exacerbating political issues is the perception of the size of the analytics team compared to other functions. Other issues may be the roles and responsibilities of the team, which can cause organizational resistance and friction from people both within and outside the analytics team. As investment in the analytics team is proposed, the growth in team members has the risk of negative perception:

- **Internally within the team:** Unless the team member being hired is the most junior member on the team, people who are more junior may think they were passed up for a promotion. Some team members may believe or feel, correctly or incorrectly, that specific team members are deficient in skills, expertise, or otherwise marginally competent. Sometimes team members just don't like each other for the unknown reasons why people don't like each other.

- **Externally outside the team:** All team leaders will likely say that their team is insufficiently resourced. Thus, issues can occur when the analytics team hires staff when other teams can't hire or are reducing force. Digital analytics is also a "hot" area, and many different teams may want to own a portion of the Analytical Value Chain. And hiring staff onto the analytics team may be perceived as "empire building" or an attempt to disenfranchise or disempower other teams, such as the BI team.

Overcoming organizational resistance due to politics and perception is one of the hardest challenges for an analytics leader. It requires, once again, going out and speaking with people and gaining mutual support and buy-in, whenever possible, for the investment you want to make. Following are some strategies that can be helpful for overcoming political resistance to funding growth of the analytics team:

- Explain what the team does and does not do—in a synergistic context, not competitive to that team.
- Identify why the role is being hired and why from an outside source.
- Present to the leaders who resist you an appropriate business case with the impact on business value that you created.
- Hold a cross-functional meeting with your managers, other senior managers, and their line of business managers across the company to present the business case and justification.

Again the key here is "communication, communication, and communication" focused on the potential business value of the investment. Let your accomplishments and plans for helping the business generate revenue or reduce cost prove the positive value of funding your team.

Creating the Analytics Team Business Justification and Investment Consideration

The time will come when you must put pen to paper, or mouse to PowerPoint, or tablet to Keynote to create the business justification. Like any business document, you should focus on your audience, senior and executive management, and follow these guidelines:

1. Write the document at a level such that a 12-year-old could understand it.
2. Don't spend time creating complexity. Keep it as simple as possible: Occam's Razor.
3. Use 20-pt. font.
4. Keep it to approximately 10 slides.
5. Include a valid financial model such as Net Present Value/ Internal Rate of Return (NPV/IRR).
6. Identify the business value from the investment by estimating savings or increased revenue or profits.

With these high-level guidelines in mind, consider the following structure for an investment consideration:

- **What is this document?** Identify the contents of the document so that people care why they should read it.

- **Executive summary:** Create a simplified reduction of the key points of the document for a senior management audience that is busy.

- **Opportunity statement:** Indicate the business value that can be created by solving the business problem.

- **Problem statement.** Indicate the business problem to be solved.

- **Explanation of what events, reasons, or causes led to this investment request:** Describe the origins leading to the proposal, such as the problem, inefficiency, constraint, and so on.

- **Review of possible options:** All possible, relevant options should be identified. From the investment proposed to doing nothing and all options in-between must be cited.

- **Recommended option:** Identify the suggested course of action you recommend based on your analysis. The rest of the facts in this document should, of course, support your recommendation.

- **Financial considerations:** List the investment required in whatever financial measurement is used by your company (from dollars to euros). If you know the budget from which the money to fund the investment is known, this is a good place to identify it.

- **NPV model and capital considerations:** Use a financially valid model to estimate the impact, such as an NPV model or other model, that leverages the best practices of capital budgeting.

- **Outcome:** Indicate the final state that will be achieved were your recommendation to be accepted and the investment made: what should be expected as the outcomes and business impact over the next several business quarters and years.

- **Summary:** Bring together the key takeaways of your investment proposal into a set of bullet points that support and prove the business case for your analytics investment recommendation.

Reporting to Executives and Other Teams about Analytics Value Generation

It is important when justifying investment to identify the business value the team has delivered during the past year. Prepare a Power-Point slideshow or some other type of narrative that documents and communicates the three to five major team contributions over whatever time period required. The longer time period, such as a year, should have macro level summary contributions whereas shorter time periods need more tactical and specific contributions. This list should include real, verifiable, performance metrics (whenever possible) that highlight specific numerical contributions and outcome of analytics work. It is ideal to use financial metrics as simple as the cost saved or the revenue opportunity identified and/or generated by analytical insights, recommendations, optimizations, and predictions. Make sure to document how the analytics team not only has impact on numbers, but also on externalities that are influenced by analysis, such as search optimization (search engine marketing [SEM] and search engine optimization [SEO]) and new customer and repeat customer behavior. Also, ensure that you communicate how helpful the analytics team has been to supporting ancillary teams that have helped (or at least tried to help) you execute analytics processes across the Analytical Value Chain.

Following is an example of a sufficient, high-level set of bullet points that show the business value of the analytics teams and can be used to help justify currently existing and future budgeting analytics team resources:

- Provided analysis and data-driven recommendations across the business that improved site performance and the customer experience, which were directly attributable to the analytics team:
  - 7 percent increase in orders
  - 17 percent increase in new customers
  - 44 percent increase in repeat customers within 60 days
  - 47 percent increase in repeat customers within 90 days
  - 51 percent increase in average order value

- 20 percent increase in the number of items placed in the shopping cart
- 30 percent increase in profitability of e-commerce product orders
- Enhanced site visibility to search engines by 13 percent year-over-year.
- Provided analytical insight and guidance for SEO across all global sites and releases, including special projects X and Y.
- Reduced cost of business activities by more than $1.5 M by guiding and leading the execution of all aspects of road-mapped projects. Doing this complex work in-house saved this business hundreds of thousands of dollars on top of the already-known, value-creating analytics recommendations and optimizations.
- Provided improved analytical deliverables, including on-demand and self-service reporting and analytical support to all teams across all global business units, ventures, subsidiaries, and partners.
- Developed an analytical framework for distributing data, reporting, and insight being rolled out to the customer service team.
- Delivered data supporting product development, privacy, legal, security, fraud, marketing, and sales teams.

Structuring an Analytics Team: The Organizational Chart

Centralization is helpful and in certain cases absolutely necessary for generating business value with analytics. The Analytics Value Chain, as discussed in Chapter 2, needs ownership and alignments across functions. The centralized analytics team provides the Center of Excellence necessary to initiate, control, track, and close analytics processes and projects. This strong statement does not preclude the addition of other analytics team structures as an ancillary component, such as hub and spoke, federated, matrixed, and so on (see the discussion earlier in this chapter). For it is true that the larger the company, the more likely inevitable that data and analysis will be created outside of the centralized analytics team because it is unlikely a centralized team exists, or if it does, is funded or resourced adequately.

The result of lack of centralization is data proliferation, Actually, data proliferation is the antithesis of centralization and can lead to inordinate issues creating analytical standards and adoption across a globally distributed organization.

This advice may seem contradictory to commonly held beliefs that the hub-and-spoke model is the preferred model for success with analytics. However, a centralized team is the core component that forms the hub. Thus, before beginning to extend or identify the "spokes" across departments and locations, you must first define and solidify the hub. On the other hand, with competencies, clusters of expertise, individual analysts, or even whole teams doing analysis, it may make sense to create a centralized analytics team from these people, or it may make sense to leave some or all of them as spokes in your centralized analytics hub. Regardless, centralization leads to improved execution from better control over analytics processes, and as such, reduces cost by eliminating redundancy. Thus, analytical centralization in and of itself creates business value. Consider the benefits of using a centralized team with three subteams:

- **Architecture and collection subteam** responsible for data collection, validation, governance, and systems configuration and administration. This subteam can be responsible for liaising with technical teams to support roadmap, ad-hoc, urgent, or process-based initiatives where deeper technical expertise is necessary than would be expected from a digital analyst who only worked with the business. (See Chapter 4, "What Are Analytics Tools?")

- **Reporting subteam** in charge of all self-service and ad-hoc reporting, including the maintenance, verification, auditing, correction, and evolution of self-service and ad-hoc systems that report digital data. (See Chapter 7, "Reporting Data and Using Key Performance Indicators.")

- **Analysis subteam** accountable for the creation, communication, and follow-up of analytics projects and deliverables. (See Chapter 5, "Methods and Techniques for Digital Analysis.")

With this structure and others like it, you create a bridge of team members and collaborative work activities and processes that helps transition analytical work from its beginnings in the business to its evolution in technology to its communication, judgment, and perception in the business. For more information about the work a digital analyst does, see Chapter 2.

Here's an example of how the teams could work together across the phased process to execute analytics:

1. A business question is prioritized to be answered after being submitted via the standard Analytics Work Request Process.

2. Within the specified period of time, the assigned point person on the analytics team responsible for assessing and managing the queue of analytics requests works with the team, as necessary, to prioritize the work by determining

   a. Whether the work is justified and feasible. Saying No is acceptable in context and with a reason.

   b. Data exists and can be self-serviced.

   c. Data exists and must be prepared for reporting by the reporting subteam.

   d. Data exists and must be presented in person by the analytics subteam.

   e. Data does not exist.

3. In Cases A to D, it is the responsibility of the analytics team to do what is necessary to execute the request and manage expectations—as long as the data requested can be and should be delivered to the person requesting analytics work.

4. Case E, where the data does not exist, presents an opportunity for a decision:

   a. Saying No for the long term with a business justification. For example, a product manager may ask for confidential financial or Personally Identifying Information (PII) data.

   b. Saying Yes:

      i. The requestor must work within the roadmap and standard life-cycle processes to assist the analyst with prioritization and working with other teams as necessary.

      ii. The architecture subteam takes the lead and works with the technology teams in the backend to the data while also working with the data governance team to ensure the data is defined and standardized.

5. Deliver the analytics work request and close it in the work tracking system. Make sure to note to whom, why, and who delivered the work and assignment of analytics value (to help identify and prove the return-on-investment [ROI] of analytics).

In the abstracted scenario, each of the three subteam verticals— architecture, reporting, and analysis—have responsibilities at various points in the process:

- A member of any of the three teams—the point person— reviews, assesses, and assigns the work with help, as necessary, from other teams.
- The reporting subteam prepares the necessary reports from already existing data.
- The analytics subteam analyzes existing reports and data, and then prepares and presents analysis.
- The architecture subteam works with IT teams and other technical teams (such as development and quality assurance [QA]) to collect data and configure and prepare the analytics systems for use by teams that have access.

By applying this process within the Analytics Value Chain, you can see in the example the entire team works together with each other, supporting teams, and external stakeholders.

Setting Analytics Team Goals

An important activity for the leaders and members of the analytics team is to set goals. Short-term and long-term planning requires goals and milestones—and because the analytics team supports ongoing business strategy and operations, it is critical that the analytics team's goals align with corporate goals. You should create the following types of goals and review each:

- **Overall team goals:** Audit these goals annually. Team goals represent the yearly tangible and intangible deliverables that create business value, which the culmination of all yearly team activities can fulfill.
- **Leadership goals:** Audit these goals bi-annually. Leadership goals establish the vision all team managers, including the

"boss," define for delivering on team goals. These goals are more tactical than the strategic team goals.

• **Team analyst goals:** Audit these quarterly. Team member goals form the basis for executing the programs and projects with which managers task them. Team goals can be strategic, but often focus on the tactical. These goals may form the basis or may actually be the goals for which people receive bonuses.

Team goals derived from business strategy should be reflected in tactical goals supported by analytics processes within the analytics value. Analyst goals are the successful execution of the projects based on tactics to deliver strategy that creates business value.

Goals are important in establishing motivation for each team member and for establishing managerial credibility. An old adage holds true for analytics teams and reminds you of the importance of goals: "If you aim for nothing, you will hit it every time." Thus, to deliver business value with your analytics, you have to set goals. The next sections discuss how to craft and provide examples of analytics goals: team, leadership, and analyst.

Creating Team Goals: Strategic Goals

Team goals are created by the analytics team leader with input from many sources: senior management, cross-functional stakeholders, analytics managers, and analysts. The best team goals, thus, synthesize the wanted outcomes from many different people for the next year's worth of analytics work. Although this task may seem daunting, it is always best to keep it simple by highlighting macro-level themes and objectives. Do not, however, be overly abstract nor make heavy use of buzzwords.

Consider the following approach to creating team goals:

1. Discuss with your manager the challenges and opportunities as they exist and are known when you ask.

2. Determine together a set of deliverables—at whatever level of detail and specificity—and a general estimate of a timeline you both think are realistic to take advantage of your current situation.

3. Set these deliverables in business terminology not using overly analytical or technical vocabulary.

4. Author three to five team goals that capture the main theme of the deliverables across the Analytical Value Chain.

For example, here is a set of useful team goals for a calendar year:

- Collect, measure, report, analyze, and predict customer behavior for roadmap projects across the following teams: marketing, product, sales, finance, research, legal, privacy, fraud/compliance, media, investor relations, and other corporate functions.
- Support the global roadmap within X company's software development life cycle and related workflows and projects.
- Provide specific, accurate, timely, and actionable data and analysis that support business strategy to increase profitable revenue, improve conversion rates, enhance the customer experience, and drive fact-based decision making.
- Bring together data from multiple systems, apply human intelligence to synthesize it, and tell stories to the business about what it means and what to do about it.
- Ensure the business impact of the key strategic and tactical decisions globally and locally is understood by key stakeholders including the executive team.
- Deliver reporting and analysis that informs about the incremental contribution of business decisions on site performance.
- Extend, maintain, and improve the global analytics infrastructure and analytics vendor relationships to enable consistency, accuracy, and provide a self-service environment.

As you can see in these team goals, they can be dissected and carved out to create leadership and analyst goals as discussed in the next section.

Creating Leadership Goals: Tactical Goals

Leadership goals express the team goals in specific tactics that managers support. Leaders may not necessarily always nor actively do analytical projects; some managers shepherd processes, whereas others review models, and others intimately involve themselves in doing the analytical work. The reality of doing digital analytics, the amount of work, and the insufficiency of resources means that leadership can't simply sit in their offices all day and mull over efficiency and track team performance to goals. Although some analytical leaders do not take such an active approach to managing analytics, the best leaders can work with analysts and managers at all levels to apply the best leadership tactics to support goals.

Consider the following approach when creating leadership goals:

1. Discuss the finalized list of team goals, and discuss what areas you both believe may be necessary to take a more hands-on managerial approach both externally with stakeholders and internally with analysts.

2. Determine a list of managerial tactics and the outcomes of those tactics (when successfully) executed. Frame, of course, in the context of team goals.

3. Document the tactics and their outcomes to capture how the leaders will deliver goals.

Following is a list of leadership goals derived from the list of team goals:

• Establish a set of KPIs that track program and project deliverability and success across each analytics team road-mapped project.

• Calculate and document every instance in which the analytics team recommendations or work activities create business value. Frame this work in business terms in the way it supports business strategy to increase profitable revenue or cost reduction.

• Establish and improve the Analytics Communication Process. Socialize analytics team goals and gather feedback from customers and stakeholders that document that the analytics team is successful.

• Focus on improving how the team maintains consistency, accuracy, and verifiable data, and provides self-service environment.

Creating Analyst Goals: Program and Project Goals

Every analyst on the team needs a set of three to five goals that focus on delivering against the roadmap and also on providing a consistent quality of service when contacting the analytics team for work outside the roadmap. In this sense, you must consider that although analysts should be measured on a timeline that makes sense for the type of work they support, it is helpful to examine the success of each analyst on a quarterly basis. That way, too much time does not pass between recognition of successful work or the need to course correct before a problem occurs. Analyst goals may focus on day-to-day activities, roadmap projects, and urgent projects (often from senior management). The best analysts need some structure amid the noise for analytical work but not too much that analytical progress is hindered. Avoid micromanaging analysts unless you have to, and if you have to, then something has gone awry.

Consider the following approach when creating analyst goals:

- Discuss the analyst's career objectives against the set of programs and projects.
- Have analysts create their own set of goals, suggesting the programs and projects for which they would like assignment.
- If the programs and projects are known in advance, it may be helpful to have the analyst rank in order the projects in terms of desirability, while clearly setting the expectation that work is delegated based on business need with an eye on personal interests.
- Identify the list of known programs and projects for which the analyst should work on (if any are known at the time of goal setting).
- Ask analysts to document their goals against the list you provided and the overall team goals.
- Review the list of goals created by the analyst, revise as necessary, and mutually agree on the goals.

For example, here is a list of leadership and team goals provided as an example in the previous sections:

- Work cross-functionally to support the following programs and projects: XXX, YYY, and ZZZ.

- Document each instance in which you think analytical value has been generated based on template X.

- Focus on establishing a standard format for delivering written analysis for each project based on input from other analytics team members.

Creating Analytics Team Roles and Responsibilities

You have learned in the last few sections the importance of the analytics team and the attributes found in successful digital analysts. You reviewed how to create an analytics investment consideration and overcome commonly encountered obstacles, generally from management, that prevent investment. You have also learned a recommended structure for creating an investment consideration and have reviewed the importance of creating sets of goals across the analytics team, team leadership, and analysts. You are well on your way to creating a powerful analytics team.

The specific roles you should hire for your team will vary based on the company, dedication to analytics, and the size of your analytics budget for hiring staff. You learned earlier in this chapter the three verticals—architecture, reporting, and analytics—that should be mapped in your organizational structure. As you plan the specific roles and responsibilities for each of your analysts, consider where it makes the most sense to create order and structure that allows the team to spend as much time as possible doing actual analysis and helping people in the business. Do not make the mistake of concentrating on the overly technical engineering of analytics when staffing a team.

The golden rule when creating roles and responsibilities for a team, whether building the team from scratch or restructuring it, follows:

Technical roles are critical and necessary, but the hard technical work for creating and collecting data is mostly unseen. What businesspeople want are analysts informed with timely and relevant answers to their business questions derived from accurate data presented to them in easy to understand ways using verifiable methods.

With that guidance in mind, Table 3-1 shows examples of the roles and responsibilities commonly seen across large analytics teams. If you work in or run a smaller analytics team, it is likely that one person's job covers many of these roles. As you can deduce, as the team grows in size, the responsibilities tend to become less generalized and more specific to particular business functions.

Table 3-1 Structure for a Digital Analytics Team

Architecture Team	Reporting Team	Analytics Team
Director, analytics architecture and development	Director, analytics reporting and data delivery	Director, analytics and optimization
Manager	Manager	Manager
Business systems analyst(s) – across all	Team leads	Team leads
Database analysts – internal data	Reporting analysts – sales	Analysts – sales
	Reporting analysts – marketing	Analysts – marketing
Database analysts – external data	Reporting analysts – finance	Analysts – finance
Systems administrators – backend systems		Analysts – customer service
Tool administrators – analytics tools	Reporting analysts – customer service	Analysts – applied analytics and data science
Project manager	...and so on, as it makes sense for your business and budget	Analysts – omnichannel
		...and so on, as it makes sense for your business and budget

Describing the Analyst: Job Posting

Analytics job postings can be difficult to write because of the all-encompassing nature of the analytics role. In a few cases, in which the analytics skill set to be hired is well known or serves a niche, a job posting can be easier to write. Nevertheless, few people sit down with a blank screen and just type out a job description for a team member. Instead, you may consider reviewing various job postings on multiple job boards and create your job posting by reassembling specific text from best, most-closely related job ads. Following is a description that provides a useful starting point for customizing a job description to meet your specific requirements. Feel free to use it or pieces of it as it makes sense for you.

The goal of the digital analyst is to use data to create analysis that helps the business generate economic value, while simultaneously becoming a well-liked, business partner and teammate critical to the analytics team and stakeholders across the business. This job is about using data, research, and analytics to tell stories to the business that help make digital experiences better! Although this job has a technical component, the digital analyst requires a sharp, multidimensional intellect that can analyze big data and use it to enable even bigger business results:

- Answer questions and provide solutions to stakeholders across the world—from executives to analysts in a multitude of groups, such as marketing, product, finance, and research.

- Analyze multichannel data from many sources—online and offline and qualitative and quantitative—including the segmentation of customers, acquisition sources (SEM/SEO/OLM/CRM), and other site, email, and social analytical data.

- Develop data-driven insights relevant to both tactical product changes and releases and strategically across business initiatives.

- Collaborate and partner effectively with a wide range of people who have different goals, projects, and ideas that need to be informed by your analysis and recommendations.

- Serve as a subject-matter expert on digital analytics as it relates to products, campaigns, promotions, brands, categories, site testing, business objectives, and strategies.

- Create written analysis and data visualizations that explain and illustrate data analysis, insights, recommendations, tactics, and strategies for improving site performance.

- Present written analysis, reporting, and research findings to internal audiences by synthesizing complex data and concepts into easy-to-comprehend, comprehensive, and cohesive presentations.

- Gather independently, creatively, and with urgency data from various systems and sources in a timely manner.

- Move beyond summary data and get into the heart of the business issue using detailed data, including helping people to ask the best questions and to recommend and understand the appropriate data.

- Define a sustainable and reusable framework for collecting, reporting, and analyzing digital behavior and Web analytics data with the goal of increasing conversion, retention, loyalty, revenue, and profit in the context of business strategy.

- Manage all phases of business requirements gathering including KPIs, data collection (including site tagging and QA testing), report creation (building and testing reporting) and distribution, but focus primarily on analysis and analytically rigorous data interpretation, synthesis, and actionable insights and recommendations.

Sample Job Requirements for a Digital Analyst

- BA/BS required; advanced degree preferred
- Minimum 3 years' experience in digital measurement and Web analytics
- Demonstrated competency with analytical tools such as IBM Coremetrics, Webtrends, and Adobe Marketing Cloud (Omniture)
- Exposure to audience measurement, competitive intelligence, Voice of Customer (VoC) and other qualitative data, and BI tools, such as comScore, Microsoft BI, and Business Objects
- Demonstrated competency writing tagging specifications, testing tagging, building custom reports, and analyzing data in a business context
- Ability to manage simultaneous projects across a wide-range of activities and scope in a time-sensitive environment with a high sense of urgency and accountability
- Demonstrated ability to work independently handling complex projects and prioritizing and managing multiple tasks under tight deadlines and time constraints
- Solid organizational skills, follow-up, and high attention to detail coupled with demonstrable ability to organize and manage projects within an unstructured environment and build new structures and process as needed
- Strong self-confidence and work ethic with a high sense of responsibility in an ever-changing environment—the only constant is change!

- Ability to exercise excellent judgment while handling sensitive matters related to corporate data and performance
- Work both independently with minimal supervision and closely in a team setting

Enhancing Your Career: Methods for Success

Many people aspire to become full-time digital analysts for many reasons. The work is interesting, innovative, fast-paced, and cutting-edge and pays greater salaries than one might expect for a given years' experience/skill set combination. Entry-level digital analysts in top companies with skills but little experience (perhaps from work-study or internships only) regularly command $60,000–$80,000 depending on the type of analytics. Competition at the entry level exists, but because there is an acute insufficiency in analytics professionals (especially at senior levels), the competition is less than you might expect for similar paying jobs in engineering, marketing, or sales. As we reviewed earlier, research proves analytics leaders can easily earn over $200,000 annually.

Digital analytics, however, is not an easy field to enter because there is no straightforward path for gaining real-world experience to help you land a job. You cannot just show up one day at work and say, "I'm no longer going to do what I am being paid to do. I'm going to start doing digital analytical work." Thus, it is hard to gain on-the-job analytics experience. And when a business determines it needs a digital analyst, it does not often look at internal resources to staff the function; it wants to hire someone who has experience elsewhere doing digital analysis, which makes it even harder to break into the field full-time without any experience.

So what is an aspiring digital analyst to do, and what do professionals who want to take their career to the next level do? Fortunately, in 2013, several avenues exist for gaining real-world practical experience under your belt to move your career in the direction you want it to go. Like many fields, the analytics industry has a "community" of professionals who collaborate and commiserate locally, nationally, and even internationally. Education opportunities exist, too. Here's a list of potential options for jumpstarting your career:

1. Get involved with analytics industry associations created by practitioners, consultants, and vendors, such as the International Institute for Analytics (IIA), the Interactive Advertising Bureau (IAB), and the Digital Analytics Association (DAA).

2. Take advantage of multiple options for analytical education, such as those available in local universities and colleges, online, or at the University of British Columbia (UBC), University of Chicago, Babson College, Northwestern University, New York University, University of California–Irvine, the University of North Carolina, and more.

3. Find a pre-existing local analytics event or create your own, such as Digital Analytics Thursdays (DAT: www. digitalanalyticsthursdays.org), Mobile Mondays, Conversion Thursdays, and so on.

4. Attend industry conferences that are privately held and/or vendor-sponsored, such as the Adobe Summit, eMetrics, eTail, and so on.

5. Install a free analytics tool, such as Google Analytics, Pwik, Open Web Analytics (OWA), and so on to gain real experience and develop skills that help you land a job.

Steps for Building a Digital Analytics Team

This chapter discussed the importance of the analytics team, what the analytics team does, how to plan and consider investment, and how to resource the team. Although this information is helpful, you may still wonder if there's an approach, or series of steps, that you can take to build a digital analytics team. Actually, you can follow this set of steps to jumpstart your creation of a digital analytics team:

1. **Understand the main points and business concerns.** Speak with stakeholders and business people to determine the current business concerns, challenges, and areas on which to concentrate with analytics.

2. **Determine the investment required.** When necessary to invest, the digital analytics leadership should quickly make that determination and propose an investment.

3. **Orient the business and technology.** After understanding the business plan and challenge, and the investment or technology to apply, you next need to communicate your plans to create your digital analytics team.

4. **Manage for process and scale.** Given the world of big data and data science, resources are hard to find and expensive when you do. Therefore, you should begin to plan for scale and process for the future state of your team.

5. **Handle the data. Big data just keeps coming and getting bigger.** The digital analytics team must keep its systems and tools in parity and alignment with the influx of ever-changing data.

6. **Get the most from the team.** By applying strong leadership and motivational skills, the team's leaders should strive to get the most from their teams.

7. **Get the most from technology.** By alignment and team-building across functions, the analytics leader must maximize working relationships and team equity with IT.

8. **Get the most from vendors.** By partnering with vendors and ensuring good relations (that is, don't always just beat up vendors), you can get the most from your vendor relationships.

9. **Produce and communicate analysis.** Critical to the perception of success is the analytics team that produces regularly occurring analysis and communicates it to stakeholders with necessary follow-ups and ongoing support.

10. **Change the business.** Through the insightful analysis and recommendations, the analytics team must work across the business to improve it by creating value from, at the most macro-level, reducing cost, creating new or incremental revenue, or boosting profitability.

Following these steps and applying the knowledge learned in this chapter to your business goals and requirements puts you well on your way to creating a world-class digital analytics team.

4

What Are Analytics Tools?

Analytics tools are the software and Software as a Service (SaaS) technologies that are critical and necessary for collecting, reporting, and analyzing data. Tools and technologies such as Google Analytics, Adobe Marketing Cloud, IBM Digital Analytics, Microstrategy, Webtrends, Localytics, SAS, and so on are all analytics tools as are other offerings from ubiquitous technology brands such as Microsoft and Oracle. Actually, many companies, consultants, practitioners, and salespeople would like you to believe that their technology is a data analysis tool—and as of 2013—a big data analysis tool that uses data science; however, not all tools are created for doing actual analysis, but instead may have limited analytical capabilities and concentrate on data collection, transformation, reporting, or visualization of existing data.

Many tools fulfill a specific role in the various phases of the Analytic Value Chain discussed in Chapter 2, "Analytics Value Chain and the P's of Digital Analytics." For example, you might use one tool to collect data, another tool to apply analytical methods to the data, and yet another tool to report the data. Depending on the number of channels you analyze, you likely have more than one tool to collect the different types of data you need, perhaps another tool to combine that data from multiple sources into one database, and yet another tool to make analytical sense of the data.

The blanket label of *analytics tools* then is broadly applied in the digital analytics industry and should be demystified by understanding that although many tools assist in creating value with analytics, few tools actually do analysis. People on the digital analytics team do analysis. Analytics tools are critical and necessary to do digital analysis but in and of themselves have little value and are considered a cost (overhead or sunk). And some might argue that tools don't actually do analysis at all ever, only people do.

My friend Avinash Kaushik is a keen advocate of the 90/10 model for allocating an analytics budget, where 90% of the money is spent on people and 10% on tools. While that ratio may make sense as a philosophy, in practicality it is hard to match that suggestion—though if possible it would be an excellent level of resourcing. He was smart and forward-thinking in setting the bar high—and in the right frame with which to resource analytics. As I said, people are the most important. Others have identified a split of 60/40 between budgeting for people and tools. The best ratio for investment of tools to people depends on your business requirements—so in reality, no ratio is going to be accurate for all cases. A 50/50 split in cases where software licenses or cloud-based services are involved could be the appropriate level. The analytics leadership needs to determine what the best and correct ratio is. In fact, the larger the corporation and more complex the data, the more likely it is that the balance of budget will tip in favor of analytics technology because it costs a lot when collecting and processing big data volumes. Regardless of the accuracy of any suggested ratio, the larger point understood is that some investment in tools is necessary, but it should be balanced against the fact that people do analysis, not tools. So how then can digital analytics tools be understood in more clarity if all tools that an analyst ever learns about are analytics tools?

The answer is by categorizing tools in the ReDCARPS framework. Tools can be understood as doing one or more of the following: **Re**quirements, **D**efinitions, **C**ollection, **A**nalysis, **R**eporting, **P**rediction, or **S**torage.

- **Requirements:** Technologies used for capturing, sorting, prioritizing, scheduling, and tracking analytics work, projects, and programs from start to finish.
- **Definitions:** All digital data must have definitions that enable understanding by the various stakeholders who create and use the data. Definitions must include a business definition, an operational definition, and a technical definition. See Chapter 6, "Defining, Planning, Collecting, and Governing Data in Digital Analytics."

- **Collection:** Technologies that collect digital data from methods such as packet sniffing, database writes, log files, JavaScript, application programming interfaces (APIs), server-to-server connections, data feeds and other methods, including extracting, transforming, and loading (ETL) data.

- **Analysis:** The application of analytical methods to data derived from the science (and art) of analysis. Analysts and analysis tools enable data science to be applied to digital data—methods such as structured equation models, an ANOVA (Analysis of Variance), determining measures of dispersion, creating regression analysis, or applying advanced machine-learning, data-mining algorithms, and statistical methods. You know when you see analysis or are using an analysis tool because the output of the tool is something you are going to consider as an input to answering a business question. To render analysis in a human-understandable way, an analysis tool enables the analyst to work with data from one or more systems to create analysis. The analyst makes sense of what can sometimes be complex data, metrics, and visualizations from an analysis tool, and then synthesizes and simplifies the key data to present to stakeholders.

- **Reporting:** Tools that take data at various granularities and present it in in a human-readable format across some device— and often allow for some level of drilling down and exploration into the data contained within the report itself. The dimensions in the data may be crossed or filters, metrics could be added, and the data can even sometimes be lightly segmented. Reporting tools include business intelligence (BI) tools that report data into pre-arranged and pre-scheduled reports, such as Cognos or Business Objects, to desktop spreadsheeting and data visualization tools (such as Prezi, PowerPoint, and Tableau).

- **Prediction:** Tools that enable data collected about past and current events—regardless the analytical method or types of data (see Chapter 5, "Methods and Techniques for Digital Analysis")—to be used to predict one or more future events. Predictive analysis and predictive analytics tools tell you "what may happen next." You know you are using a predictive analytics tool when the output informs you about a possible future state—and isn't focused predominantly on explaining what can be understood about the current or past data or its trends, movements, and patterns—and often only so much so as to investigate past data to create the variables from data collected in the past for input into the predictive model.

- **Storage:** Tools that take data and put it on some type of storage medium, such as a storage area network (SAN) or local disk or storage in the cloud in a SaaS. Storage is the disk space needed for recording and persisting your big data. Typically a minimum range for storing digital data is 13 months in order to allow for year-over-year comparative analysis.

The line between *analysis-only* tools and *predictive-only* tools is not a clean line in a similar way to how *reporting* differs from *analysis*. (See Chapter 7, "Reporting Data and Using Key Performance Indicators," for a detailed discussion on the differences between reporting and analysis.) Prediction involves analysis and analysis involves reporting. Thus, prediction, of course, involves reporting the results of the predictive model that applies analytical methods. These different concepts should then be understood in the context of how each helps to create value as part of the Analytical Value Chain. You can use analytics tools to predict, but you would not necessarily use a predictive tool to make sense of data you've already collected or to explain a change in a time-series. But current and past data always serve as inputs to predictive models.

The referenced tools tend to do more than one thing, and vendors often sell complementary tools that enable you to do any of the ReDCARPS, as shown in Table 4-1.

Table 4-1 The ReDCARPS Framework Applied to Common Digital Analytics Tools

	IBM	Adobe	Webtrends	Google
Requirements	X			
Definition	X	X	X	X
Collection	X	X	X	X
Analysis	X	X	X	X
Reporting	X	X	X	X
Prediction	X	X		
Storage	X	X	X	X

Every analytics practitioner and team has a number of tools they prefer. For example, many digital analysts are familiar with Google Analytics or Omniture; however, other types of digital analytics (such as email, customer, and advanced) require knowledge of larger and different toolsets (SQL, SAS, R, and so on). The more familiarity you have with the different historic, current, and emerging analytics tools, the more career options you will have.

Although an analyst may prefer a type of tool, many tools perform similar functions. Thus, don't get too tied to and involved with any one tool. An overemphasis on one tool can bias how you conceive and understand digital analytics. What may be difficult and require "guru" skills in one tool may be as simple as a few clicks in training from another tool.

Familiarity with tools is helpful and explains why people have preferences for their specific tools, but different tools are necessary to create different types of analysis. You would not commission a sculptor of bronze to paint a watercolor, just as you would not hire a SAS programmer to socialize business analysis to an executive audience. Instead, of course, you would hire the right horse for the right course; thus, it is likely that to successfully execute on an analytical vision, you need more than one tool to do so, just like an analytics team needs people with different, but complementary skills to execute the analytical value chain.

To help you further understand the landscape of analytics tools beyond the ReDCARPS framework, analytics tools can be divided into the following types:

- **Internal tools:** These are always deployed in a software environment—perhaps in a data center or in a cloud—that is controlled, managed, and configured for all intents and purposes by people employed by the company for which you work.
- **Site analytics tools:** Site analytics tools collect data from a digital site via a number of methods, store and aggregate it, and then report it. Some tools enable data exploration, such as crossing of or drilling down or filtering of dimensions in the data and the usage of analytical methods.
- **Business intelligence (BI) tools:** BI tools tend to exist under the control of IT and technology and include the databases and systems that support data storage and processing. Analytics

teams make use of BI data and may combine BI data with other internal or external data. BI tools also have capabilities for ETL, storage, reporting, visualization, and analysis—and in some cases, the analytical capabilities that can be applied directly to the data can be very advanced.

- **Advanced applied analysis tools:** Applied analysis tools operate off of existing data that may require data to be specially transferred or prepared to be modeled and analyzed within the tool. Advanced analysis tools allow the user to apply statistically rigorous models and algorithms to digital and other types of data. A common example is SAS.

- **Desktop analytics, reporting, and testing tools:** Many analysts use tools available in common desktop publishing programs or programs created by smaller software companies to perform a specific task. For example, analysts can use Excel to manipulate, format, and visualize data and may use a browser-based tool such as Fiddler or Charles to test data collection. As the power of computing increases, desktop tools can also contain an impressive set of statistical methods, such as regression, on data.

- **Homegrown, internally created tools:** Sometimes, off-the-shelf tools and BI tools just don't do what may be required to analyze data; thus, companies customize off-the-shelf technology or build software solutions from scratch to deliver analysis. These solutions can be fully homegrown or cobbled together from multiple vendor systems or even highly customized versions of off-the-shelf enterprise software products.

- **Online advertising and marketing tools:** This category of internal tools includes technologies for analyzing online display, (re)targeting, optimization, bidding, planning, executing, fulfilling, emailing, Customer Relationship Management (CRM) tools, and more. These tools could be deployed and managed by your company—in other words, an ad-server you host, not one that is provided by another company.

External tools include the following:

- **Competitive intelligence:** Many tools exist that help a company understand the competitive landscape, who are the competitors, where they are located, and, of course, key metrics and data related to market share, share of wallet, corporate performance, and a host of other metrics specific to the business and industry.

- **Data enhancement:** Tools that provide data not available to the company. This new data is joined with internal data to create more meaningful and valuable data. Companies include Choicepoint, Experian, Rapleaf, and so on. For example, a company may have a customer list of other businesses and may purchase mailing data from a data enhancement company to improve customer information quality.

- **Audience measurement:** Tools for competitive audience measurement include a number of companies who collect data directly from digital experiences, by observing a statistically significant audience and estimating digital behavior and metrics (panel data collection) and by a combination of both census and panel data. These companies include comScore, Nielsen, Compete, Quantcast, Google, and so on.

- **Cloud-based and SaaS online advertising and marketing tools:** SaaS technologies for analyzing online display, (re)targeting, optimization, bidding, planning, emailing, CRM, and more. These tools are hosted in the cloud by the vendor.

To Build or to Buy?

A core question about analytics technology and available tools is whether it makes sense to build or buy? In other words, do you spend capital to purchase analytics technology for collection, reporting, analysis, prediction, and storage usually by investing in a software license or a SaaS technology? Or do you and your engineering, IT, development, quality assurance (QA), and business teams create from scratch the analytical tool ecosystem you require using custom software development and engineering?

To build or to buy seems like a simple question, but it is not. Software that everybody can buy if they have the money means that everyone may have the same measures and data with which to analyze an experience. Take for example Google Analytics, IBM Coremetrics, and Webtrends: These tools all report visitors, visits, and time-based metrics and enable custom metrics to be collected and reported. Such commonality among tools is useful for particular industries and activities in which a common vocabulary is helpful for enabling commerce. However, the counts of data from these three vendors will all differ, regardless of their name, due to the differences in how the tools collect and process data.

The online advertising industry in which the buying and selling of audiences requires shared metrics to evaluate advertising success is important. Proposed metrics standards available across tools include types of Gross Rating Points (GRP) and other reach-and-frequency measures. In these cases in which the industry demands shared metrics (typically defined according to some standard published by an industry association such as the Interactive Advertising Bureau for online ads), it is useful to have a set of tools that at least share some common metrics defined in similar (preferably identical) ways.

Then why, might you ask, would companies build their own analytics technologies using internal resources? The reasons are numerous and generally focus around the requirements for specialized data for unique and specific business purposes often highly specialized and even only applicable for that company, as shown here:

- **Business secrets and proprietary knowledge.** Many companies operate using trade secrets and proprietary knowledge that could cause potential business challenges and financial risk if shared in any way with an external party. Take, for example, the case of a Fortune 500 company that is named as a direct competitor by a much larger and more powerful company that also provides a popular analytics tool where users are allowed to share their business's data with the vendor. Does it make sense for the business to use this vendor's tool? What if most people knew about the tool and wanted to use it? Despite such desire and advocacy for usage, the business risk is just too great.

  This abstract example is a real example. Google provides Google Analytics, which enables users to opt-in to sharing their data so that Google can use it in other products and services. It also named Kayak (recently acquired) and Monster Worldwide as competitors in its Securities and Exchange Commission (SEC) statements because each business provides search technology on top of data that Google does not have (travel data and jobs/employment data, respectively) in industries in which Google does not operate. Thus, it would make little sense for the analytics teams at either Kayak or Monster to deploy a large-scale implementation of Google products without data and technical assurances of confidentiality (such as Google Premium or Google Universal).

• **Technical requirements and standards.** Many businesses have specialized technology models in which new data specific to the nuances and uniqueness of their business has never before existed and must be created, collected, and stored. For example, consider a company that I advise, Yieldbot, which has a marketplace built on their proprietary technology for understanding Intent and matching it to relevant content and other concepts that help people fulfill their intention to do something online, like buy a product or become a member. Yieldbot reports conversion rates in excess of the highest conversion rate from paid search. Where would Yieldbot go to buy data for replicating Intent? It simply can't buy this technology off-the-shelf because the company ideated, innovated, and invented it. In this case, not only are the Yieldbot data models proprietary and confidential trade secrets and intellectual property, but they are also necessary to build the product based on the business idea and product requirements that require innovatively complex engineering.

Another example of where technical requirements and standards compel companies to build their own analytical data solutions is when data must be analyzed across channels. Companies may have purchased and be successfully using site, search, email, and online advertising technology across the business but do not have a single analytics platform on which to analyze the multichannel data to understand it as a single, unified data set—called Omnichannel Analysis. Although vendors are starting to sell solutions for the omnichannel analytics vision as of 2013, companies tend to use BI teams to build out these types of data architectures—often with the help of professional services teams from the hardware or software vendors. (See Chapter 12, "Converging Omnichannels and Integrating Data for Understanding Customers, Audiences, and Media.")

• **Complexity in the data, reporting, and analysis required.** Out-of-the-box software or SaaS means that a product team put the "stuff" in "the box" it thinks customers will need. For analytical tools, certain data collection, reporting, and analysis/prediction capabilities can be easily achieved by putting a "tag" on every page or by making a particular API call to an analytics service. Vendors over the last several years offer ways to extend the "in-the-box" data model to include custom-defined business metrics and dimensions, called Events. Although all these feature enhancements and vendor-based analytical innovations are necessary and helpful, there are still many cases in which the business wants a particular slice of data served in a specific way that was not put "in the box" and thus must be internally engineered.

Consider the example in which an insurance company tracks the starts and completes of the quotation process (for example, quote starts and quote completes), which seems simple to do at first glance. Then consider that the necessary reporting must be longitudinal and segmented by various metrics or dimensions available in other, disconnected systems. Vendor tools may not store sufficient data at the granularity you need or enable the type of data exploration, drilling-down, and crossing-dimensions to fulfill the business need. The technology teams may have never considered that anyone in the business would ever want to look at data in the way you want to look at it. Data models may not support the relationships you want to query and analyze. In these cases, the right option may be to periodically extract the data into an internal database and join it with necessary data to be reporting in another tool. Take the example of the insurance quote start and complete; add to it four different types of starts/completes each with five types of start/complete options across 50 states and the need to include customer-level data. These requirements necessitate data integration or new data modeling and reporting before analysis can even begin.

- **Strong beliefs and politics that "building" is always better than buying.** It may seem ridiculous and absurd to think that people may simply have a bias for building technology as opposed to buying it—even when both the finances and functionality point to buying not building. Resistance to new technology tools often comes from those people entrenched and invested in the success of previously purchased or created tools. Politics may cause people to not want to consider alternatives that their political opponents in business present. SaaS can take away some IT responsibilities and reduce the criticality of IT in the Analytics Value Chain; some IT executives may create obstacles to what they saw as SaaS technology taking over their team's work and marginalizing their responsibilities. Regardless of why people have strong beliefs or the causes for their entrenchment, the analytics team and its leaders will definitely learn about them.

It goes without saying that the decision to build-versus-buy is nuanced. With the exception of start-ups, most corporations have analytical and data "baggage" that needs to be considered. You should assess your current analytics technology against the following states listed below. These states comparatively identify how much direct analysis your team is doing against how much time the same team is spending not doing analysis and working on other aspects of the Analytics Value Chain that occur before analysis:

- **Needing nothing—keeping all existing tools with no replacement.** Analytics teams that spend more than 90 percent of their time on analysis not tool usage for reporting and socialization.

- **Needing something—keeping all existing tools and enhance with new tools.** In this case, between 70 percent to 90 percent of an analyst's time is spent on analysis and socialization with the rest on tool usage, configuration, and reporting.

- **Replacing some existing tools and maintaining some existing tools.** In this case, between 20 percent to 70 percent of an analyst's time is spent on analysis and socialization with the rest on tool usage, configuration, and reporting.

- **Replacing all tools with new tools.** When 80 percent to 100 percent of analyst's time is spent maintaining and handling tools, correcting data, and just keeping the lights on—and stakeholders are not happy—it may be necessary to consider replacing all tools.

Next, this chapter reviews in more detail the business considerations and indications for understanding which option may be preferred for your given situation.

Needing Nothing: When to Keep Your Existing Analytics Tools (Without Replacing)

The perfect state in which the analytics tool(s) are ideally suited in almost every way for helping the analyst create analysis and deliver against business requirements are rare to find; therefore, those teams that reach this ideal state deserve congratulations because their company has achieved the highest echelons of analytical competitiveness.

Following are some other reasons—beyond phenomenal achievement and success—for needing no additional analytical tools:

- **Cost to replicate is prohibitive.** In mature companies, considerable investment and development cycles have already been used for building analytics systems that work for a given purpose. They may not be perfect and may even be severely deficient in some ways; however, given available budget, the decision can be made to keep the existing system because the cost to re-create and enhance does not make financial sense at the current time.

- **Contains custom Internet Protocol (IP) or Personally Identifiable Information (PII).** Due to legal and privacy concerns, analytics tools can contain PII that may be perceived as not being able to be securely stored with minimal risk and maximum confidence in analytics systems external to the company, such as a SaaS vendor's tool. Thus, the legacy systems that have always collected and stored this data continue to be used.

- **Created specifically for a point purpose.** Legacy analytics tools often serve a particular niche business function and can be heavily customized to do that function. For example, the CRM team self-develops an attribution tool for identifying the sources and cost of its CRM performance from all marketing channels using complex, highly specific, and nuanced business logic proprietary to the business. As such, the attribution tool can't be quickly or easily re-created using available resources nor may it be understood fully by the engineering team—and since it works effectively for the job, there may be no need to replace it with the latest and greatest attribution technology that uses entirely new or different attribution models.

- **Report unreplicatable data.** Accurate digital data collection as a site, app, and other digital experience is always challenging to implement and even more challenging to maintain as time goes on. When complex data collection implemented over many years works and the reports from the data collected are accurate, why replace the technology?

- **No investment available.** Facing the facts that no investment is available for analytics is unfortunate, but it happens all the time.

- **Lack of available resources.** Sometimes you want to change and improve, but resources are tapped out on already existing work.

Needing Something: When to Keep Your Existing Analytics Tools (Without Replacing)

The most common state in analytics teams is where tools never die; they just fade into disuse or become so bloated with confusing and erroneous data that they are only resurrected or examined at various times by employees who know the nuances of the data and maybe even that these tools exist at all. In some cases, it may take years to decommission a business tool, such as moving from Brio to Microsoft. People also tie themselves to the data and tools that work for them; thus, tools are hard to replace, and new team members usually want to buy the tools they already know or want to know. In one company, at least six different reporting systems often with similar data across various geographies were used, which had to be consolidated, optimized, and enhanced.

Following are several reasons why the analytics team may need more tools:

- **Data collection is broken.** The process for collecting digital data can be complex. Many tags need to work in unison. When these tags break or are insufficient, data collection needs to be optimized. Perhaps a Tag Management System (TMS) is needed. Code may need to be rewritten. The type of data collection may need to be reengineered to use APIs or a web service.

- **Insufficient staff to maintain.** As companies evolve and resources shift, systems can become orphaned without ownership—and as such often wither on the vine and die a slow death as the data becomes more corrupt and eventually useless.

- **Cost.** Cost may be too expensive given alternatives, or the use of free or low-cost tools may not provide necessary capabilities.

- **Reporting is not flexible.** The capabilities required for data exploration, analysis, and visualization are not sufficient.

- **Unsupported.** Over time, tools change. New versions are released. Products are sunsetted.

- **Inability to extend with other systems.** Emerging and new standards for orchestrating and working with data can be essential for creating the pools of data necessary for reporting and analysis.

Replacing Something but Not Other Things: Surgical Reengineering

The second most common state is one in which the analytics team has one or two core tools and is in the process of trimming as well as growing its tool usage around the edges of analytics. Take the team that uses Google Analytics and a BI solution for core analysis work; but for more specialized work, the team uses SAS, Kissmetrics, Monetate, and Sysymos.

Following are several reasons why the analytics team may need to replace some tools:

- **Occurs in larger environments when teams are centralized.** When companies centralize analytics, it can become hard for that team to meet the needs of all stakeholders if the team is not sufficiently resourced. As a result, people can go around the analytics team and deploy free tools, such as Google Analytics, as they wait for the centralized analytics team to deliver.

- **Always upgrading and maintaining.** Tools need to be upgraded to take advantage of new capabilities. When running multiple tools, it can be difficult to provide the same features (or even the current feature) of the tool.

- **Requirements to create Data Marts and Operational Data Store (ODS) using data warehousing best practices.** It may be possible to put all data into a single data mart. Often multiple tools provide access to data and views on that data that can't be found in one tool or location. As such, the business may want to move data and join it together to create new relationships between data that allow for it to be explored in new ways. One model is to create an Enterprise Data Warehouse (EDW) with all key analytical data alongside a functional specific ODS and Data Mart (DM) for each business unit: for example, an ODS/DM for finance, another for marketing, another for sales, and so on.

- **Requests for something become repeatedly and humanly unsustainable.** Despite the best mix of tools and talent, the business can request the creation, collection, reporting, and analysis of new reporting, and the need to sustain the reporting automatically can't be maintained by the current staff or tool set.

- **New product and channel needs.** Tools have limited functionality that may not be applicable or extensible to new products or new data that needs created or required by the business.

- **Inability to get engineering support.** Tools wither not only when they don't have an owner, but also when the tools do not receive support or extension from IT.

Everything Needs to Go: Ripping It All Out and Replacing Everything

It is fortunate that most analytics professionals never experience a tense moment when they realize that the analytics engine and all the tools that support it need to be shut down and totally replaced. In this case, the company has realized that it has totally failed with analytics or maybe has never before tried to "do analytics," and to not miss the boat, it must hurriedly arrange transportation to the dock. I experienced this situation just once in my career: A complex BI system built from Java for processing server log files needed to be entirely replaced across more than 200 websites with a highly customized implementation of SaaS technology for digital analytics. In this case, less than 20 percent of an analyst's time is spent on analysis and socialization with the rest on tool usage, configuration, and reporting.

Following are several reasons why the analytics team may need to replace all tools:

- **Broken and, despite best efforts, can't be repaired at all or fast enough.** A company may have dedicated significant roadmap space and time to repairing an existing tool, but it is still failing to meet the needs. Often older tools don't have newer technical features or the company can't manage to fix a tool and use it at the same time.

- **Insufficient staffing.** Due to organizational structure and investment, staff may not exist to manage and maintain the tool—and the cost to replace, augment, train, or hire new staff is prohibitive or deemed to not be a worthwhile investment.

- **To instill confidence when perception of the analytics tool and its output is poor and investment is available.** When an existing tool has poor perception, it can help to just kill or replace it to improve the perception. Sometimes people have had bad experiences, for one reason or another, with a particular tool, that it just makes sense to eliminate it and start fresh with a new tool not bound by the bias of previous perception and judgment.

- **Vendors make a product change to new, underlying, core technology.** Mandates to move from one main vendor to another can compel speedy infrastructure change. For example, a company may choose to use only open source software or technology provided by a specific enterprise software vendor or another that supports a certain required technical capability.

- **Doesn't answer the business questions.** As a business changes, the business reason why the tool was purchased may have shifted and no longer makes sense. The tool simply no longer has relevancy in the data that it collects, reports, visualizes, analyzes, predicts, or optimizes.

- **Significant vendor issues (such as training).** Complex tools require training staff or hiring trained staff. Training can be costly, so companies can skimp on the cost and require employees to self-learn how to use a tool. This can lead to the tool not being leveraged fully and expectations not being met. As a result, the perception is the tool is not useful, when it may simply be that the company has not invested in the right amount of training for the staff, or alternatively given them enough time and support to learn it on their own.

Balancing Management of Analytics Technology: Should "the Business" or IT Run It?

As has been shown throughout this book, an analytics team requires *some* given level of support from IT, engineering/development, and QA. The level of support from these groups is highly dependent on what the digital analytics team is being asked to do.

Depending on the orientation and positioning of your team within the organizational chart, you will likely be part of either "the business" or "IT." As such, you may be responsible for running analytics technology that builds or provides a user interface (UI) for reporting. Or you may be a consumer of reporting and dashboarding provided by the people who run the technology and provide a business service to you. As a result, it is likely that misunderstanding and inefficiencies exist in your Analytical Value Chain caused by friction from possible misalignment of expectations, goals, and vision.

Note

My professional background is solidly grounded in business, and I have spent my entire career in software technology and the Internet. The culmination and experiences I have had have taught me that it always makes sense to align a business leader at the helm as the top manager. An analytics team can easily become operational and transactional supporting engineering technologies in a laggard reporting-only approach. On the counterpoint, business-only focused analytics teams may not have the technical knowledge and experience to understand the software development life cycle and the feasibility of data collection and reporting. Thus, it is necessary to ensure that your analytics team doesn't fall victim to this polarity by balancing business and technology.

In some sense, I might be describing the notion that technical BI teams can provide analytics, and business teams can manage technology for providing analytics. Neither team can provide maximum value without the other. The solution for analytical team balance is thus to combine teams that include sufficient expertise across business and technology led by "the business."

A business leader at the top level leading the analytics team ensures that analytics is focused on answering business questions against business priority, not the technical roadmap or technology. Technology serves the business, not the other way around, so the business must make technology accountable for the parts of the Analytic Value Chain for which it is expert, such as system maintenance, networking, data instrumentation, and QA.

Several methods exist for the business to ensure technology teams are accountable:

- **Organizational methods involve team structure and defined roles:** For example, it may make sense for the BI team to report to the analytics leader either in a direct or dotted-line capacity. A quantity of available IT hours can be allotted to analytics for IT work. Retrain, hire, and replace staff to create accountability. Available points in Agile sprints can be allocated for supporting analytics.

- **Strategic methods:** It may be necessary to train, educate, or develop new ways or work to accommodate for the nuances of analytics into the technology process.

- **Financial methods:** Compensation and bonus incentives for IT can be tied to satisfaction ratings.

Selecting an Analytics Tool

Digital analytics tools are, obviously, important to any analytics program. Tools are numerous and varied and the options for digital data collection, reporting, and even analysis are all advancing daily, release after release. In 2013, the landscape from digital analytics vendors placed a lot of emphasis on mobile, social, multichannel and omnichannel, optimization, and prediction using data science on big data—whether enabled by software run by IT teams on-premises or in the cloud, as SaaS, or from third-party data vendors, such as audience measurement firms.

The idea of multichannel means that data exists across more than one channel. Omnichannel (see Chapter 12) means analyzing data across more than one channel in a unified way focused on the customer. In traditional media, a channel would be TV, radio, billboards, direct mail, newspapers, magazines, and so on. In digital media, a channel would be paid search (Search Engine Marketing [SEM]), organic search (Search Engine Optimization [SEO]), display advertising, Quick Response (QR) codes, or a hyperlocal mobile campaign or targeted social media campaign. The best tool vendors aspire to bring together all this data, organize it, allow for querying and reporting, and the application of advanced statistical techniques that can predict the future (indeed, see Chapter 13, "Future of Digital Analytics"). By moving all these data from where they exist to databases, it is expected that the data can be mined for relationships that help understand how to create new or incremental business opportunities.

At the time of this writing, for those closely immersed in the "tool battle," it is hard to compete with free...but it is done all the time. It is a commonly held belief that a large corporation can get by using the free version of Google Analytics. This could be true or false. As the saying goes, "It depends." The more complex business environments could benefit from free tools. Or perhaps Google Analytics Premium or Universal would make more sense. Or an offering from Webtrends, IBM, or Adobe?

Following is a framework for selecting an analytics tool, and the key questions you should answer before considering purchasing a new tool, extending your existing analytics tool, or just using a free tool:

1. How much money can I spend?

2. What resources do I have?

3. Do I have the organizational capability and maturity to run an in-house software solution?

4. Do I prefer to eliminate overhead and technology expense by delegating control of my digital analytics technology and infrastructure to a hosted solution run out of a vendor's data center (that is, SaaS or in the cloud)?

5. Do I want to bring together analytical data from multiple channels (cross-channel data integration)—either within my own systems or outside of my company? If so, what systems have the data I need (CRM, Ad Server, and so on)? And what method for extracting, transforming, and loading the data can my IT team support (such as, web services, API calls, and flat files)?

After discussing and agreeing upon the answers to these questions, you can identify a set of vendors to consider.

The framework for vendor selection evaluates products across critical attributes of the product and vendor selling it. The following list of criteria is not exhaustive—and is provided only as a sample in this book. These criteria are discussed in the context of how they are relevant to your business needs and goals.

To synthesize and work with these criteria, create a matrix where the criteria is on the left axis, and the companies you select are on the top axis. Fill in the cells with your custom information evaluating a vendor (each vendor is a column in the spreadsheet) according to these guidelines and more:

- **Business value:** Include the key business initiatives and KPIs for the project.
- **Stakeholders:** The business teams and people impacted and involved with the project.
- **Architecture:** What are the vision, standard tools, Service Level Agreements (SLAs) required, and backup requirements?
- **Structure of the deal:** Indicate the preferred financial, invoicing, and payment terms.
- **Company description:** Describe the company using publicly available sources. How long has the company existed? How solvent is it? What do customers say about the company?
- **General technology description:** Explain the technology and how it works. What happens to the confidence level and confidence interval (that is, margin of error) when drilling down on the data? Can you report on every dimension and attribute of available data about a segment or is the reporting limited? How about when exporting?
- **Product and service capabilities:** Assess the overall capability of the vendor's technology and services organization when compared to the industry. What percentage of the company's customers successfully deploys tags and gets complete tag coverage across every page from day one? Or successfully transfers and correctly parses customized log files from day one?
- **Product(s) required for a solution:** List the product or products required to support the full solution. Can I run identical queries and get identical answers across all company technologies?
- **Ease of use:** Indicate the complexity of interacting with and navigating through the interface and reports. Assess the user experience of the UI from a usability and information architecture perspective. Can you simply find the data you need to gain analytic momentum?

- **Product updates and difficulty:** Indicate difficulty of product updates and the general migration path for upgrades. Does taking advantage of new functionality in a release usually require upgrading the tagging and other data collection?

- **Real-time reporting latency:** Identify the delay or lag in availability of the data within the technology. Continuous processing? Batch?

- **Time to implementation:** Indicate the time to deploy the baseline, out-of-the-box solution. What percentage of the company's customers have successfully tagged all site pages and processed logs within one month after beginning? Three months? Six months?

- **Ease of implementation:** Indicate the difficulty level of implementing the technology. What percentage of the company's application can you use if no changes are made to the JavaScript page tag?

- **Data collection model:** Identify data collection methods. Does the company's data schema simply roll up and report "unique" counts across time periods and delete the underlying data (even if you don't buy an additional product)? Does it cost more money to retain full, unsummarized visitor data for 13 months? Twenty-six? Longer?

- **Data retention and ownership:** Indicate if you retain ownership of your data. If so, for how long and at what level of granularity? For what duration does the company retain visitor data? Is that the same across all applications (not just a data warehousing component)?

- **Integration:** Determine and describe the number of data sources, formats, dimensions/facts, data retention and update frequency required, metadata, history, and classification of data as well as the transformations required on the data. Identify features and methods for integration with external systems. API? Web services? Summary extracts? Just Excel?

- **Innovation:** Indicate the level of innovation perceived by looking into the company when compared to industry competitors. What do the analysts say? How large is the company's engineering organization? What percentage of overall expense does the company spend on R&D? Partnerships?

- **Security:** Identify the security model. Does the tool support integration with directory services and enterprise software for managing users? If so, how? What is the cost per seat or license?
- **Segmentation:** Identify the flexibility and ease of segmenting data. What is the total and maximum number of segments available for use out-of-the-box? How much more does it cost if you want to increase segments or filters? How are segments created?
- **Advanced analytics:** Identify the statistical, predictive, data mining, machine learning, and other complex analysis requirements.

More attributes exist. More questions should be asked. Truly understanding an analytics technology means asking hard questions and assessing the way a company answers those questions to frame your subsequent analysis and guide your selection.

Social Media Tools

Social media tools refer to the ever-growing and vast collection of technologies that exist as software or SaaS for free or for cost that collect, store, measure, report, or analyze data from social media whether in real time, latent in detail, or aggregate in one or more geographies. Social media tools can be provided by the Social Media Platform (Facebook Insights and Twitter Analytics) or not (comScore and Compete.com or Salesforce.com).

Social media tools are (as of 2013) as numerous as grains of wheat in an American wheat field. As such, your business will more likely benefit from a social media expert, who farms out the data with a statistical scythe, rather than social media ninjas who show their kicks to influencers and hitting critics with nunchucks. Thus, the best social media tools help the digital analysts (and the subset named social media analysts) separate the wheat in the social data from the chaff.

In the preceding section, we reviewed criteria helpful to consider when selecting a digital analytics tool. Much of the same criteria can be applied to selecting a social media analytics tool as well. When selecting a social media tool, however, you also want to consider features that support the uniqueness and new concepts in social media.

Following are some helpful criteria to consider when evaluating a social media analytics tool:

- **Users:** Determining how the analytics team will use the social media analytics tool is common sense—or is it? Does the tool need a dedicated administrator? Are the user roles customizable? How many users should you have in what roles? How is user security handled?

- **Listening and engagement features:** Discover the way social media analytics listening and engaging can be measured. Are conversations threaded? Is data capture in real time? Can you respond to social media channels within the tool itself? What type of metadata or other data from different social sources is available to use?

- **Search:** The heavy textual nature of social media communications (and even the transcripts of videos and tagging of objects, like pictures and web pages) requires an excellent search capability. Make sure to learn about the nuances of social media search analytics features in each tool. What technology is used for search? What languages? Automatic categorization, clustering, text analysis? What about strange words with multiple meanings in different languages or geographies? Query language? Cost per search? Use lists of keywords? Filter results? Drill-down? Save? Rerun? Email results? Natural language? Boolean?

- **Sentiment and text analysis and categorization:** Identify the features for text mining and analysis and how customizable it is. Discuss with customer references if the tool for text mining are helpful or lacking in some way. How does the tool handle linguistic nuance and cultural differences? Text mining is an area that can easily "wow" people because it is so easy to understand—and the potential to help business is so powerful—yet, the best text analysis does not come out-of-the-box (yet), so dig deep on text analysis and how it is handled when words have multiple meanings, in different cultures (with different semiotics), and across different languages (in one, multiple, or within one country). Make sure the tool can be tuned to your local and regional linguistic and spoken nuances and slang.

- **Data access and integration:** Social media data alone has value, but the value can be truly unlocked only by integrating it with other data. Integration with CRM systems, third-party data vendors (comScore and Rapleaf), data enhancers

(Experian), data from large platforms (Google and Facebook), and customer data (in CRM systems) is possible, but social media tools are nascent in support as of 2013. Determine how the data, when collected, is stored and summarized. For how long? At what cost? Who owns it? Can data be accessed without leaving the tool and by the tool itself? What partners exist and proven use-cases are demonstrated where data was accessed, extracted, transferred, and loaded either to and/or from the social media analytics tool?

- **System integration:** At a more macro level than data integration, entire systems can be linked together and their operations orchestrated to generate business values. Adobe Genesis, Webtrends Connect, comScore Social Analytix, Salesforce.com, are all examples of systems integration that are possible at the vendor or customer level.

- **Customization and growth:** Social media is dynamic and evolving organically; thus, social media analytics tools must provide features that enable extensibility and scalability of data collection, processing, reporting, and analyzing data. In addition, the features for listening, participating, engaging, and managing social media analytics must continue to evolve. How is the tool supporting the inevitable fast pace of change in 21st century social media?

- **Tracking, reporting, and analysis:** Can the social media team's time and activities be tracked in the tool? Message archiving? Scheduled engagement? Dashboarding? Scheduled reporting? Usage of other data from third parties?

Mobile Analytics Tools

Mobile analytics tools are similar to digital analytics tools—and should be considered using the same criteria for them as outlined earlier in this chapter. These tools enable data collection, processing, reporting, visualization, and possibly even analysis on mobile data collected directly from handheld mobile devices, and the apps and software programs installed on them. The best tools enable the mobile data to be extracted from the tool and even integrated with other digital or traditional data, such as qualitative and Voice of Customer (VoC) data. Other mobile analytics tools integrate with marketing tools to provide mobile marketing features or capabilities, like in-app messaging or in-app purchasing or in- and across-app mobile marketing platforms.

Tools for mobile analytics are divided into the following:

- **Internal mobile measurement tools:** Deployed either via software installed and maintained by IT in a data center, or provided by a vendor such as SaaS, for example, Webtrends and Localytics.

- **External mobile measurement tools:** Third-party data vendors who collect, aggregate, report, and sell analysis and access to analytical data to customers from proprietary systems, for example, Nielsen and comScore.

Because mobile analytics is another digital channel, many of the same principles apply for determining how to select a mobile analytics tool as apply for selecting a digital analytics tool or social analytics tool (see the discussions in the preceding sections of this chapter). Nuance on the mobile channel makes it worth identifying the following challenges to collecting, reporting, and analyzing mobile data:

- **Data collection:** Not all mobile browsers execute JavaScript, so the most common method for collecting Web analytics data doesn't work across all devices. Thus, vendors offer choices for data collection. Current mobile analytics offerings include image-based data collection methods, packet sniffers, server-side "no tag" implementations, web services, log files, and more.

- **Unique visitor identification due to lack of cookie support and the changing of IP addresses:** IP addresses on mobile browsers can change as they switch from tower to tower. In addition, many mobile devices take the IP address of the gateway, making all the devices look like the same "person."

  Compounding the difficulty in assessing "uniqueness" is that not all mobile devices support cookies. As many of you know, in Web analytics, cookies are helpful in defining uniqueness, and in mobile analytics, they are helpful in weaving together sessions when the IP address changes mid-session. The fallback method in analytics, when you can't use a cookie, is IP address/user agent. Thus, if you can't set cookies and the IP address and user agents are identical, then how do you identify uniqueness? That's the challenge. Interestingly, packet sniffing as a data collection method has an advantage here because some devices pass unique IDs (such as the phone number) in the hypertext transfer protocol (HTTP) header. When you can detect a unique value in the header, you can easily detect uniqueness.

- **Handset capability detection:** Companies that want to identify whether the device supports pushing, streaming video, ringtones, downloading video clips, and so on need to carefully select a measurement tool to ensure these attributes are available.

- **Phone and manufacturer identification:** Databases and mobile Direct Data Repositories (DDR) that use Wireless Universal Resource FiLe (WURFL) such as DeviceAtlas can be used to identify phone and manufacturer device attributes. Larger vendors are further behind on integrating this data into their current offerings, whereas the smaller niche players are making use of it.

- **Screen resolution detection:** The Mobile Marketing Association's standards for the four "standard" screen sizes might carry enough weight to push this disdained piece of metrics trivia available from JavaScript-based tagging in Web analytics into a brighter spotlight for guiding user experience and interface design for mobile applications.

- **Traffic source detection:** Determining the source of traffic, such as search, email, direct entry, display advertising, other mobile apps, app stores, browsers, and marketing campaigns can be challenging in the mobile space.

- **Geographic identification:** Where are the visitors viewing your site coming from? And what does the mobile audience environment "look like" in each country? From this information, you can extrapolate country-specifics for mobile site and application optimization and localization. But not all devices enable geographic detection because the gateway's IP address is used, not a global positioning system (GPS) signal. If geographic data is important to you, make sure you ask vendors that you are researching how they collect it and what are the limitations.

Although there are still many challenges in collecting and reporting mobile analytics data, the industry is much further along than ever before in delivering solutions in this emerging area of analytics. Still there's a lot more work that vendors need to do to improve the precision of the data they are collecting and the overall data about the mobile experience that they are reporting.

As you look toward purchasing the best solution for your company's needs, carefully consider the data you need to collect and report for analysis, and judiciously choose the vendor that provides the most appropriate and extensible data collection and reporting capabilities that fit your business goals.

Succeeding with Tool Deployment

Here is a simple framework for success with tool deployment:

- **Consider doing an Request For Proposal (RFP).** Sure, vendors will always say "Yes" and can claims do everything, which is not what is meant to be uncovered by an RFP. RFPs act as artifacts around which to capture explicitly in writing not only the requirements of the tool, but also the requirements of the business. An RFP can act as a centroid for documenting requirements in a reflective and recursive way. In addition, the process of interacting with a vendor is identified early in the business relationship. You would be surprised how often the behavior of a company in the RFP process (ideally its best behavior because it wants your money) is an indicator of future behavior that will indeed be different (after it has your money). Thus, the RFP process not only helps to identify, document, socialize, and gain cross-functional approval for both tool and business requirements, it also acts as an artifact for understanding and predicting the organizational behavior of the vendor. This is key in digital analytics; when talent and resources are so scarce, consultants are often necessary at all phases in the implementation, execution, maintenance, and optimization of a world-class 21st century analytics program.

- **Interact in person with the vendor's team (at all levels).** Although sales relationships may get you some free food and meals, drinks, sports tickets, and otherwise good fun, the sales guys generally run to cash their commission checks before the ink is dry. By that point, you will already have been assigned a client partner after the sales cycle (and baseball games) who you may have never met and may have no idea about your business, you, and your team's goals. Thus, quite simply, ask to meet the people whom—were you to sign the contract—you would be interacting with as a customer. This includes the professional service engineers, client's partners, project managers, and even phone calls with the support engineers. This is no time to be shy; ask about the people before you sign the deal.

- **Demand that the vendors use their own resources.** Given the talent shortage in digital analytics, it is not uncommon for vendors to use partners from other companies, which may or may not be disclosed. In other words, you buy X software and expect the X professional services team to deploy your implementation, but the vendor is too busy. Thus, the vendor contracts Y boutique consultancy and sends Y worker to handle your deployment. Although this might not make sense, be aware this can happen. Although many of the best have their own consultancies, the tool vendors who create the tools have "bench strength" in professional services and direct access to the product engineering teams.

- **Don't settle for ambiguous scope.** Scope can be defined as all the work required to do a project. Scope is essential for the successful delivery of any analytical deliverable—from the simplest and most common basic report to the most erudite, complicated, and sophisticated analytical deliverable. Don't settle on reduced scope as a businessperson. Businesspeople dictate analytical scope to IT—not the other way around—and successful businesspeople control, refine, shrink, and expand the scope of analytics deliverables to ensure they do what is best for the business...or else.

- **Demand a project manager on both sides.** Analytics teams require support from project management professionals (PMP). This isn't about the analytics team using Microsoft Project or some online software to manage the actions, items, risks, and issues of a project in a quasi-PMP fashion. Digital analytics projects can benefit from the full or at least part-time allocation of a real PMP. A project manager handles the details of the projects and can help the analytics manager and analysts successfully execute the project.

An analytics manager may be the best project manager that has ever existed in corporate history, but her job is not as a project manager. Her job (and why she gets paid) is to analyze data and tell stories to the business based on mathematical fact, not manage an ever-changing array of constantly shifting tactical details related to the execution of projects on which her team is working and for which she is accountable. In other words, analytics managers need to manage rigorously, relentlessly, and in some cases ruthlessly the analytics team, the macro-level projects, senior management, peers, stakeholders, themselves, and project managers.

- **Relentlessly track project success (yourself, Mr. Bossman).** A manager, even one working as a world-class PMP, needs to keep track of managerial indicators for every project your team is currently executing, planning to execute, and asked to execute. This means that you, the analytics vice president (VP), should work to aggregate into a common format all the internal operational, tactical (and strategic) work that you and your team executes. This master file should be kept current, history should be recorded and maintained, and this file should be requested to show what your team did in the past, is currently doing, and will do in the future.

- **Ensure cross-functionality.** Last but not least is a tip that is useful for succeeding as an analytical manager. You may think you know what it takes (and you may be right); you may think you can do it all yourself (and you may be right); but businesses are organizational and cultural entities. Rarely in the course of human events has the tide turned positively in the best direction with a single person's sheer effort, willpower, brute force, might, and intelligence alone. Businesses are societal entities that take teams for creating value. As such, the best analytics VPs will create value with data, research, and analytics by leveraging business, technical, and social skills to create cross-functional consensus essential for competing on digital analytics.

Business Concerns: Maintenance

The maintenance of an analytics function is complex, hard, and challenging, but is also very rewarding and interesting work. The Analytics Value Chain reviewed in Chapter 2 has multiple phases. Each phase from data definition to collection to verification to reporting needs to be executed correctly and accurately. Thus, analytics requires support from many different functions. If any of the teams supporting the work in the phases of the value chain happens to fail or not deliver to requirements or agreed-upon scope, then the downstream data will be inaccurate and useless for analysis. As such, it is the responsibility of the analytics leadership, from the SVP to VP to Director to Manager to analysts at all levels to work together to maintain analytical excellence. Maintenance of a digital team can be divided into the following macro-level maintenance areas:

- **Architecture, infrastructure, data collection, and data governance:** This maintenance area refers to the engineering, IT, and technical work, processes, and teams for maintaining the successful, ongoing operations of the technology supporting the tools that report data. Data collection, such as tagging and using API calls, as well as the related tagging specifications and data collection testing (QA), should be categorized and resourced here. Finally, the data must be accurate, and that accuracy must be maintained as digital experiences change release by release.

- **Reporting and data distribution:** Reporting is critical and necessary. The production and distribution of reporting is a necessary and inherent part of analysis. Maintaining reporting is never a "set it and forget" activity. Reporting and the underlying data supporting it need to be audited and reviewed periodically to ensure the data has not drifted and soured. Actually, the potential likelihood for reporting to "go stale" is one of the reasons why automated reporting and other scheduled reporting needs to be maintained judiciously and often for brief periods. In other words, strive to provide analysis to answer business questions—and don't just pump out reports autosent by email.

- **Analysis and analytical communication:** Those who apply analytical techniques and methods for data analysis in new ways that incorporate digital data in a timely manner are absolutely essential to value creation with analytics. IBM cites that 90 percent of the world's data was created from 2010–2012, which proves the organizational capability and business competency of the proverb of "competing on analytics." Winning with analytics requires, of course, analysts who spend the time investigating, observing, exploring, slicing, dicing, and drilling up and down on the data to answer business questions. Stakeholders use analytical answers to take action on the analysis to create new or profitable revenue and decrease costs. Additionally, the analytics team must communicate and socialize the analytical deliverables, recommendations, conclusions, and research. Analysis work can involve modeling data and applying analytical methods and techniques, site and landing page optimization, predictive modeling, customer experience management, and so on.

When maintaining an analytical program, you must have team members who have skills that apply to more than one of these maintenance areas. For example, you want an analytics team who in general understands all the work involved in executing the Analytics Value Chain even though each team member will likely have a specialized function, such as primarily working in data collection, but will also have related skills such as doing analysis and presenting data.

Why Do Digital Analytics Tools and Data Decay?

Deploy a tool based on business requirements, customize it to fit your needs, and start analyzing the reports—and it all goes perfectly, right? No. Actually, it is common to find corporations on their second, maybe third, analytics tool over the last several years. Or they have deployed multiple tools in an attempt to arrive at where they need to be. So why then is it so difficult to find a tool for delivering comprehensive and systematic analysis to a business community and helping to drive action from insight? Several factors impact the promise of a tool and the successful use of a tool, which can cause the potential risk of failure:

- **Inability to customize to business needs:** As sites create more and richer dynamic experiences across more than one digital channel, the tool needs to accommodate for multiple channels or omnichannels. Business stakeholders can innovate new products that need specialized methods for tracking, or stakeholders can require types of data collection, reporting, analysis, optimization, or prediction not capable in the current tool or set of tools.

- **Training:** A corporation must hire or train people who understand how to use a tool. It doesn't always follow that because people know how to use Tool X, they can easily move over to using Tool Y. If a corporation doesn't budget both the time and money to extend its team's ability to use a tool, the tool will not be effectively wielded and will likely fall into disuse and ultimately fail. You must allocate resources to ensure your staff has the most current training available; otherwise, the tools you have could be considered useless because they can't be employed effectively, which leads to the exploration of alternatives and the subsequent purchase of other tools.

- **Lack of analytical resources:** Not a tool problem per se, but this issue reflects itself in an inability to quickly and agilely respond to business requests to extend the tool, provide data, or, worse yet, analyze the data. If a company can't dedicate sufficient resources to using and extending a tool and analyzing the data collected, it can quickly conclude the tool, rightly or wrongly, has little to no value and seek alternatives.

- **Too much detailed or too little detailed data:** Because of big data, the time it takes to query and report data from terabyte and petabyte data sources can take longer than expected. And just throwing more hardware at the big data doesn't necessarily speed up processing. Thus, to reduce the time to report raw data, the analytics team may create indexed or aggregate views of data. Over time, the business need for raw data or detailed data can change and, as a result, so might the toolset used to do the analysis.

- **Inordinate complexity:** The idea of analytics tool deployment and extension being "easy" is somewhat of a joke in the analytics industry. Tools, and digital analysis, are never easy, and are more hard or complex or a number of other more colorful adjectives. The difficulty and complexity in taking full advantage of an analytics tool is in how you extend it to meet your business needs. And many tools make it less than intuitive or, in the worst case, way too hard to extend a tool across an enterprise. From challenges with tagging, to orchestrating changes to data collection, to testing data collection and building reporting, and to building out a custom schema to requiring the configuration and integration of additional applications to deliver against requirements to working with multiple variables to build various types of statistical and predictive models: When these things go wrong, companies get frustrated, seek alternative solutions, and often abandon a tool in the process.

Many other reasons exist, of course, for why tools fail (cost, infrastructures, data availability, and so on), but the previous list contains items to keep in mind as you evaluate, select, implement, use, maintain, change, upgrade, or decide to augment, extend, or replace your set of analytics tools.

5

Methods and Techniques for Digital Analysis

Analysis is defined by Wikipedia's sources:

Analysis is the process of breaking a complex topic or substance into smaller parts to gain a better understanding of it. The technique has been applied in the study of mathematics and logic since before Aristotle (384–322 B.C.), though *analysis* as a formal concept is a relatively recent development.

As a formal concept, the method has variously been ascribed to Alhazen, René Descartes (*Discourse on the Method*), and Galileo Galilei. It has also been ascribed to Isaac Newton, in the form of a practical method of physical discovery (which he did not name or formally describe).

Digital is defined by Wikipedia's sources:

A **digital** system is a data technology that uses discrete (discontinuous) values. By contrast, non-digital (or analog) systems represent information using a continuous function. Although digital representations are discrete, the information represented can be either discrete, such as numbers and letters or continuous, such as sounds, images, and other measurements.

The word *digital* comes from the same source as the words *digit* and *digitus* (the Latin word for *finger*), as fingers are used for discrete counting. It is most commonly used in computing and electronics, especially where real-world information is converted to binary numeric form as in digital communications, digital audio and video, and digital photography.

Analysis, by common definition, is inherent in the representation of digital systems. Thus, if you were to combine these two definitions together into a neologistic mashup to define digital analytics, you could postulate that digital analytics is simply:

The process by which people apply technology and method to the unified understanding of information and behavior across one or more digital experiences.

This definition is generalized with the intention to not include financial concepts such as cost, revenue, and profitability. Digital analytics, of course, can be applied to nonbusiness functions (as discussed in Chapter 1, "Using Digital Analytics to Create Business Value"), such as nonprofit, content-driven, and mission-driven digital experiences beyond conversion and revenue-focused digital experiences.

The general theory and concepts for digital analytics will be discussed in the companion ebook text to this book named *A Digital Analytics Primer*, and this chapter reviews several concepts that are useful for applied analysis of business data. While examples are provided wherever possible, the review here is at a higher level, focused on an audience that has had an introductory level of exposure to analytical concepts, such as data visualization and mathematical and statistical methods. The content of this chapter is non-exhaustive and certainly does not cover every method or technique that can be applied to digital data; however, this chapter can be a helpful reference for understanding what is possible. I wrote this chapter to give the reader an orientation about analytical techniques that is hard to find in one spot. This chapter:

- Overviews past and current academic theory on analysis, which is relevant, useful, and applicable to digital data and digital analysis
- Discusses the techniques for examining and interrogating data when extracted from source systems using appropriate data extraction tools and methods
- Reviews important and helpful data visualizations that can be applied to digital data to go beyond data tables and spreadsheets
- Provides a high-level review and description of useful statistical data mining and machine learning techniques for digital data analysis

By the end of this chapter, you should have confirmed and expanded your knowledge about the fundamentals of analysis, so that you are prepared to apply these techniques and methods to the analysis of digital experiences such that you find the insight and signals from which to create business value.

Storytelling Is Important for Analysis

The importance of narrating a compelling story about what the data can tell you is critical to analysis. When telling a story with data, answer the business question posed and demonstrate insights and knowledge derived from data that includes a solid set of relevant and useful outcomes-focused recommendations. Fulfilling the goal of delivering accurate analysis that helps to create and drive business value involves applying the methods and techniques in this chapter; however, the way you deliver the message in the data may even be more important than what the data says. Keep in mind that if you present analysis that in any way differs, changes, or presents a perspective different than is commonly understood or if your analysis shows business performance in any way that is not positive, it is likely that your data and analysis will be challenged. The analyst must ensure that analysis is presented in the most humanistic way possible focused on organizational behavior, motivation, and human emotion. Thus, instead of blasting up data only with numbers and slides with charts and graphs, make sure to weave a narrative through the data. Do not make the mistake of presenting only data and visualizations. Tell stories with the data.

Following are several guidelines when forming a story to tell from data. Consider applying these techniques when socializing analysis in the form of story-based narratives:

- **Identify why the analysis has occurred and why the story you are about to tell is important.** Businesspeople are incredibly busy and require context for reporting and analysis. Explain why they should care.
- **Indicate the business challenge you want to discuss and the cost of not fixing it.** By clearly stating what business issue

necessitates the analysis and framing the recommendations, you can eliminate confusion.

- **Identify any forewarnings.** If there are any errors, omissions, caveats, or things to discuss, clearly indicate them in advance.

- **Depersonalize the analysis by using fictional characters to help humanize the data you are reporting.** Using fictional characters helps to depersonalize analysis and lowers political risk. Creating fictional scenarios and abstracting concepts when narrating an analysis helps to eliminate the risk of offending a specific stakeholder or group.

- **Cite important events that help to illustrate a narrative.** When presenting time-series data with changing metrics, make sure to annotate the data with the events and activities that co-occurred with the change in data. Externalities, market events, and other things that happen in the business can help to clarify changes in the data.

- **Use pictures.** They are worth a thousand words. Save valuable time by using charts, graphs, trendlines, and other data visualization techniques. When possible, use illustrations to communicate concepts.

- **Don't use overly complex, wonky vocabulary.** Esoteric and scientific vocabulary is best left within the analytics team. No one will really be impressed if you use words like "stochastic." Try to make the communication and presentation of analysis as simple as possible, so that is easily understood and acted upon by your stakeholders.

- **Identify what is required.** Clearly indicate what you think needs to be done in written language using action-oriented verbs and descriptive nouns. Say what you think and what you want to do. Set expectations as early as possible for cost and new resources needed to support analytics.

- **Identify the cost of inaction.** Clearly indicate the financial impact of doing nothing—and compare it against the cost of doing something. It may help to present comparable costs from other alternatives.

- **Conclude with a series of recommendations that tie to value generation (either reduced cost or increased revenue).** Although you may not be an expert at the same level as the person requesting the analysis, analysts should express their ideas and perspective on the data and business situation.

Recommendations should be made that are clearly and directly based on data analysis—and these recommendations must be able to withstand the scrutiny and questions.

Tukey's Exploratory Data Analysis Is an Important Concept in Digital Analytics

John Tukey authored the (in)famous book in 1977, *Exploratory Data Analysis,* and was the first person to use the term "software" and the word "bit" or "binary digit" in the modern lexicon. Most digital analysts could learn a thing or ten from Tukey and his EDA. Apply EDA to digital analytics.

Exploratory data analysis (EDA) is more of a mindset for analysis rather than an explicit set of techniques and methods; however, EDA does make use of several techniques contained in this chapter. Tukey's philosophy on data was one that favored observation, visualization, and the careful application of technique to make sense of data. EDA is not about fitting data into your analytical model; rather it is about fitting a model to your data. As a result, Tukey and EDA created interest in non-Gaussian and nonparametric techniques in which the shape of data indicates it is not normally distributed and may have a fat head with a long tail. Sound familiar? It should. The idea of the long tail is a Pareto concept that Tukey probably would have favored for understanding big data. After all, much Web data is not normally distributed, so using basic statistics that expect a normal distribution would not be optimal.

The reason Tukey is referenced in this text is not only because he has been hugely influential on using mathematics and statistics to understand what the data is saying, but his paradigm for data analysis is based on a set of philosophies or tenets that are useful to consider for digital analytics, which involve:

- **Visually examining data to understand patterns and trends.** Raw data should be examined to learn the trends and patterns over time and between dimensions and concepts in the data. Visual examination can help frame what analytical methods are possible to apply to your digital data.

- **Using the best possible methods to gain insights into not just the data, but what the data is saying.** Tukey espouses getting beyond the data and its details and understanding what the data is saying in the context of answering your questions. This approach is integral to digital analytics.

- **Identifying the best performing variables and model for the data.** Digital analytics is filled with so much big data, but how do you know what is the right big and small data to use for solving a business problem? EDA helps ascertain what variables are influential and important.

- **Detecting anomalous and suspicious outlier data.** Digital data has outliers and anomalies that in and of themselves may be important, highly relevant, and meaningful to the business or just random noise that can be ignored and possibly excluded from analytical consideration.

- **Testing hypothesis and assumptions.** Digital analytics emphasizes the approach to using insights derived from data to create hypotheses and test hypothesis-driven changes within digital experiences. The idea of using data to test hypotheses and assumptions is crucial to EDA.

- **Finding and applying the best possible model to fit the data.** Predictive modeling and analysis requires an EDA approach that is more focused on the data rather than the model.

Tukey's principle helps simplify the creation of digital analysis; it emphasizes the visual exploration of the data as the first step in the process of analysis, instead of first determining the statistical method to apply to the data and fitting the data to it.

The philosophy of EDA is well aligned with digital analysis. One of the first things to do when examining a data set is to identify key dimensions and metrics and use analytical software to visualize the data (using the techniques reviewed in this chapter) before applying any statistical method. This way, you can use the tools and your pattern recognition abilities to observe the data relationships and unusual data movements. By visually examining and exploring the data, it is possible to help focus your approach to the work of analysis. Then after looking closely at the data, you can determine how to analyze it and the appropriate applied analytical method to use to generate value from it.

Digital analytics combined with Tukey's EDA approach (or modality) to data analysis can be used alone or with other techniques. EDA can be used in combination with, perhaps more well-known, modalities for understanding data, such as classical statistics and Bayesian methods. Fortunately, all three modalities for data analysis provide frameworks for finding insights in data that can be applied to digital analytics; EDA, however, imposes less formality than either classical or Bayesian approaches. This flexibility is helpful when analyzing all the different types of digital data from those that exist now to those that may exist in the future.

EDA advocates that you look at the data first by plotting a data visualization and then analyzing the data using the best possible techniques for that data, which may be classical, Bayesian, or not. Classical statistics, unlike EDA, would first instruct the analyst to fit the data to the preferred model, perhaps trimming data to make them fit. A Bayesian approach is an extension of the classical approach where you would first look at prior data. EDA recommends creating data visualizations first before selecting a model or reaching any conclusive insights. Classical and Bayesian analysts would likely view data visualization as a supporting artifact created during or after analysis (not as the first step to start an analysis). EDA would consider Gaussian and non-Gaussian techniques equally valid based on the data and would encourage the analyst to explore the data and make simple conclusions based on useful visualizations. The advanced applied analysis in EDA comes after the simple conclusions.

When conducting digital analysis, keep classical, Bayesian, and EDA approaches in mind and remember what Tukey said in his book *Exploratory Data Analysis*:

Following is a short suggestion of exploratory data analysis:

It is an attitude AND a flexibility AND some graph paper (or transparencies, or both).

No catalogue of techniques can convey a willingness to look for what can be seen, whether or not anticipated. Yet this is at the heart of exploratory data analysis. The graph paper and transparencies are there, not as a technique, but rather as recognition that the picture-examining eye is the best finder you have of the wholly unanticipated.

Types of Data: Simplified

Data typing is a useful concept to apply to digital analytics. *Data type* refers simply to the types of data that an analyst runs into in the digital world. My goal here is to not overwhelm you with complexity nor confuse you with unusual and uncommon words. Data type doesn't refer to the common computer science and engineering terms (such as integers, Boolean, floating point, and so on). Instead, it is a simple way to understand data types and data subtypes in a practical business way:

- **Quantitative data:** Data that is numeric. The data is a number, such as 2 or 2.2—whole or floating point integers in engineering parlance. Quantitative data can be further subdivided into

  - **Univariate data:** Like the prefix "uni," this data type deals with one single variable. The analyst uses this variable to describe the data to stakeholders using methods to examine distribution, central tendency, dispersion, and simple data visualization techniques like box plots. A question of univariate data might be, "How many unique visitors have we had on the site by month for the last 24 months?"

  - **Bivariate data:** The prefix "bi" means "two;" thus, this data type deals with two variables. The analyst uses these variables to explain the relationship of one to another. The methods' used include correlation, regression, and other advanced analytical techniques. A question of bivariate data might be, "What is the relationship between marketing spend and product purchases?"

  - **Multivariate data:** Data that has more than two variables. Many advanced analytics techniques, from multiple linear regressions to automate-tested, targeting, and optimization algorithms and technologies use multivariate data. Most, if not all, analytics systems create multivariate data. Big data is multivariate data.

- **Qualitative data:** Data that is not numerical but text-based. Traditionally, qualitative data could be pass/fail (P/F) or multiple choices (A, B, C, D) or text-based, verbatim answers derived from market research.

Quantitative and qualitative data can further be divided into subtypes such as

- **Discrete data:** Data that can be counted separately from each other, for example, the number of unique visitors.
- **Nominal data:** Data where a code or variable is assigned as a representation. Nominal data can be quantitative or qualitative, for example, using Y or N to represent whether a particular marketing campaign is profitable.
- **Ordinal data:** Data that can be ranked and has a ranking scale attached to it. For example, Net Promoter Scores or the star-rating on a mobile application are examples of ordinal data.
- **Interval data:** Data that is based on two points where the count starts does not matter. Interval data can be subtracted and added but not divided or multiplied, for example, the recency of two distinct segments of data (as expressed in days).
- **Continuous data:** Data that can take any value with a specific interval, for example, the time a customer spends on a mobile device on weekdays compared to weekends. Or the size over time of your website's homepage.
- **Categorical data:** Data that is, as the name implies, represented by categories. Think of search categories, inventories, taxonomies, and other classification systems that need to be represented in analysis.

The reality in digital analytics is that an analyst often runs into each type of data—often when solving for the same business problem. Take for example, the analytical project where a search-referred visitor's online opinion data about a mobile application is joined to his digital behavior. In this case, the search keyword (and related ad group) is known, as is the person's either positive or negative opinion about the relevancy of the digital content to his intent—and the person's behavior that led him to his conclusion.

It helps digital analysis to categorize these data types, especially the data used for Key Performance Indicators, into leading, lagging, or coincident indicators. A leading indicator signals a future event whereas a lagging indicator occurs after an event. A coincident indicator occurs at approximately the same time as the circumstances signified. For example, interest rates are leading indicators whereas unemployment rates are lagging indicators. The index of the stock market at any given time is a coincident indicator.

Looking at Data: Shapes of Data

When first beginning a digital analysis project, it helps to look at the shape of the data to understand what method may be appropriate. *Data shape* is likely a familiar concept to you due to the popularity of concepts like the bell curve in the normal distribution. A perfectly normal distribution is shaped like a bell. In digital reality, most data is not perfectly shaped; instead, it is usually skewed *negatively* to the left or *positively* to right.

At the ends of the distributions, you can find outlier data. Outliers are data values that fall outside of where most of the data is located. The traditional statistics rule is that an outlier is indicated by a data measurement at or more than two standard deviations away from the average. When data has many outliers, they are considered to have *kurtosis* such that the ends of the distribution may be fatter and turn up at the ends.

Shape is important when analyzing data because it is an easy way to immediately infer the type of data and the possible methods or approaches for dealing with the data. For example, if you notice that the shape of your data is Pareto with a long tail, it may not make sense to use a model for normally distributed data. Perfectly symmetrical data would be ideal to work with, but it never exists; thus, analysts attempt to use various techniques to turn skewed data into symmetrical data.

Understanding Basic Stats: Mean, Median, Standard Deviation, and Variance

Digital analytics is complex in many ways—from people to the process to the technology—and even the analysis. Classical statistics, like that taught in business schools throughout the world, is helpful for making sense of digital data. Actually, after plotting that data using the visualization techniques described in this chapter, you should also use basic analytical methods such as the following:

- **Mean or average of the data.** By summing all the observed values in a dataset and dividing by the number of observations, you can calculate the average. Averages are perhaps the most commonly used technique for making sense of data.

They can also be one of the most misleading because the mean can be skewed by the outlier data. Averages can hide detail in the underlying distribution and should be used carefully, not casually.

• **Median or stated in another way—half of the observations were above this level and half below.** The median basically takes the statistical midpoint in the data. It is the middle of the dataset, the median. In distributions where the mean is skewed by outliers, the median is helpful to assess.

• **Mode is the often neglected or forgotten concept.** Generally speaking, mode is the value most frequently used in distribution. For example, if 29 out of 50 people got a score of 88 and 21 people got scores that were not 88, then the mode would be 88 (because it is the most frequently occurring value).

• **Standard deviation is a measure of the spread in a dataset.** The standard deviation measures the dispersion of the values in the data. For example, if analytics showed that people spent between 3 and 27 minutes on website A and between 13 and 15 minutes on website B, then website A would be considered to have a larger standard deviation because the data is more dispersed.

• **Range is another useful concept used in digital analytics.** It is the measure between the highest and lowest values in a data set. As such, it is highly influenced by outliers. For example, if one month a mobile app has 200,000 downloads and the next month the app has 500,000 downloads, the range would be 300,000 (500,000 – 200,000).

• **Outliers is a common term in data, which are measured by an observation in a dataset that is equal to or larger than two times the standard deviation.** In the real-world practice of digital analytics, outliers can be trimmed from the dataset to shape the data for application in the model. Or in a truer EDA-esque approach, outliers can be investigated to determine whether an unusual insight exists in the outlier.

For example, if a person deposits one million dollars into her bank account instead of her usual thousand dollar paycheck, the one million dollar deposit would be considered an outlier. Banks use outlier data detected by analytics systems as input for targeting and promotional offers. For example, the person's bank may offer a financial instrument for investing those million dollars upon next login.

These rather simple statistical concepts are the foundation for understanding how to analyze quantitative data. Make sure to comprehend these concepts and their definitions, and apply them in your analysis.

Plotting Digital Data

One of the simplest, lowest risk, quickest, and highest value analytical activities is plotting data. Data plotting requires a minimal effort and is a common data visualization supported by most analytics and reporting tools. By taking the data in raw or detailed form and applying it to a set of coordinates and related visualizations, an analyst can see what the numbers say. In EDA (previously reviewed), the graphical interpretation of data is central and primary. In digital analytics, plotting data using the techniques described next can help the analyst identify the best model for analyzing the data. Plotting may reveal outliers and other anomalous data that should be closely investigated as a part of a digital analytical plan. These plots are the block, lag, spider, scatter, and run-sequence plot discussed here.

Block Plot

The *block plot* is an EDA tool that attempts to replace the Analysis of Variance test (ANOVA) used in Bayesian statistics. The block plot is a graphical technique that enables the comparison of multiple factors on a particular response across more than one group. Block plots are useful in digital analytics for comparing data generated from testing and experimentation where multiple combinations of elements on a goal are being analyzed.

The block plot can help you determine whether a particular variable impacts your goal and whether the impact is significant. By using a block plot to visually examine the results of testing and experimentation, you can identify the best possible combination of variables meeting a goal and how much current performance may be impacted by the various experiments.

For example, you could use a block plot to visualize the impact of a business plan on an average order value (a common e-commerce metric) where the plan experimented with marketing channel, site speed, time of day, and the user's persona. You can then use the block plot to determine if the average order value were significantly impacted by the people being exposed to different advertising at different times of the day and the impact of speed on the business model.

The block plot helps you quickly identify the impact of your experimentation without using an ANOVA or other method. The challenge when trying to employ this basic EDA technique is that most commercial software can't create block plots.

Lag Plot

A *lag plot* is a more complicated type of a scatter plot. It is used for visualizing whether a dataset is random (stochastic) or not over a particular lag (time). After all, random data should look random and not actually take any noticeable and definable shape. For example, if you plot data and notice the lag plot shows data points in a pattern (like a line), you could quickly surmise that the data was linear or quadratic and apply the appropriate analytical method. Although you won't get into the importance of random data in research, the lag plot is one easy way to check for randomness—and also notice if any outliers exist in the data. Use a lag plot to check the shape of data and visually inspect it to determine a suitable model to apply for analysis.

You may ask what the difference is between a scatter plot and lag plot. The difference is that the two variables measured in a lag plot are plotted over time displacement. If you don't understand what time displacement means, use a scatter plot.

Spider/Star/Radar Plot

A *spider plot* is a type of plot for multivariate data where the analyst wants to understand the impact of one variable across a visually complicated display, but one that presents a considerable amount of data visually. This visualization can also be called a *star* or *radar plot*. The easiest way to understand a spider plot is to look at one (see Figure 5.1).

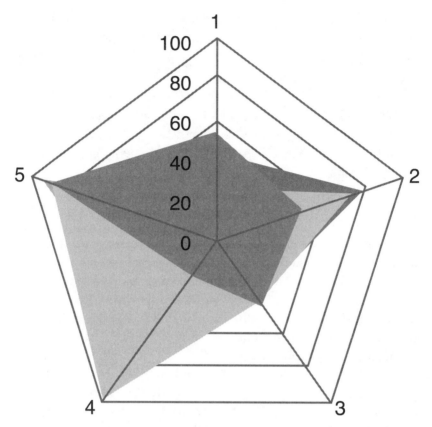

Figure 5.1 An example of a spider plot, also called a star or radar plot.

As you can see in Figure 5.1, each variable is connected by lines between a set of spokes. Each spoke is a variable, and the length of the angle is in proportion to the impact of that variable (against all other variables). As such, the data looks like a star or spider. This type of data plot is especially useful when you compare a number of observations across the same scale. The angles visually demonstrate if any variables impact more than others and can also help comparing whether similarities or differences exist when comparing different subjects across the same attributes. Just remember not to use too many variables, or the plot can get messy and unreadable.

For example, you may use a spider plot to visualize the performance of a website across geographies, visits, visitors, time spent, and conversion rate.

Scatter Plot

A *scatter plot* is fundamental data visualization when analyzing a data set. It quickly helps to show relationships between variables. You would plot one variable and all observations on the x-axis and the other value on the y-axis. Metrics such as conversion rate and dimensions such as marketing campaign and time can be scatter-plotted to reveal relationships, such as linearity or nonlinearity. As with most EDA visualization, the noticeable relationship between the data in the scatter plot can help the analyst understand correlation (visually) and helps for selecting the best analytical model to use for analysis. As with other analytical techniques, be careful not to over-interpret a correlation noticed in scatter plots.

Probability Plot

The *probability plot* is a powerful EDA technique for determining the type of distribution of your data. For example, it is helpful to know whether you are working with a normal distribution or another non-Gaussian type of distribution. The mechanics and mathematics of creating a probability plot are well beyond the goal of this book; however, probability plots are easy to understand and interpret. The analyst plots each data point in a straight line (or at least attempts to do so)—and any data point that falls outside the line is considered to not fit the hypothesized distribution based on a correlation coefficient. Because of the flexibility of seeing if the data fits into the plot (and thus the hypothesized distribution), this technique enables the analyst to run tests on the same data against different distributions. The probability plot with the highest correlation coefficient indicates the best-fitting distribution for the data.

Run Sequence Plot

The *run sequence plot* is among the most common data plots because it is applied to univariate data. That is, an analyst needs only one variable plotted across time to create this simple, but powerful, data visualization. It is the data summarization technique that helps to detect changes in the data. This plot enables a data set to be examined on a common scale and across the distribution to determine outliers, the scale of the data, the location of the data, and the randomness. The response variable, such as conversion rate, is always plotted on the y-axis.

Four Plots and Six Plots

Four plots and *six plots* are, respectively, sets of four and six EDA techniques for graphically and visually exploring your data. The main difference in the presentation is that a four plot uses the run-sequence plot and the six plot uses scatter plots. The four-plot technique is more frequently associated with univariate data, while the six-plot is more associated with multivariate data. Both visualizations are in fact useful for digital data. Table 5-1 shows the four- and six-plot techniques.

Table 5-1 Four and Six Plot Methods

Plot Grouping	Methods
Four Plot	Run sequence, lag, histogram, probability plot
Six Plot	Three scatter plots (independent, dependent, and residuals), lag plot, histogram, and probability plot

Histograms (Regular, Clustered, and Stacked)

Histograms are graphical representations that show scale of one or more observations to summarize the data distribution. They help an analyst visually comprehend the spread of a distribution along with its center, skew, and any outliers. Typically, the y-axis shows the measurement and the x-axis shows the variable measured. Histograms are flexible visualizations in that you can custom-define both measurements you want to show. Showing more than one measured variable is simple with a histogram because the analyst can create the groupings (called classes) based on their own rules—or using classical statistical methods (such as dividing into 10 equal classes).

Histograms show scale on the y-axis and different data on the x-axis based on type. Histograms can be different types:

- **Regular histograms** show one or more similar measurements, for example, displaying the count of unique visitors by month for 2013.

- **Clustered histograms** show scale on the y-axis and a grouping of variables along an interval. For example, you may use a clustered histogram to show the count of unique visitors by month for four different sites.

- **Stacked histograms** show the components (the detail) in a distribution. For example, you may stack marketing spend by month by campaign.

Pie Charts

Pie charts are an extremely common visualization in data analysis. They are circular and divided into sections where each section represents a portion of the total measurement. Pie charts do not, however, make all analysts happy. Actually, the pie chart is quite disdained as an insufficient or unnecessary technique. Pundits claim that a data table can show, more easily, the slices of a pie. A histogram shows the exact same data as a pie chart—for these two visualizations are interchangeable. The pie chart starts to get messy and hard to read when divided into more than six sections.

Pie charts are easy to understand and are a common dessert metaphor, which explains their popularity. Everyone understands how to slice up a pie, and it's an easy leap for students and new analysts alike to put their data into this familiar image. Pie charts are of four types:

- **Standard pie charts** are circular and show the proportion to scale of each piece in the total measurement.

- **Expanded pie charts** are where the sections of the pie are dislocated from the entire pie and then showed adjacent in space. By using white space to separate sections of the pie, the analyst is visually highlighting the data.

- **New types of pie charts**, such as the *3D pie*, the *pie ringchart*, and the *doughnut chart* are evolutions of this visualization and have their own parameters and applications that further break down the pie chart to communicate and highlight more data.

- **Harvey Balls are** not actually pie charts according to the traditional definition, but are highlighted because of similarity in shape. A Harvey Ball uses either a hollow, solid, or sectioned circle to communicate information about the applicability of an object to criteria. For example, you could use Harvey Balls to illustrate whether the speed of a web page meets a given threshold.

Line Charts

A *line chart* is a visualization for communicating trends in data that occur, most typically, over time. Because the chronology of experience can be charted using a line, this chart is frequently employed by analysts to show trends and time-series. By plotting data points in a distribution and then connecting them with a line, the scale and pattern in a trend and temporality can be communicated. Outliers, trends, and anomalies can be seen using a line chart. By comparing lines representing the same measure across different intervals, changes in data can be observed. Line charts are created by plotting the measure for which you want to trend on the y-axis and time on the x-axis.

The "line" in the chart in most cases represents the trend exposed by connecting the data points. In other cases, an analyst may present a line on a chart that "fits" that data. The "best-fitting" line when plotted, typically within another type of chart, is meant to show the general trend in a large number of data points where it is not possible to draw a meaningful line by connecting the data points. In these cases, the best-fitting line can be created using many statistical methods, such as linear regression or other methods where the best-fitting line may not necessarily be a straight line, such as quadratic or exponential techniques.

The most common line charts an analyst produces are the following:

- **Area charts** are used to show portions of a total or to compare more than one variable across the same measures (generally scale and time). Like the stacked bar, the area chart can be used to show the distribution and movements of sections of data against other sections and the whole.

- **Sparkline charts** are popular because they are so simple to understand, visually powerful, and easy to create. Unlike the standard line chart, the sparkline is never bivariate or multivariate. It's always univariate. In application, the sparkline is loosened from the "chartjunk" and "infoglut" such as axes, gridlines, words, and numbers to concisely and quickly communicate a small amount of information.

- **Streamgraph charts** are an evolution of the area chart where more than one variable is trended across time (or another measure) against some scale. Each "stream" in the graph represents a portion of the total in the same way that a bar in a stacked bar chart represents a portion of the total. The difference in the stream is that the axis is displaced such that the lower and upper bounds of the chart are not limited or trimmed. Each stream touches the bottom of the higher stream and the top of the lower stream.

Flow Visualizations

Flow visualizations have their roots in operational management and other phased processes that result in an outcome. The metaphor of a "flow" is suitable for digital analytics where customers are coming and going from many channels, on many devices, to many different digital experiences. As these prospects and customers flow through a digital experience, it is important to understand if the customer is creating value by measuring whether the customer completes the goals you have defined either in one visit or across time.

The idea of "flow" should sound familiar to those who already work in the digital space. One of the most common constructs for representing customer flow to create value is by using a data visualization to show the discrete steps in a user's behavior that make money. Take the well-known notion of the "conversion rate" where three to five pre-identified steps such as entry page > search > product page > checkout > thank you page define the conversion flow on your website. Customers may not convert when they begin the conversion process, may jump between steps, abandon the process, or complete it at a later date via different marketing channels. To help visually communicate these complex digital experiences and the customer flow over time, the following flow visualizations are useful:

- **Bullet chart:** A flowdata visualization technique whose closest offline analog is a thermometer you might have found in the Austrian Alps in the 1960s. Bullet charts display not only scale of a univariate observation, but also use color to highlight a qualitative judgment of success and enable plotting a goal. Bullet charts are a type of histogram—and can be categorized as such; however, because they can be associated with a goal and a target, they can also be used to visualize conversion—and thus can be considered flow charts. By showing multiple bullet charts in an adjacent space, you can illustrate a sequence of steps.

- **Funnel chart:** A graphical technique for illustrating the sequence of steps that lead to a macro or micro conversion within a digital experience. Funnels can be custom defined to begin at any point in the customer life cycle. For example, a multichannel funnel may start with exposure > acquisition source > landing page > product page > checkout. A site funnel might simply represent the steps taken to purchase a product or to sign up for a newsletter. Other funnels may be in page funnels representing the fields a user must fill out to complete an action.

  Funnel charts are often represented linearly such that each step in the funnel immediately occurs sequentially before the others. It is also valid to show a nonlinear, nonsequential funnel where steps are jumped, skipped, or entered from other parts of the site. The funnel has no formal structure or creation rules except that the last step in the funnel is the point at which value is created. Advanced funnel visualizations, such as Webtrends, attempt to visually demonstrate funnel linearity and nonlinearity including step-jumping, interpolation, and abandonment in a single chart.

- **Tumbler chart:** A newer concept, which you may be reading about for the first time here is the Tumbler. See the Unified Customer Analytics Lifecycle model discussed in Chapter 12, "Converging Omnichannels and Integrating Data for Understanding Customers, Audiences, and Media." The Tumbler expresses flow as a series of step-jumping in and out of various states. In the context of e-commerce, a person goes through the following states: seeking (where they look for a product); shopping (where they buy the product); and sharing (where they talk about the product with other people). The Tumbler is a visualization that shows the flow as people move in and out of these purchasing states.

Analyzing Digital Data Using Statistics and Machine Learning

Digital analytics is exploratory, observational, visual, and mathematical; yet, there are common data analysis methods encountered in today's analytical companies. These quantitative techniques are applied judiciously to data to answer business questions. When executing on an analytical plan, certain techniques exist for understanding data to determine what is important and represented in a distribution. You can determine whether there is a correlation between two or more data points. An analyst can use tools to automate different types of regression analysis to determine if certain data can predict other data. The details of distributions and assessments of probability can be calculated. Experimentation can be evaluated, and the hypotheses on the data can be tested to create the best-fitting model for predictive power. While statistics and machine learning are complex topics beyond the scope of this book, many of the quantitative techniques underlying algorithms in advanced analytical tools are discussed in this section.

Correlating Data

The statistics adage is that "Correlation is not causation," which is certainly true. Correlation, however, does imply association and dependence. The analyst's job is thus to prove that observed associations in data are truly dependent, relevant to the business questions, and ultimately whether or not the variable(s) cause the relationship calculated. Correlation is whether two variables move together. For example, if every time a visitor comes to your site they buy something, you could consider a strong positive correlation between a site visit and a purchase. This insight may lead you to conclude that all a person needs to do is visit a site and she will always buy. Although you might want this relationship to be true, it's more likely that the person has already decided to purchase the item before coming to the site and is just fulfilling her desire. Thus, although the mathematics may show a positive correlation between data, common sense indicates that causation does not imply causality—and that there is only an association between a site visit and revenue. Thus, there is no true causality, and the conclusion that a site visit always creates revenue would be a specious and arguable conclusion at best.

The most common measure of correlation you find in an analytics practice is a type of correlation named Pearson's correlation. Pearson produces a measurement between 1.0 and −1.0. The closer the measure is to 1.0, the stronger the positive correlation; whereas the closer the measure is to −1.0, the weaker the positive correlation such that a negative correlation coefficient indicates that the data moves in the opposite direction from one another.

In a world of linearity, Pearson's correlation is useful; however, if the data relationship for which you are calculating causality is not linear, Pearson's correlation should not be used because the conclusion based on the measure will be wrong. Test for linearity (using a number of methods) on your data set before using Pearson's correlation. If you determine that the relationships in your data are not linear, the world of statistics has other quantitative methods for determining correlation.

Rank correlation coefficients, instead of Pearson's correlation, can be applied to data sets where the distribution is not linear. If you use correlation on a set of predicted variables, you can use a partial rank correlation to understand the data. Rank correlation also indicates the relationship where one variable increases or decreases in proportion to one another.

Nonlinear dependent correlation calculations, such as Kendall's and Spearman coefficient, express the same type of positive or negative data relationship but for non-normal distributions. An analyst, however, should be careful when testing data to determine the correct correlation coefficient. Although it may be possible to substitute a linear correlation measure for a nonlinear correlation measure, these calculations are measuring differently. Such difference needs to be understood in the context of data and explained in your analysis.

Regressing Data: Linear, Logistic, and So On

The phrase *regression analysis* means applying a mathematical method for understanding the relationship between one or more variables. In more formal vocabulary, a regression analysis attempts to identify the impact of one or more independent variables on a dependent variable. There are many different approaches to completing a regression analysis based on all sorts of well-known and not-so-well-known methods. The more common methods are based on Bayesian statistics and probability distributions, such as single linear regression and multiple linear regression.

Analytics professionals and the people who ask for analytical deliverables often talk about regression, regression analysis, the best fitting line, and ways to describe determining or predicting the impact of one or more factors on a single or multiple other factors. For example, the impact of various marketing programs on sales may be determined through regression analysis. The most common regression that you see in business is the linear regression. It's taught in business schools worldwide, and many of widespread spreadsheet and data processing software support regression analysis. In the ubiquitous Excel by Microsoft, the complexity of calculating a regression is reduced to a simple expression on a data set.

In digital analytics, the regression analysis is used to determine the impact of one or more factors on another factor. Like in formal statistics, regressions in digital analytics have one or more independent variables and at least one dependent variable. In some cases, the application of a multiple linear regression analysis is possible with digital data. It is far more likely the other types of regression analysis such as exponential, quadratic, and logistic regression are a much better fit for your data. With regression analysis in digital analysis, your mileage can vary due to the interplay of relationships in big data.

Although this book and particularly this chapter are not meant to be an exhaustive coverage by any means of the mathematical principles behind the application of various models to digital data, true understanding of the application of advanced applied analytical techniques like regression, ANOVA, Multivariate Analysis of Variance (MANOVA), and various moving average models, such as autoregressive integrated moving average (ARIMA), require comprehending the underlying small data underneath.

In the purest form, as explained when discussing correlation, the type of distribution impacts the model you select. In true EDA fashion, an analyst must first look at each factor proposed to be used in a potential regression analysis. Multicollinearity, kurtosis, and the other shapes and measures of dispersion help the analyst determine if classic, Bayesian, or nonparametric techniques are the best fit for the data.

For digital data, such as the keywords and phrases from search engines to the frequency of purchases of various customer segments, digital data is most often not normally distributed. Search keywords data may follow Zift's law, while frequency may appear to follow Pareto. Thus, much of the classic and Bayesian statistical methods taught in schools are not immediately applicable to digital data. That does not mean that the classic methods you learned in college or business school do not apply to digital data; it means that the best analysts understand this fact and accommodate for it in their digital analyses. Fortunately, so do the engineers and product managers who create analytical software whose applications assist analysts in pre-processing non-normally distributed data to fit classic methods all the way to applying the best nonparametric model to the data.

The remainder of this chapter discusses frequently mentioned types of regression analysis and exposes newer thinking by current academics and reviews techniques that you can explore to understand how to fit your data to a model if you choose to go that route—or if you choose to fit your model to the data, like in EDA. Remember that regression analysis is not appropriate with all types of variables, such as discrete variables where alternative regression must be used.

Single and Multiple Linear Regression

The underlying math behind simple and multiple linear regression can be studied in detail in books such as *Applied Regression: An Introduction (Quantitative Applications in the Social Sciences)* by Michael S. Lewis-Beck (1980). For the purposes of digital analytics, a simple linear regression is used when an analyst hypothesizes that there is a relationship between the movements of two variables in which the movements of one variable impact either positive or negatively the movements of another variable. See the discussion on correlating data earlier in this chapter for more information.

Multiple linear regression and other forms of regression where the dependent variable—that is, the variable for which you are predicting—is predicted based on more than one independent variable are used in digital analytics. Understanding the marketing mix and how different marketing channels impact response is often modeled using multiple logistic regression.

Logistic Regression

Logistic regression enables predicting a categorical variable based on several independent (predictor) variables. The output of a logistic regression is binomial if only two answers are possible or multinomial if more than one answer is possible. A 0 or 1 may be the results of binomial logistic regression, whereas an output of "yes, no, or maybe" may be the output of a multinomial logistic regression. The predictor variables are used to create a probability score that can be used to help understand the analysis.

Logistic regressions are used frequently in predictive modeling for digital analytics and marketing analytics data. The best predictors should be tested for their impact on the model; however, the output is easy to understand. Take for example how a logistic regression could be used to segment data into a 1 or 0 where 1 meant to sell that product online and 0 meant to sell it only in stores. Logistic regression is one type of predictive data analysis.

Probability and Distributions

The shape of data and observing shape can help an analyst understand the data and the type of analytical methods to use on the data. After all, the way an analyst applies a method to a normal distribution versus a non-normal distribution is different.

Probability simply stated is the study of random events. In analytics, you use statistics and math to model and understand probability of all sorts of things. In digital analytics, you are concerned about probabilities related to whether a person will buy, visit again, have a deeper and more engaging experience, and so on. And using digital analytics tools, you can count and measure events related to visit and purchasing behavior and patterns related to the path to purchase and conversion. Measures of probability are used to determine if events will happen and then to help identify or predict the frequency of those events.

Probability analysis in digital analytics can be done mathematically (using existing data) or experimentally (based on experimental design). Simple and compound events occurring discretely or continuously either independent of or dependent on other events are modeled in probability.

A digital analyst should be familiar with the following concepts:

- **Modeling probability and conditionality.** Building a model requires selecting (and often in analytics, creating/collecting) accurate data, the dimension, and measures that can create your predictor variables. Central to the tendency to create models is statistical aptitude and an understanding of measures, probability, and conditionality. *Conditional probability* may sound complicated (and it can be), but the term simply means understanding the chance of a random event after something else has occurred previously (that is, a condition).

- **Measuring random variables.** A random variable is a type of data in which the value isn't fixed; it keeps changing based on conditions. In digital analytics, most variables, whether continuous or discrete, are random. Because the nature of random is not possible in mathematics, random variables are understood as probability functions and modeled as such using the many techniques discussed in this chapter.

- **Understanding binomial distributions and hypothesis testing.** A common way to test for statistical significance is to use binomial distribution when you have two or more values (such as yes or no, heads or tails). This type of testing considers the null hypothesis is done using Z and T tables and P-values. The types of test are one-tailed or two-tailed. If you want to understand more than two variables, you would use a multinomial test and go beyond simple hypothesis testing to perhaps chi-squares.

- **Learning from the sample mean.** Measures of dispersion and central tendency (such as those discussed in this chapter: mean, median, mode, and standard deviation) are critical to understanding probability. The sample mean helps you understand the distribution and is subject, of course, to the central limit theorem, which indicates the larger the sample population the more closely the distribution will approximate normal.

Thus, when modeling data, the sample mean, and the related measures of standard deviation, variance can help you understand the relationship between variables, especially with smaller data sets.

Experimenting and Sampling Data

Experimenting with digital analytics means changing one element of the digital experience to a sample of visitors and comparing the behavior and outcomes of those visitors to a control group that received the expected digital experience. The goal of experimentation is to test hypotheses, validate ideas, and better understand the audience/customer. In reality, though, digital is not biology, and it is often impossible to hold all elements of digital behavior equal and change just one thing. Thus, experimenting in digital means controlled experimentation.

A *controlled experiment* is an experiment that uses statistics to validate the probability that a sample is as close as possible to identical to the control group. Although the boundaries of a controlled experiment may be perceived as less rigorous than a true experiment where only one variable changes, that's not actually true because controlled experiments, when performed correctly, use the scientific method and are statistically valid.

The data collected from controlled experimentation is analyzed using many of the techniques explored in this chapter, such as applying measures to understand and work with distributions. The type of data analysis you do on the data can be as multivariate as the experimental data itself; however, controlled experiments typically have the following elements:

- **Population:** The aggregate group of people on which the controlled experiment is performed or which data already collected is analyzed. The population is divided into at least two groups: the control group and the test group. The control group does not receive the test, whereas the test group, of course, does.

- **Sampling method:** The way you select the people, customer, visitors, and so on for your experiment is important. And it depends on whether you want to understand a static population or a process, because different sampling methods are required. Sampling is important because a poorly or sloppily sampled group can give you poor results from experimentation.

Ultimately, you want to randomly sample your population to create your test group. Every person in your group should have the same probability of being selected as the other. When there is random, equal potential for selection in the data, then you have created a truly random **sample**.

You can also break a population down into segments that each have their own attributes you define, for example, all customers who are male, below the age of 30, and make more than $100,000 a year. Breaking a population down by its attributes is called *stratified sampling*.

When measuring processes in digital analytics, such as a conversion process, it is likely that they change over time. Thus, you can't hold the population static. In cases like these, in which you analyze a process, you must consider process-based sampling methods, such as systematic sampling.

In *systematic sampling*, the first datum is chosen randomly; then the next one is chosen based on some algorithm, such as every 50th visitor is selected for the test. This type of sample selection method approximates random and incorporates the dimension of time, which, of course, is important in the analysis of digital behavior. An analyst can also look at sampling subgroups. Basically, the analyst finds a common dimension in a set of customers and then picks the population from various subgroups according to best practices for sample size and at a sampling frequency that creates the necessary sampling size:

- **Expected error:** When analyzing the results of experiments by applying the methods discussed in this chapter, you need to go into your experiment with an idea of the expected amount of error you are willing to tolerate. There are various types of errors (such as type 1 and type 2). Confidence intervals and confidence levels are applied to understand and limit expected error (or variability by chance) to an acceptable level that meets your business needs.

- **Independent variable:** What you are holding static in the population or is shared among the population or subgroups are the independent variables. Not all of them matter, but some (hopefully) will.

• **Dependent variables:** The predicted variables that are the outcome of the data analysis. For example, the conversion rate is a common dependent variable around which experiments in digital analytics are intended to inform.

• **Confidence intervals:** Commonly stated at 95 percent or 99 percent. Other times they could be as low as 50 percent. The meaning of a confidence interval is generally said to be the "99 percent of the population will do X or has Y" but that interpretation would be incorrect. A better way to think of confidence intervals in digital analysis is that were you to perform the same analysis again on a different sample, the model would include the population you are testing 99 percent of the time.

• **Significance testing:** Involves calculating how much of an outcome is explained by the model and its variables. Often expressed between 10 percent and 0.01 percent, the significance test enables you to determine whether the results were caused by error or chance. Done right, analysts can say that their model was significant to 99 percent, meaning that there's a 1 in 100 chance that the observed behavior was random.

• **Comparisons of data over time:** Such as Year over Year, Week over Week, and Day over Day, are helpful for understanding data movements positively and negatively over time. Outlier comparisons need to be investigated.

• **Inferences:** What are made as a result of analysis. Inferences are the logical conclusions—the insights—derived by using statistical techniques and analytical methods. The result of an inference is a recommendation and insight about the sampled population.

Experimentation in digital analytics is often executed through advanced testing and optimization, which are discussed in more detail in Chapter 8, "Optimization and Testing with Digital Analytics: Test, Don't Guess."

Attribution: Determining the Business Impact and Profit

During the last few years, the concept of attribution has become important within digital analytics. In digital analytics, "attribution" is the activity and process for establishing the origin of the people who visited a digital experience. Attribution is a rich area being explored by data scientists worldwide right now as you read this book. The roots of attribution for digital analytics come from traditional web and site analytics where business people, primarily in marketing, wanted to understand the reach (that is, the number of people), the frequency, and the monetary impact of marketing programs and campaigns. Going back even further, the idea of attribution has roots in financial management and measurement.

Attribution enables an analyst to identify from data that an absolute number of visits or visitors came from a particular source, such as paid search, display advertising, or from an email campaign. By understanding the sources that send people who convert (and thus create economic value), businesspeople can then fine tune and optimize their work to produce the best financial result. For example, if attribution data shows that the highest converting source is paid search, then a conclusion could be to test the impact of increasing the spend on paid search and then ultimately the financial impact of doing so.

Attribution can be complex and always includes the measure of time as an important component. Temporality in attribution can be set to "windows" at which to "look back" at when the person or cookie was first identified. For example, you may set an attribution window to 90 days or longer, or 30 days (which is common). In this case, the person will only qualify for attribution for a source if they were exposed (or touched/clicked) that source within the attribution window (that is, the lookback time period).

Years ago there were few models for attribution. In recent years, new (or existing) models have been created from a number of other scientific disciplines and from new thinking about digital data analysis. The mainstreaming of the Internet; the widespread availability of Internet-enabled devices, like mobile phones; the rise of social networking; linking across digital experiences; and the rise of multi-screen behavior have also catalyzed the creation, evolution, and adoption of attribution models.

Attribution in digital analytics includes the click, but also goes beyond the click. Interactions with digital experiences that may not require a click (think of a touch-enabled smart device) can be attributed, as can exposures to events, types of content, or advertising (as in the case of view-thru conversion). Common attribution models are listed below, where I use "click" to describe what could also be an interaction or exposure:

- **First click (or interaction or exposure):** This model frames the attribution calculation on the person's first click prior to conversion or creating economic value. In first click attribution, if you first visited a site through Google Paid Search and then visited the site again through a display ad, then the credit for the purchase in this model would be associated with Google Paid Search, not organic search—because the first click that led the person to the site was Google.

- **Last click (or interaction or exposure):** This model is probably the most common form of attribution because it is supported by most analytics tools and is the easiest to understand. Last click is the equi-opposite of first click. In the scenario from the previous bullet, where the person first came from paid search and last came from organic search before the purchase, then organic search would receive the attribution credit.

- **Last non-direct click (or interaction or exposure):** In cases where a person has come to a digital experience during the lookback window from more than 2 sources (such as direct, organic search, and via an email campaign), this model would give the attribution credit to the last non-direct source of traffic, whatever that may be. In the case where the first visit was from organic search, the second visit from paid search, and the final visit where the conversion occurred came from direct traffic, then this model would give attribution credit to the last non-direct click.

- **Last N click—where N is a digital channel, such as search, mobile, and video:** This attribution model is used to validate the impact of certain sources of traffic by assigning the credit for attribution to the last source as defined by your business. For example, in the case where the first visit was from display, the second visit from paid search, and the final visit occurred from a link in a video, then this model would give attribution credit to the source you define, such as paid search.

- **Linear:** This model allocates an identical amount of credit to every source of attribution. All observations are collected and aggregated to create a linear attribution from factoring the equal weightings. If, for example, a person came to a site via four different interactions, then each interaction would be given 25% credit. By tallying all interaction types and averaging all credits given to those types, linear attribution can be identified.

- **Time Decay, Time Lapse, and Latent:** The time decay, time lapse, and latent attribution models are similar and often considered almost or totally identical. In this case, more credit is given to the sources closer in time to the conversion event. For example, if a visitor came from five different clicks (paid, organic, display, online ads, and direct), then this model might give 70% of the credit to the last click, 20% to the second to last click, and so on. The weightings in time decay attribution can be customized.

- **Construct-based, such as position:** Popularized in paid search where geo-spatial position on-screen or on-device is important to the revenue model, the concept of attribution from a particular construct is important, such as position. Construct-based attribution can be used to determine the impact of screen location and design. And in the case of cost-per-click, the bid and position help identify the attribution.

- **Event-based click (or interaction or exposure):** This model provides attribution credit to specific, custom-defined events that may be a click, interaction, exposure, or another concept related to the movement of people into a digital experience. In this case, it is possible to associate the impact of behavioral events on the credit given to sources.

- **Rules-based click (or interaction or exposure):** In this type of attribution, rules are created by the business and assigned to clicks, interactions, exposures, and events related to the revenue being generated or another metric. The rules assigned can change the lookback window, the weightings of the sources given credit, and other rules as developed for your business context.

- **Algorithmic:** This catch-all phrase for attribution modeling references those created using machine learning, data mining, and statistical methods—some of which, like regression, were reviewed earlier in this chapter. Algorithmic attribution can be identified as the model when it is proprietary within a closed, commercial system. The underlying algorithm is the trade secret or the intellectual property; hence, algorithmic attribution, though real, is often a term used to describe models where the details might not be explained to the users.

Three Best Practices when Building Models

Here are three best practices when analyzing complex and large data sets:

- **Discard outliers.** The common rule in statistics is that an outlier is any data observed to be two times the standard deviation. Techniques like the box plot can help you visualize outliers you have identified by applying descriptive statistical measures. Because outliers can skew data to the left or the right and generally pull the distribution in one direction or the other, you may want to remove them to focus on the center of the distribution. Although these best practices are useful in many cases, you don't want to do them in all cases. For example, in digital analytics, if you remove outliers without actually thinking about the implication, you may be throwing away the most important data. Remember that there is a chance for outliers and anomalies in data to have meaning and be worthy of deeper analysis, but first prove the outliers were not created by error.

- **Pick the best variables.** In digital analytics, there are so many different data types, dimensions, measures, and values, it can sometimes be overwhelming to determine the best variables. Every variable could be an independent one, so how do you select the right variables? One common approach is to use stepwise regression to determine which variables are best for the model. That being said, stepwise regression is a garbage-in/garbage-out approach.

- **Don't overfit models.** Overfitting a model occurs when it becomes too complex by having too many variables. As a result, the output of the model yields questionable results, and in many cases, can produce inaccurate results. When creating a model, it is better to be as simple as possible, not as complex as possible. The idea being that simplicity in analysis creates better outcomes and insights than being complex.

- **Don't let the model dictate the data; let the data dictate the model.** Taken from Tukey and his EDA, too many analysts learn about a cool new model like a logistic regression, and then want to fit the data they have to the model. Although that approach may work in some cases, regardless, it can be the wrong approach and is not preferred in digital analysis.

The best analysts take the time to study the data and understand the relationships in the dimensions and measures not only within the data itself but also against the business questions from stakeholders and the overall strategic business context. Data visualization before applied analysis is the right order of work for digital analysis. As such, the best practices and ideas presented in this chapter are suggested and can be helpful for you; however, your mileage could vary. Regardless, it is certain that by focusing on the business questions, visualizing and exploring the data, determining the best model and most appropriate set of analytical techniques, the analytical outcomes and insights resulting from your analysis will be highly effective, useful, and profitable.

6

Defining, Planning, Collecting, and Governing Data in Digital Analytics

The Analytical Value Chain discussed in Chapter 2, "Analytics Value Chain and the P's of Digital Analytics," illustrates the phased process by which the analyst goes through from start to finish when creating business value with digital data. You should read Chapter 2 before tackling the detail of this chapter because it will be helpful for framing how these concepts fit into the overall picture of doing digital analytics. The start of the analytical process requires understanding why you are doing analysis and the audience for the analysis. From the business questions from which the team identifies the need for answering with digital analysis, the analyst next needs to identify the data, map it out, and understand the gaps and how to fill them in order to create an analytical plan. The analyst verifies existing data that is accurate and usable and determines new data that may need to be created. Data can only be proven accurate if it is evaluated against definitions. And new data can only be created if it is defined. Analysts may need to create definitions for existing data when it has not been previously or clearly defined. Detailed data definitions, when they exist in a corporation, help the analyst find out if the data is applicable, accurate, and relevant to the business questions and should be used in your analytical plan.

Data definitions are just what they sound like—descriptions of data that identify the details of data. For a corporation to use data and the resulting reporting and analysis, people and groups who use the data must understand it; thus, the creation of data definitions also has some element of organizational politics. For example, consider whether it would be easy for your company to identify the definition for a "customer" or "user." Definitions answer the following question about data, "What are you looking at?" whereas the analysis of defined data answers the question, "What is meaningful in the defined data, and when and why; what should I do next?"

Data definitions serve the needs of different, various audiences whether they are businesspeople or technical people. To meet the needs of all stakeholders who want to understand data, the best analytics teams actively maintain a data dictionary, often in Excel, that lists the definitions for the data used in analysis. Technical teams maintain data definitions in other artifacts from which definitions can be created, such as schemas, Entity Relationship Diagrams (ERDs), technical design specification, and other documentation that supported the engineering and product creation process. Businesspeople who create product specifications and other artifacts and documentation of the product creation and innovation process often define, in some form, the data they think should exist (but may not).

After the data definitions and verifications are captured in your analytical plan, data needs to be collected. An existing data collection, when maintained, may be extended or modified to accommodate for new data requirements. Changes to data collection need to be tested to verify it is accurate. New data collection must be verified to ensure it does not impact functionality. Change management related to the code or systems supporting data collection may be necessary. In corporations, the idea of change management may be rigorously "Waterfall" or more "Agile." In structured, formally rigorous environments for data collection, changes may need to be planned months or quarters in advance, whereas more flexible technical environments may allow for quicker changes to be introduced to data collection. In more controlled change management, the resources to make changes quickly to data collection (if possible) are likely already being used (so changes are that much harder to allocate resources and schedule). In more Agile environments, formality in data collection may be so loose such that it becomes hard to manage and sustain common code that controls analytics data collection across multiple releases.

Data collection for digital analytics that adheres to agreed-upon, shared definitions is never simple. The larger and more global the organization, the bigger the data, the more complexity in business requirements for data, and the different types of analysis, the more challenging and harder it is to control data collection and ensure conformance to data definitions. Thus, the concept of data governance has emerged over the last several years.

The idea of *data governance* is just what it sounds like: A person is in charge of the data named the Data Governor who may or may not have direct reports. The Data Governor and the Data Governance team function horizontally across the business to ensure that established rules for data are followed. Common jobs for the Data Governance team include ensuring that data definitions exist for all data and that those definitions make sense and are relevant. The Data Governance team members work across projects that touch data to make sure that all teams work with common data. When data is thought to be inaccurate, the Data Governance team gets involved and often leads the data investigation and is held accountable for final resolution.

Defining, collecting, and governing data is absolutely essential for success with digital analytics. This chapter takes you through the following:

- Digital data definitions and how to create business, operational, and technical definitions. Also reviewed are how to create and maintain definitions with examples and commentary about existing definitions.
- Data collection in the digital world and a review of how to collect and integrate data across digital sources including site, mobile, social, and marketing campaigns.
- A broad overview of data governance for digital analytics including suggested roles and responsibilities of the Data Governance team and how the data governance process works across programs that involve multiple teams.

Defining Digital Data: How to Do It

Data definitions create meaning and relevancy that is shared and understood commonly by a group of people. Digital analytics requires data definitions. Data definitions seem simple in concept but are much more challenging to create, maintain, and control as the environment changes in which those definitions were created.

Taking a step back, definitions in digital analytics have three audiences, and thus take three structures for the three audiences: business, operational, and technical. A common example that illustrates the difference of data definitions is the metric and dimension named "unique visitors." The "unique visitor" is a highly misunderstood concept in digital analytics. Most people who ask the digital analytics team about unique visitors want to use the number as a fact about the number of people visiting a website or other digital experience (such as a mobile app). To the experienced analyst, it is common knowledge that a unique visitor number, as implemented in mostly all Web/digital analytics tools, is not representative by any stretch of the imagination as an accurate count of people. Web Analytics 101 teaches you that the number of unique visitors is simply the count of deduplicated cookies within a given time frame (or in digital analytics, a visitor could be identified in other ways, non-cookie). Then you learn that a time frame is necessary to calculate uniqueness.

You can't simply sum up the number of daily visitors and get a weekly, monthly, quarterly, or yearly number of unique visitors. The "hoteling problem" comes into play. If a person comes to a hotel every day for 30 days, she is one person who stayed at the hotel—one monthly visitor. But she is also a daily visitor every day. Adding up the daily visitors would count one person 30 times. When cookies are deleted and re-created and then deleted ad infinitum, each new cookie that has never been seen before by the analytics tool becomes a new person or unique visitor. Meanwhile, the engineering and business intelligence (BI) teams have databases, data structures, and queries used to render the number of unique visitors within an interface of your favorite reporting tool: from Omniture to Microstrategy.

In this example of unique visitors, you can find three audiences: the businessperson, the digital analyst, and the analytics platform engineer, all thinking and working to create the concept of unique visitors in different ways. Thus, in the complexity of the environment, the usefulness of a definitional format/structure that accommodates for the needs of these various participants in the Analytical Value Chain is helpful. Following is an example of a simple definition for "unique visitors" suitable to create understanding across the business, operational, and technical audiences:

- **The business definition:** The number of people who came to the site in a month
- **The operational definition:** The count of duplicated cookies within the monthly period
- **The technical definition:** The database, key, table, and canonical query for retrieving the data

The formality of the details in definitions is up to your identification of the business need.

What Are Business Definitions for Digital Data?

Business definitions are explanations that make sense to businesspeople who are not necessarily analysts in laymen's terms. Your college buddy or spouse should understand these definitions. If you were going to a cocktail party or general industry event, you would talk about what you do in business terms. At family dinners, when your relatives ask you what you do, how you explain your job is basically a business definition.

Humor aside, the business definitions for digital data are the most important type of definition. Business definitions are the vocabulary of communication and the language of the business. They help communicate how the business understands the performance of the business, so communicating in the language of the business is critical. Business definitions enable the digital analytics team to do so.

Simply put, business definitions express the metrics in vocabulary specific to the company in which those definitions were created. The vocabulary guides perception of data—and the perception of data is the reality. You must cater your data for communication in clear business terms based on agreed-upon definitions.

What Are Operational Definitions for Digital Data?

Operational definitions are more complex definitions to create because they are nuanced. As the intersection between the technical and the business, the operational definition serves to unify both. The operational definitions establish the criteria and conditions for usage of the data within business processes. For example, when a stakeholder asks for the number of people who in the last month used a certain mobile application, the stakeholder is not thinking, "How many deduplicated people can I count from an assortment of unique identifiers or cookies and other methods for visitorization?" Yet the operational definition of a unique visitor is "a count of deduplicated cookies or other unique identifier within the defined time period."

The preceding example clearly illustrates that the operational definition for data is different than either the business definition or, what is discussed in the next section, the technical definition. In summary, operational definitions are more detailed in their relevancy to a particular topic, tool, or process than a business definition. Operational definitions make sense to experts in the field and people who do analytics work; however, the operational definition does not get into the details of the underlying technology, database, or more engineering elements of analytics. Save those details for the technical part of the digitial data definition.

What Are Technical Definitions for Digital Data?

Technical definitions for digital data are understood by the engineering and research and development (R&D) teams. When the business says the number of people, and the operational teams say the number of cookies duplicated in a given time period, the technical definition specifically cites the technological method for accessing the data. In some cases, this could be the structured query language (SQL) or other technical method used for the data retrieval of a particular field's value in a database. In other cases, a technical definition may be a description of the name value pair and whatever necessary encoding is sent when an analytics tag is executed. The point of having technical definitions is that the teams creating and maintaining the implementation work necessary for data collection can develop a technical understanding of what has been and may need to be implemented to collect data. In the same sense that both business and operational definitions have a common formatted structure, a technical definition should also have a common format. All technical definitions are maintained by engineering teams and the appropriate technical specialists, but should be available for review and verification by both the operational and business teams. Just keep in mind, that due to the technicality in this aspect of data definition, it should not be expected that business operational teams may understand the technical definition.

Creating and Maintaining Data Definitions

The creation and maintenance of data definitions is a cross-functional task. Multiple teams from across the business must be involved in the creation of data definitions. After all, multiple perspectives are needed to identify and agree upon the formalities of technical, operational, and business definitions.

At a bare minimum, three teams need to be consulted when determining data definitions: a business representative, an analytics team member, and a technical member. By including all necessary teams, the potential for confusion is reduced. Clarity is gained through the alignment of multiple teams that each provides input to the Analytics Value Chain.

In some forward-looking corporations, a person or even a small team may be responsible for data governance. The details of this function are discussed later in the chapter. But it is important to note that the Data Governor or Data Governance team plays an important role in creating, modifying, and approving global standard data definitions. In many cases, the Data Governance team authors and maintains a data dictionary, which lists the data definitions for key business data.

In the absence of a formal Data Governance team, the analytics team often leads this function and can even be held accountable for the accuracy of data. In cases where no Data Governor exists, then make sure to gain support for definitions from the leaders of the teams that are impacted by the definitions. Without alignment on definitions, the analytics team will face challenges analyzing data.

You should create a data definition by asking the following questions:

- **What will the businessperson do with this data?** Gain clarity and find out what the stakeholder will do with the data after they receive it. You want to find out what the downstream activity will be for the data and how the analysis will be used to solve a business problem. Find out what the vocabulary is in the situations in which the data, analytics, and research will be used.

- **How does the analytics team collect and use this data?** Elaborate on how the digital analytics team defines the requirements for data collection, and specify the teams that the analytics team needs to work with to collect the data. You must also identify what downstream usage data will have—from reporting, to usage as a variable and a model, to automation.

- **What are the technical details necessary for accessing this data?** Work alongside a technical partner. The detailed information about the location of the data, how to access the data, the relevant database, querying information, and other technical specifics deemed relevant by your business are helpful to consult when creating data definitions.

- **Is there anything special or nuanced about this data?** You may want to consider answering the question about whether there's anything special or nuanced about the data. For example, the data was provided by an external vendor or the data may exist in a production database with limited availability for querying. In each of these cases, it could be helpful in the future to document these facts about the data. Also, the people who originally created the data and/or definition and made any updates to the data can be identified and listed in the definition.

- **How does the business create value from this data?** One extremely useful question to ask is how the business creates value with the data you are defining. In some cases, the answer will be clear. In other cases, in which data about behavior is being collected across every single click in every single page, the usefulness of the data may be questioned after it is defined. In other words, when there is not a clear linkage to generating revenue, reducing cost, or increasing efficiency, in some way or another from analytics, the collection of that data and other activities associated with the data can be considered overhead (and so can the people who work with that data).

As a result of answering these questions, you may create a format for definitions as shown in Table 6-1. From this framework, you can deconstruct the details of the data to create the following definition for a unique visitor (ahem, person).

Table 6-1 Framework for Digital Data Definitions

Metric	Unique visitor
Business Definition	A count of the number of people that has visited a digital experience within the last month. This metric is used by the business to understand customer behavior and is used in reporting and analysis provided by the global analytics team.
Operational Definition	A count of monthly duplicated cookies and other parameters used to identify uniqueness across digital experiences.
Technical Definition	Location: XYZ Database Connection String: Foobar SQL Statement: SELECT this FROM that WHERE
Notes	This metric is met skeptically due to cookie deletion.

This example definition may help to frame your own definitions, or you may decide to follow a framework that you have developed or found from another source. Regardless, proactively (and even reactively) defining data, verifying its accuracy over time, and establishing formal data governance helps analytics.

Definitions Are Not Standards: Industry Initiatives

Many associations, such as the Digital Analytics Association (DAA) and the Interactive Advertising Bureau (IAB), have created a set of definitions that are often perceived as standards by practitioners in the industry. In reality, definitions are not standards. Definitions by third-party entities are helpful because they describe concepts within digital analytics, but they do not unify the activities and operations of vendors and practitioners under any common manner or method as consensus-based standards would.

The big three definitions from the IAB are the definitions for a unique visitor, visit, and page view. Meanwhile, the DAA has a long list of various definitions. You should applaud the activities of both organizations as steps in the right direction from community effort. Standards, however, are consensus-based and widely agreed-upon where tools and technology conform to the standard. Standards are practiced and adhered to by vendors, academia, and other analytics professionals. When multiple organizations have different definitions, you might wonder if having analytic standards across the industry is possible. Until the analytics community stands up and demands standards from vendors, they might not exist. Right now, the best the industry may get is the involvement of vendors in initiatives of industry organizations that aim to define some types of digital data.

Counterpoint to the perspective that standards are necessary for analytics is, of course, the idea that even if standards exist, nobody would adhere to them because the industry changes and evolves so quickly. In addition, the absence of standards enables an almost limitless combination of innovation in the types of data available to understand digital behavior. In that diversity and that metrical ecosystem lies the opportunity to profit from new ways of data-driven commerce. Thus, standards can be considered by the analytics industry to be a double-edged sword. In one case, having any consistent set of widely applied standards adhered to by the vendor community can help to increase efficiencies and reduce the complexity of analysis. On the other hand, standards can begin to trim the edges of innovation in the industry potentially limiting the types of data in structures that can be created to support new, evolving, and innovative digital business models. For example, is a Klout score a standard, can it be standardized, and if so, why and is it worthwhile to standardize?

Planning for Digital Data: What Should You Do?

One of the P's in analytics, as discussed in Chapter 2, is planning. Planning is the exercise or process of conceptualizing, thinking, and organizing about a particular topic to deliver work that meets pre-identified business requirements at future periods of time. To deliver analytics, you must always plan. If an analyst does not plan, then they will not deliver the best possible work and will likely fail. The same fact can also be applied to businesspeople because, of course, digital analytics doesn't just happen in a vacuum. The businesspeople and their ideas are part of the planning process. In fact, the best digital analytics teams have formal processes for planning, prioritizing plans, reviewing plans, and approving plans with other supporting teams.

The process for planning for digital data collection includes:

- **Gathering the business requirements and business questions:** Expectations and questions may not always be as specific or refined in the way they are asked as a digital analyst might require. Part of an analyst's responsibility is helping businesspeople ask the best possible business questions. I always recommend a pre-engagement session with the various business stakeholders requesting analytics work. For a detailed review of pre-engagement, see Chapter 2. Regardless of how you choose to gather business requirements, whether using a pre-engagement session or another method for gathering requirements, you can't focus digital analytics teams around business goals without aligning the analytics team's work with the business.

- **Determining what is possible (and what isn't possible):** People will request analysis for data that exists, data that could exist, data that will never exist, and data that exists only in their minds. Make sure to do a comprehensive feasibility analysis to determine whether the analytics data and analytics work requested is feasible and can actually be accomplished. Generously ask questions of the requester to make sure you fully understand the difficult request; then, if it is truly difficult (or at worst impossible) to execute, propose alternatives when you explain the reality.

- **Organizing and prioritizing the data available from what's already been collected:** When considering how to approach an analytics project, you should map the data sources available to the data required to support the analysis. Organize the relevant data into categories that help you effectively prioritize the data: for example, behavior, financial value, or referring source. Then prioritize what is available and rank the prioritized data by level of effort required to use it. This prework can help make your analytics planning easier.

- **Planning for future data collection requirements:** Businesspeople won't necessarily ask for exactly what they want, so the digital analytics team can help to refine the "asks." The digital analytics team can help business stakeholders enhance the questions they ask about, and by doing so lay a framework for understanding how to ask for data in the future. When creating analytics, make sure to go beyond what the request is saying and consider the potential for similar requests in the future.

- **Aligning with stakeholders:** Conduct a pre-engagement meeting with analytic stakeholders to determine their requirements. There are other ways to align with stakeholders such as phone calls, email, and other virtual methods of communication; however, the in-person pre-engagement meeting is always preferred. For more information, see Chapter 2. When you have identified a preliminary plan, it is a good idea to review it in advance with the people who will approve it. That way, you will overcome any resistance to the plan before the meeting. Often times, the result of this meeting is a reduction in the number of analytics projects and the establishment of a rank order of priorities.

- **Socializing and communicating the plan:** A meeting hosted by the analytics team and held with all relevant business stakeholders can function as the setting for socializing and communicating the analytics plan. In this meeting, all concerned parties discuss their overall thoughts about the analytics plan, which at this point should not be the first time anyone in the meeting has seen the plan. In fact, the best planning meetings are when everyone has already individually agreed to the plan in one-on-one meetings with the analytics team. Then in this meeting, an overall alignment with every stakeholder is reconfirmed. Timelines need to be discussed as well as the format for deliverables.

Collecting Digital Data: What You Need to Know

Digital data collection is one of the primary activities you find the digital analytics team constantly involved in. The theory of digital data collection goes something like this: A businessperson provides requirements to an analyst or the specific business questions they want answered. The analysts then write a data collection specification. The specification is delivered to the analytics implementation team. The quality assurance (QA) team with the assistance of the analytics team validates the data collection is accurate. Analysts then verify the data is being collected accurately in the analytics tool, cascading its way into reports, and is finally verified as suitable for use in public reporting and for analytical activities.

The reality of digital data collection can be very different. Business requirements may or may not exist. Typically, they do exist but often are not in the format or the level of detail that is immediately useful. Thus, the digital analytics team often needs to clarify data collection requirements, sometimes realigning with stakeholders or the technology team. Digital experiences and devices may have specific data collection limitations. For example, JavaScript may not be supported in mobile environments. Data can be collected on the digital channel in a number of different ways:

- **JavaScript:** Commonly in digital analytics and Web analytics tools, the JavaScript page tag is applied to collect page-level, click-level, and event-level actions. A JavaScript file that may be in the site code or called from an external server or cache is what typically controls the data collection in site analytics environments. By working with event handlers and listeners and modifying the Document Object Model (DOM), JavaScript provides a very flexible language for asynchronously collecting and defining many different digital data.

- **Log files:** Traditionally, log files from web servers or other flat-files or comma-separated files were processed by analytics to track behaviors and metrics such as unique visitors, visits, and pages. Today, remarkably, despite what you may hear about new types of technical advances for digital data collection, the log file is still commonly used as the final format that analytics tools ingest to process. Log files are used by audience measurement vendors, Web analytics systems, BI tools, and as a format for integrating data for multichannel or omnichannel analysis. After all, a log file is simply a set of named relationships in a structured format, and it can be created to follow common log file standard formats and customized for proprietary needs.

- **Application programming interfaces (APIs):** At the most basic level, APIs allow for getting and setting data in digital analytics systems using a number of protocols, including hypertext transfer protocol (HTTP). Developers often use APIs within other application code to send the data specified for collection. It is more common to see digital analytics APIs that allow for getting data from analytics systems and then sending data to those systems—or data extraction APIs. These are more common than data insertion APIs (though both exist). Common languages for APIs include REST and JSON. APIs have limitations in their extensibility and applicability to data collection. It is common for companies to slow down (throttle) API calls that are deemed excessive (thereby limiting the use of APIs for certain use-cases in data integration), or to charge either dollars or some virtual currency (such as tokens or credits) to use the API.

- **Programming languages:** Custom programming can be created using the necessary language for enabling the data collection. Both compiled and uncompiled programming languages can be used to collect digital data. Commonly encountered programming languages for digital data collection include Python, C++, Objective C, JAVA, and so on. These languages can be used to glue together other application code and result in more extensive and coordinated data collection across different systems to support complex and often proprietary business requirements. For example, data can be collected in a registration system and passed to a customer relationship management (CRM) system. Programming languages can be used to write events directly to databases (as can APIs and Web Services).

- **Web Services:** Using almost exclusively HTTP, Web Services can leverage APIs and also be instantiated using traditional programming languages. In the modern Web of 2013, Web Services are used very commonly by large and small websites—from Facebook to Google. Technologies, like hypertext markup language (HTML) 5 and rich Internet applications (RIAs), that have presented challenges to traditional digital analytics data collection are able to be instrumented for data collection using Web Services.

- **Server-to-server connections:** Another less common, but more recently supported, method for collecting digital data is via connections that are established securely between servers. These server-to-server communications enable the automated and scheduled transmission of digital data between systems. Server-to-server connections are supported between online advertising and analytics platforms and between tag management systems and so on. Such connections can result from development partnerships between vendors or as a result of custom programming or creative use of APIs.

Multi- and omnichannel digital environments, such as those found on mobile devices, may require the analytics team to use a combination of digital data collection methods. Keep in mind that when more than one channel is involved, data may be collected from the device itself (such as the smart device, tablet, or kiosk). Then the applications and programs that run on that device may collect data, sent not only to the device manufacturer (like Apple) but also to the developer of the application or the owner of a mobile website. Take into account the social media data collection from the social platforms and companies providing data aggregates and derivative social data, then consider that data collected from various types of Internet transactions can be stitched together from multiple sources into the totality of a person's digital experience across multiple devices and screens—the reasons for the existence of many different types of data collection becomes clear. Analytics vendors are offering software solutions for bringing together visitor-level data across multiple screens and devices, understanding it, and attributing the visitor behavior to some catalyst (like an advertising campaign), using the data collection methods described above.

When considering the number of different devices and systems directly wired or indirectly wireless, no single data collection method will likely suffice for collecting all digital data. No single technology can possibly cover all analytical use-cases across all apps, sites, social networks, interactive billboards, set-top boxes, and the interfaces that power Web-based and online technologies such as Internet music streaming and radio services. Thus, it is becoming more common for digital analytics teams to understand all these data collection methods to make sense of them as a unified pool of data.

Governing Digital Data: The Data Governance Function

Data Governance refers to the process of identifying, participating, influencing, and helping business teams adhere to previously established internal or external standards and definitions for data— from the physical infrastructure to the logical infrastructure to the cognitive structures related to data collected and used by the business for analysis. In a real sense, the Data Governance team actively participates as a policing and auditing team that ensures data conforms to business requirements from its roots in infrastructure to its application in business context.

In the case of financial data, the Data Governor may work to ensure that regulations for the Sarbanes-Oxley Act in the United States or Basel III in the European Union (EU) are followed. The sales process depends on accurate information related to current and future customers, so the Data Governance team may work with external vendors who provide data for sales enablement to correct inaccuracies or expand the internal data set managed by the governance team. In the general business, when new data must be created from literally nothing (other than hopefully well-defined business requirements), the Data Governance team can work to ensure that the data definitions are agreed-upon, shared, and socialized across teams. When there is redundant or duplicitous data or if the data changes, the Data Governance team gathers input from the various stakeholders in order to make the final call about which of the multiple, conflicting data is accurate. The Data Governor has the final say in all issues regarding data definitions. As you can imagine, the Data Governance team's job is not easy; however, it is a critical one for companies that want to compete and win with analytics.

The role of the Data Governor is likely new to you. The role has little precedent and has likely emerged from technical disciplines related to enterprise data warehousing where the importance of well-structured and defined data is essential for operations. In data warehousing, the importance of data structures and underlying technical definitions is what makes the entities and constructs work. Technical disciplines like master data management and pricing optimization created the need for bridging the gap between the product catalogs and inventories and the databases that run point of sale and inventory replenishment systems. These ideas gave rise to Data Governance. Like most technical roles, the business has some level of influence in steering the evolution of technical business projects that needed commonly defined and standardized data; therefore, the idea of Data Governance emerged as a way to control drift and inaccuracy in existing and new data created in complex, distributed environments. As such, the Data Governor role was created to lead the business function.

The Data Governance Team: What Do They Do?

Data governance is a new business activity, and as such it has a different definition depending on who you ask. While I have described in the preceding section some work scenarios in which the Data Governor may participate, it is helpful to understand data governance at a more macro-level. In a nutshell, data governance brings together concepts like master data management, data synchronization, data policies, business process management, and data quality and verification to improve and enhance business activities. Because a critical part of the data governance role is ensuring that data is used at the highest and best level of the corporation, the Data Governance team gets involved with the creation, modification, and overall definition of data within the enterprise. As a result, the analytics leadership and analytics team often works with the Data Governance team were one to exist. Common responsibilities for data governance include the following:

- **Verify data conforms to business requirements and data definitions for specific projects and across large programs.** The Data Governor should have a seat at the table in the project and program planning meetings. As the person on the team responsible for ensuring that data conforms to business requirements and data definitions, the Data Governor acts as an aggregator of data definitions and an advocate of the end user. The Data Governance team should ensure that data definitions are standardized and carried successfully and accurately across all corporate programs and projects.

- **Eliminate redundant and duplicitous data so that there is one metric that represents a mathematical business fact—not several numbers named identically and purported by various teams to indicate the same data but that do not match each other.** The Data Governance team should be called in when the data audit occurs to help steer and guide the elimination of redundancy and the correction of any problematic data. The Data Governor has the final word for data definitions and data reconciliation issues about what data should exist.

- **Reduce data proliferation by reducing duplicitous systems that collect and report data and by auditing the list of people who have access to systems that contain data.** As the data steward and champion of accurate data in the corporation, the Data Governor should restrict access to various systems and databases so that data does not proliferate. As a result, only people who need access to data can have access to data, which can help eliminate confusion and competing analyses. The Data Governor may control authorizations and approval for accessing systems that contain data. In other cases, the Data Governance team may audit the systems used to collect and report data—and reduce and consolidate data systems.

- **Create data definitions that make data meaningful for business, operational, and technical audiences and usages.** The Data Governance team is in charge of the corporate data governance playbook. The playbook should identify the process under which the Data Governance team operates. An important section of the playbook is a common set of data definitions across all three types (business, operational, and technical) that have been created at the company. The Data Governance team owns this document that requires relevant and necessary input from the business.

- **Establish formal processes for auditing, conforming, maintaining, and extending data.** Discussed in more detail next, the Data Governance team creates processes that ensure data quality and governance steps are in place to ensure that data and handling of data is standardized across the business. Like analytical process, the processes that support data governance must be cross-functional and aligned with and supported by other teams.

- **Participate in projects where data is created or modified to ensure conformance to existing data definitions and standards.** For companies that fund projects that create or modify data, it is helpful for the Data Governance team to be involved at some level. When a new project for new data is created, it is more important for the Data Governor to be involved at the beginning of the project. In projects where existing data is meant to be maintained and modified, the Data Governor has likely already established definitions. And as a result, the Data Governor may begin around the same time the analytics team begins verifying data. In this case, the Data Governor and the analytics team should work closely together to ensure data matches analytical and governance requirements. If they do not, then the two teams can work to enable compliance.

The Process for Data Governance Across Programs, Projects, and Teams

The process of digital data governance has never been formally established by any consensus that has defined a set of working principles and guidelines. While entities like the Data Governance Institute provide helpful knowledge bases for understanding data governance, what you're about to read is my take on the process of data governance within the modern corporation, derived from practice and experience. As you've concluded by this point in the chapter, data governance ensures data meets business requirements across multiple simultaneous programs and projects in a way that is aligned with tactical and managerial goals and strategic objectives. Thus, the data governance function must act as a steward for the data and keep aligned with how data ties to the business mission and vision.

Data governance and the process supporting it have a technological perspective. At the heart of data governance is the importance of data quality within the business process. This means that people, management, and teams must be compliant with data governance processes to succeed. Technology teams must ensure that data governance is implicit in their database development and other engineering work that touches data.

The Data Governor must take a broad, cross-functional perspective when creating a data governance process. The perspective must include business strategy, finance, technology, analytics and reporting, and human organizational behavior. The data governance process may look like the following:

- **Determine data management principles.** The principles behind data management involve data quality, master data management, data synchronization, data architecture, data extraction transformation, and the way the business handles metadata. These functions are often technical and illustrate areas in which data governance must work with technical teams.

- **Identify business processes.** By determining how the business assesses feasibility, designs products, models data, executes on programs, monitors performance, and optimizes digital channels, the Data Governor learns the work activities to govern across business teams.

- **Create ways to audit and manage compliance.** The Data Governance team as part of its process creates policies and standards that help to secure the privacy of business data. Business rules will be applied to not only creation but also the accessing of different data sources. The idea here is to manage this risk in a way that is sensitive to the data needs of the business.

- **Organize people to support data governance.** Although the operative word in data governance may be data, the other word is governance. Governance involves working with people. Therefore, as part of developing a data governance process, the Data Governor needs to figure out how to manage the people that help manage the data. The data governance process must take into account people's roles and responsibilities in the business. The data governance process should involve identifying owners of the different types of data, who is accountable when data changes, who should be contacted when critical decisions need to be made about data, and for the people that should communicate and execute change management for data.

Although the actual process of executing data governance in a corporation is new and evolving, the principles outlined in this chapter can help you create whatever data governance process is necessary at your business to support digital analytics. At the end of the day, the data governance function is an important one that helps ensure data has standard treatment, definitions, handling, correction, and presentation to both internal and external stakeholders. The best digital analytics teams support and work with data governance.

The Difficulty of Testing and Verifying Data

The work activity of testing and verifying data may seem simple at the highest level. But it is a task that is fraught with difficulties and challenges. Data often exists without any of the definitions discussed in this chapter. Data can often be scattered across the corporation in various different types of databases and source systems both internally and externally, which the analytics team may not have access to or knowledge of. Teams that control data may not want to support or work with you. It goes without saying that the larger the corporation, the more data it will generate and the more complex and matrixed data governance and analytics management can be required. Defining, reconciling, controlling, and sustaining "big data" is almost impossible to sustain without data governance.

Take for example the simple sequence of data verification steps outlined below. The steps are similar to the work that a Data Governor, data tester, or analyst may perform in day-to-day work:

- **Identify the different redundant and competing sources of data.** In most corporations with more than one database, there will be redundant data contained within multiple systems. One of the main goals of the Data Governance team is to eliminate data redundancy and standardize definitions in systems in which data is collected, stored, and reported.

- **Extract common data across these different sources.** The Data Governance team will be part of cross-functional program and project teams that work to extract data from these different data sources to create a single source of truth. The Data Governance team may actually manage the resources that do this type of work, or they may do it themselves. They can certainly ensure that this work adheres to the definitions required.

- **Assess any existing definitions for differences.** When a situation exists in which redundant data occurs, the Data Governance team is in charge of auditing the existing definitions of the data and determining which of the data is accurate and should be used by the business. The data assessment function of the Data Governance team should be the final decision on the subject.

- **Step through the process from which the data is collected to understand the logic and rules applied to data collection.** When verifying data, it may become necessary to actually step through the code, the logic, or the flows in the digital experience that create the data that's collected. By understanding the logic in the business, rules for data collection, data processing, and data verification is easier. In order to do this type of data investigation and reconciliation, the governance team may hire contract staff or use internal engineering resources.

- **Use mathematics, computer software, and custom programming to compare potentially redundant data.** After potentially erroneous, redundant, or duplicitous data has been collected into the various file formats, the work all needs to be consolidated and analyzed. To do this, software programs and mathematics is used. Custom programming and applications developed internally to support governance may be created.

- **Summarize the conclusions of your data verification exercise and present it to business stakeholders.** Only the analyst or the Data Governance team knowing the answer resulting from the data investigation is never enough; the results of the data audit must be communicated to concerned people and teams. Thus, after gathering the data, verifying the logic, and doing the analysis on the data, the governance team, possibly in coordination with the digital analytics team, needs to take the next step to summarize the analytics findings to the business. It is in the step of summarization and communication where politics can ensue—but that can be reduced by having a Data Governance team with the final say (which reduces political risk). After all, if the data is not showing positive performance or confirming commonly held beliefs, the data will be challenged, which may be the reason for the data verification exercise in the first place.

Although the scenario for data verification described above is fairly straightforward, the reality of such an exercise can be different. In fact, the simple set of steps previously described may not be performed for a number of reasons:

- **The gatekeepers to the data do not allow access to the data.** Certain data can be considered company confidential and even top-secret. Other times data can exist only in production databases, which typically can't be queried without the risk of impacting critical business operations. As a result, it may be difficult and next to impossible to get permission to access or the credentials to query the data necessary to verify and compare data source and its definitions against another.

- **The data has no commonality or integrity to it.** In cases in which there is a question as to whether data is accurate across multiple sources or which data source is accurate, the analyst may find out that the two data sources have nothing to do with each other and have no commonality. In this case, the confusion may lie in the way the data is named or presented. One solution here is to change the name, effectively creating two data definitions from the single one that existed previously. In other cases, data thought to be related may actually have a looser and unrelated relationship that previously understood.

- **Definitions do not exist, and the people who created the data have left the company.** In less mature analytical environments, you rarely find data definitions. It is only after a business has learned the importance of defining the data that it uses standard artifacts like data dictionaries created by teams that use data. It is not uncommon to find the beginning of data definitions, or at least some descriptive information in product requirements, and functional specifications. Given employee attrition, the people who authored such documents may no longer work at the company. In this case, another area to investigate for data definitions are transition plans and other communications left by people leaving the company so their existing work can be maintained.

- **The data was created from a black box process that you can't re-create.** In established corporations, some systems that create data may have less documentation than the analytics team would like. In some cases in which multiple platforms exist and in highly technological environments, data can be created by systems that the engineering teams no longer touch. When data is required to be extracted from these systems, it may be difficult to get the technical support to do so. It is entirely possible for a company to maintain a system that creates or reports data that is largely misunderstood or not understood at all.

- **The logic that runs the data processing is not known or understood by engineering teams.** It is entirely possible that the engineering team does not know or may need to learn or better understand the logic behind the data collection or data processing of analytical data. In this case, you can expect to take some time to verify data, and you can also expect to work with the technology teams to do so. This situation presents an excellent opportunity for the analytics and Data Governance teams to participate and get involved collaborating with technical teams.

To avoid or at least mitigate the potential impact of some of the data verification challenges and reduce the chance for data proliferation and the analytical confusion and problems that can result, consider doing the following:

- **Create a Data Governance team.** Without a doubt, companies that are complex and data-rich environments should allocate resources to data governance. If you don't have a Data Governance team or don't have the budget to create one, you can find a home for data governance as a part-time or ad-hoc role as necessary for projects and initiatives that touch data.

- **Have the analytics team act as the Data Governance team.** In companies in which resources do not exist to formalize the Data Governance team, the analytics team may inherit the responsibility. It can, however, be a burden for the analytics team to also maintain data definitions and perform the data governance role. Choose judiciously based on the business impact if it makes sense for the analytics team to not do analysis and instead do governance. Also consider the Project Management Office (PMO) as a good candidate for data governance, since the PMO and its project/program managers already work cross-functionally on technical projects.

- **Communicate the importance of accuracy of data and the data verification process.** To accurately collect, verify, manage, sustain, and optimize a data governance function, cultural change may be necessary and organizational resistance may need to be overcome. Cultural change may be necessary. In these cases, the analytics team can be the advocate for the benefit of data governance. Regardless, the analytics team should champion the necessity for clean and accurate data to enable business decision making every day. All teams that expect clean, accurate, and usable data for analysis should be consulted and their voices leveraged to communicate the importance of data verification and governance.

- **Create formal processes called "verifying data" and "governing data."** When creating your set of formal analytics process, you should create one for data verification and one for data governance. See Chapter 2 for more information about process. These processes should approximate the tactical work necessary to verify data and support the data governance process. Include feedback and integrate the concerns of other teams when creating these processes (or they may fail). It may be necessary to get formal signoffs on these processes due to their cross-functionality and importance.

- **Create a data dictionary and data governance playbook.**
  A data dictionary includes the business, operational, and technical definitions that have been created about the data used to run the business. The data governance playbook identifies the set of processes the Data Governance team uses to do its job—and can often accompany the data definitions document. Use the data definition framework in Table 6-1 to help lay a foundation for your data dictionary.

- **Make data a part of everyday decision making so that people understand how important it is for data to always and entirely be accurate.** By producing and communicating analysis to answer business questions and help people succeed in their jobs, the analytics team will quickly become a valued team. As a result, people in the company will want to ensure that the data they are receiving is accurate and fits their business purposes. At this point in the maturity of the analytics team, people already understand the importance of accurate data, and their opinions (and positional power) can be leveraged to sustain accuracy. If the analytics team can create a demand for their work and services, then a chorus of businesspeople can help the team do whatever is necessary to maintain data accuracy.

Consider the lessons imparted in this chapter when executing the Analytical Value Chain reviewed in Chapter 2, especially to data definition, data collection, and data governance activities. By integrating the lessons learned in this chapter into your work activities, you can succeed more quickly by having improved data quality and accuracy. Do not underestimate the need for clear, relevant, maintained data definitions for key business data nor miscalculate the resources necessary to maintain data definitions across the business, operations, and technology. Establish a data governance function informally or formally to ensure that the digital analytics team, business stakeholders, and company benefit from the highest and best use of clearly defined, standardized, and accurately governed digital data for reporting, analysis, insights, optimization, and prediction.

7

Reporting Data and Using Key Performance Indicators

Data in technology systems and within databases has limited value to a business. It doesn't matter if the data is the most appropriate data for answering business questions. It doesn't matter if the business intelligence (BI) team has created the most high-performance and scalable architecture known to exist in the entire world. It doesn't matter if the data has the best design and most applicable definitions ever created. If the data is just sitting in a database, it is mostly useless. Thus, analytics teams are necessary to create value from data. As you reviewed, the highest use of data is when humans have applied analytical methods to understand the data and then determined how to use the data and their social skills to communicate answers to stakeholders about the data. But before a team can even think about doing analysis, the data needs to get out of the database and into some format with which it can be worked by analysts.

The most common way data is communicated in a business is through reporting. In fact, the core statements of a business—from the Income Statement and Balance Sheet to complex Securities Exchange Commission (SEC) filings and other legal documentation that contains numbers—are reports. Reports are everywhere. You may even laugh when I say that you must make sure you have your cover sheets on your TPS report. While the jokesters in the movie *Office Space* ended up burning down the office and TPS report cover sheets, by the end of this chapter, you may want to burn your reports.

Reporting, of course, is critical and necessary but in many cases is almost obsolete as soon as it is produced and distributed. Automated reporting emailed to people often gets neglected. The set of self-service tools for reporting may fall victim to a lack of data governance, and as a result, the reporting may contain inaccurate data or grow so large with reports it becomes unwieldy. Companies then are constantly in the process of reinventing reporting, transforming, and loading data from across multiple systems to create the type of reporting that the business wants. As the business grows in size, complexity, and the number of consumers of reporting, the challenge of governing and maintaining reports can become onerous and troubling for the analytics teams.

Vendor technology helps in the sense that the problem is often the solution. The reason reporting is problematic is that vendors may not have offered customers full solutions, or the solution provided may be outdated. You may be a low-value customer and not get assigned a direct engagement manager to help the business fully leverage and learn the vendor's tool. Some technologies come out-of-the-box with hundreds of reports (such as Web analytics tools), but when looked at deeply, the data contained within them may be too general or not applicable. It is a catch-22 that the most appropriate way to fix the reporting problems that exist in many companies, or in new companies with no or limited baggage, is to deploy vendor solutions or, in some cases, open source solutions, and in others open source solutions that are complemented with vendor professional services of value-added extensions (such as R and Hadoop).

This chapter reviews the following topics, which by the end of reading, should enable you to go back to your office and better understand why you are in the current state of reporting you are in and what options you may have for improving and fixing your current state:

- What is reporting and how does it happen?
- The five elements of excellent reporting
- The difference between reporting and dashboarding
- What is dashboarding and how does it happen?
- The five elements of excellent dashboarding
- The difference between dashboarding, reporting, and analysis
- Key performance indicators (KPIs) explained
  - Peterson KPI Model
  - Kermorgant/Manninen KPI Model
  - Phillips KPI Model

- Where does reporting and dashboarding fit in the Analytics Value Chain?

- Example KPI formats and example KPIs: averages, percentages, rates/ratios, Per X, and derivatives

What Is Reporting and How Does It Happen?

Reporting is a set of one or more information documents and an online representation of data items in a format appropriate for the business. Reporting can be either of two types, but not both:

- **Ad hoc reporting:** This type of reporting is what is created when people ask for data for a one-time business use or ask for modifications to existing reporting. The nature of an ad hoc request is that it occurs, in principle, just one time. In reality, when ad hoc reporting keeps being requested, it should be accommodated not as ad hoc reporting but as sustaining reporting. Ad hoc reporting is often completed manually.

- **Sustaining reporting:** A set of reports automatically produced accurately in a timely manner and distributed to the business via some method (often self-service, email, in binders, and so on). Sustaining reporting is the type of reporting created to support roadmap projects and other work that may be supported by program and project managers with formal life-cycle development processes. Sustaining reporting is the type of reporting consistently produced with no errors for the business to self-service. From sustaining reporting, analysis can be created and stakeholders can ask "What about this?" questions that can be answered in ad hoc reporting on analysis. Sustaining reporting can be provided in self-service environments.

Now imagine this scene. An executive is sitting at his desk looking at a report. It's the same report he saw last week that contains data about how effective online marketing is at generating online sales from the company's digital channels: a website and a mobile application. The data looks similar every week, so the executive understands the patterns in the data as well as any analyst and knows when a fluctuation in the data in this report is indicative of something of which to be concerned. Today he notices that the Average Order Value (AOV) has declined. Because the metric is tied to profitability, the executive is concerned about the decline. He is so concerned that the vice president of analytics gets a mobile call from him at 7 a.m., a call from his secretary at 7:05 a.m., and two emails by 7:10 a.m. The executive wants to know why the data has changed and has gone down significantly by the end of the day.

Such scenarios running digital analytics organizations are not uncommon. Depending on your level of maturity (and expectations you set and manage), they may occur frequently or not at all. The level of effort and time it takes to answer this executive's question may take longer than one day. The executive, however, does not care about the obstacles you may have to remove to get the answer.

Taking a step back, the executive received a report and is, in layman's terms "freaking out." What the executive did not receive was analysis. The data was not interpreted for him and the executive was left to his own devices to understand the reporting. When the data in reports does not do one of the following, it will be questioned, sometimes ferociously:

A. If the data does not meet expectations, it will be asked about and challenged. This mantra is most important to understand when analytics shows negative trends in data. As a result, the data gets highly scrutinized and questioned.

B. If the data does not support commonly held beliefs, it will be challenged. People and corporations have common beliefs or even false beliefs and ideas not based in reality about how the business operates or what the data "should look like" even when they have no basis or foundation for such opinions or beliefs. When the digital analytics team's accurate work changes commonly held views, the data and conclusions can be highly challenged.

Accuracy is the most commonly questioned subject in a report. People always want to know how accurate are the reports and, often, how the analytics team can prove the reports are accurate. Data Governance, of course, helps to improve and sustain accuracy in business reporting. In the previous simple case, B occurred and the executive wants to know why. Unfortunately, commonly cited ideas about the highest paid person's opinion (HiPPO) and explaining that analytics is the "What" not the "Why" does not work at a certain level. It's just too basic. Although an analytics team could argue over the nuances of the difference between data elucidating the What versus the Why, executives expect the analytics team to get deeper into the data to understand more than just the What. So what are reports in digital analytics? Reports are artifacts delivered in hard copy or soft copy from any number of existing technical systems that provide lists of data and, commonly, visualizations of data. Reports are commonly seen as spreadsheets in Excel or more dynamic reporting based on cubes in tools such as Cognos or Microstrategy. Reports are meant to be used to identify types of data and express trends and relationships between data points. Delivered on paper in binders or via traversing a complex hierarchy, reports are the documents used as a primary means of providing physical evidence about data.

Reports in analytics are necessary and in many cases, such as financial reporting, they are absolutely critical and legally required. People use reports for providing evidence that their programs were successful and for planning the next set of actions. The data in reporting is often clipped out, repurposed, and transformed into other reports. Reports are useful, but they are artifacts within the larger analytics process and simply provide the detail of the data to complement analysis. In some cases, a report may even be considered analysis, but reports are not analysis and may quickly become outdated from the moment they are released and even less valuable as time goes on.

Before discussing reporting, you must identify why reporting is important to a business. Following are a list of reasons for spending time, effort, and money to create and distribute reporting:

- **Reports provide a central artifact to consult in the decision-making process.** As physical evidence, a data service has been performed; reports help the business understand what's going on in the data.
- **Reports can be custom built using a variety of methods to custom requirements of the business.** There is no one-right-size-fits-all approach to reporting; however, there are best practices and perspectives on reporting developed by experts that are important to consider.

- **Reports enable stakeholders to anchor on physical evidence that the data and the support infrastructure exists.** Similar to the preceding information, collecting data in databases is mostly useless unless the data is extracted and reported in a business context against goals and benchmarks.
- **Reports enable conversation by forming a centroid for thinking.** Reporting can provide a central focal point for framing a business discussion by not only depersonalizing business performance, but also providing for often-needed quantification of business results.
- **Reports can be used to track performance over time against goals in a way that humans can understand and use.** By using reports to trend data, people can understand the ever-changing and evolving movement in data and how the data changes from business activities.

So how do reports get created by the digital analytics team? The process for creating reports follows the Analytics Value Chain (discussed in Chapter 2, "Analytics Value Chain and the P's of Digital Analytics"); however, a significant amount of underlying technical work must be executed successfully by technologists for report creation:

1. Data is stored somewhere in a database or set of files.
2. Data is modeled to create a logical data model that expresses the relationships between data objects.
3. The data model is implemented in a database, typically by a technical BI team. The database and data model act as the logical structure into which the data will be housed.
4. Raw data from files or perhaps another database is extracted, transformed, and loaded (ETL) into the database you choose based on the data model and your mappings of the source data to fields in the data model.
5. Technical transformations of data are executed; BI tools are deployed. For example, a fact table will be created, and you create a set of canonical queries used as the technical definitions for extracting the data from the database.

6. The raw data is available as dimensions, measures, and filters that can be used to create reports.

7. Reports are built within the BI tool using available dimensions, measures, and filters in the data model.

8. Reports are then automated for creation and scheduled for delivery.

9. Users then access the reports within the BI tool, export or link the data to spreadsheets (such as Excel), or query the raw data and export the data into various file types.

Sounds easy, right? It can be, but in most cases, it is complex to pull off without any snags. Now take a look at what can go wrong with reporting, which may be the case of decline in the AOV detected by the executive in the vignette at the beginning of this chapter. In other words, the data can sometimes be wrong and thus inaccurate! And inaccuracy is always a problem whenever it occurs. It may, however, be hard to pinpoint the source of inaccuracy in reporting, such as the following:

- Source data is incomplete or missing.
- Source data is not as expected.
- Source data is in an unsupported format.
- Source data is too large for the servers to handle.
- Source data takes too much time to download to be timely and useful to the business.
- Source data is coming in from multiple locations and isn't synchronized.
- The data model is incomplete.
- The data model doesn't provide for the relationships needed to understand the data.
- The data model doesn't support viewing the data in the way you want to view or report it.
- The team working with the source data and data model do not share the same timelines, priorities, or goals.
- The Extract Transform Load (ETL) is wrong.
- The ETL fails.

- The ETL takes too long and must be subdivided.
- The data fails to process for many systemic reasons.
- The servers have outages, bandwidth issues, or other unforeseen technical obstacles.
- Computational power is insufficient for either local or shared disc or memory.
- The dimensions, measures, and filters are not as specified by the business.
- The data is incomplete or partial.
- The report was built incorrectly or had an error.

As you can determine from the previous list of 19 items, a lot can go wrong—and this list is incomplete. For each issue listed, there could be many causes for it. In most cases, the analytics team is a downstream consumer of the technical work necessary to report data, which is where many of the problems in reporting accuracy tend, in my experience, to originate, but this isn't always the case. Traditionally, an engineering, research and development (R&D), and BI team supported by entire teams of release engineers and networking teams will be needed to ensure that the source data is being collected, ETLed, processed, and made available in the tools used by the analytics team. These supporting teams will not necessarily be a part of the digital analytics team but could be matrixed into the team. Or the supporting teams may have some allocation of hours or points (in Agile) dedicated to the analytics team.

The digital analytics team may or may not provide input into the data models being developed and will likely provide little input into the infrastructure underlying the reporting tools. In some cases, the analytics team will even have no input into the reporting tools used, which could be legacy-implemented or the responsibility of technology teams. It may be surprising to hear that the analytics team may not choose the database or even the reporting tools used to provide reports. The reason is that in many traditional companies, the work necessary to produce reporting is executed solely by technology teams or teams that have deep technical expertise, not by the teams who consume or analyze the data. That said, digital analytics is different—and requires the analytics team to work more closely with technology teams in identifying the need for and developing data models for analytics. It is also helpful for the analytics team to have input into the tools used. The support required from technology teams will vary significantly as will the processes to support in-house tools and infrastructure versus Software as a Service (SaaS) tools and cloud-based infrastructure.

Digital analytics and the reporting necessary to support it needs specialized treatment by a company, similar to how financial systems are treated in modern corporations. It is absolutely incorrect to think that analytics consumes only the data downstream from the BI and other technical teams. Modern business in 2013 requires that the analytics team works "on both sides of the fence": technology and the business. That's why the analytics team needs input into the detail behind the data, data model, tools, and infrastructure.

A "middleperson" is a good way to describe the role of the digital analytics organization when it comes to reporting. The team can take on the following modalities:

- **Broker between IT and the business:** Teams can take requirements via a process, ensure the requirements are business justified, communicate them to the technology teams, and then communicate the reports (and analysis) back to the business stakeholders.

- **Data and report creators:** Teams manage the collection of data by writing tagging specifications and other documentation that defines data collection and acts as artifacts in the report creation process. The team may then manage or execute the creation, release, and support of the reports they create.

- **Provider of reporting to distributed analytics teams:** Teams can provide a centralized reporting service for the business by taking control of the reporting process; working with existing reporting systems; and helping to improve existing reporting and the way reports are requested and communicated to the business, adding analytical value (of course).

- **Data validators and business acceptance tester:** Teams may verify data collected against the business requirements, which they may have defined, and then determine if the reporting meets the business need for user and business acceptance testing.

- **Data investigators and governors:** Teams are often called in to help investigate strange movements, oddities, outliers, and anomalies in the data contained in reports. In other cases, teams act as the owner and approvers of the creation of new data and work to ensure the conformance of existing data to definitions established.

What modality you operate in depends on seniority of the leadership and the positional power and influence your team has, as well as its available skill sets. The level of empowerment and autonomy provided to the analytics team at your company will also vary by the perceived criticality of reporting and analytics, both within projects and as an overall function. The interesting thing about digital analytics is that the team may serve all these roles simultaneously or during specific projects. When creating reporting, the analytics team is often tasked with gathering requirements, which it or others have written, synthesizing the requirements into cogent lists, and prioritizing what needs to be done. Often the team will communicate requirements to technical teams within the appropriate development model (such as Agile or Waterfall). These activities generally occur regardless of any of the preceding modalities into which the team fits. When a new digital experience is created and the analytics team is in charge of the technology, such as what might occur with Google Analytics or Omniture, the digital analytics team takes on the role of the data and report creator.

When the analytics team acts as the broker, it is in instances in which the data exists in systems not directly controlled by the analytics team (but influenced by the team). A good example of where the analytics team acts a broker between IT and the business is when data in internal transactional systems is necessary to report. In this case, the infrastructure that produces the data is likely in production systems. It is rare for an engineering team to allow or support the analytics team to querying production systems because its risk of catastrophic failure is too high. If the production database goes down because of the work of the analytics team, then the business could stop working. The analytics team, then, works upstream with business stakeholders to determine their reporting needs. This work is performed in a similar way to the process-oriented approach used when data and report creators translate the business requirements into data collection specification. The BI or engineering teams then work to execute on the requirements, which can be accepted only by the analytics team. In this modality, the business implicitly trusts the analytics team to do what is required.

Sometimes the responsibility for ensuring the availability and accuracy of the data falls on the technology teams. In this case, the analytics team receives what should be "clean data" for analysis, which is a rare modality in which to operate. In most cases, the analytics team gets its hands deep and dirty in some level of technical work with technology teams, ensuring data conforms to definitions and accuracy is maintained. At the least, the business expects that the analytics team has looked at the data in the reports, investigated any outliers, strange trends, anomalies, and has accepted the work as applicable to the business goal and fulfills requirements. Regardless of whether the team wants to get involved with the technology underpinnings of the reporting, a time will come when the data doesn't look right to stakeholders. It fails to align with the two guiding principles that if the data does not show positive performance or support commonly held beliefs, then the analytics team becomes the Sherlock Holmes of data, wasting time trying to prove data is accurate instead of doing analysis.

Whether an analytics leader likes it, the analytics team often becomes the primary data investigators, reconcilers, and governors of the data for reporting. Inevitably, the data will change, and people, like the executive with his AOV question at the beginning of this chapter, will want the analytics team to look into it.

The analytics team may be tasked with investigating, governing, and fixing data problems, but the work to do so, in many cases, can't be done by the analytics team. Thus, the analytics leadership needs to ruthlessly set expectations and identify who is accountable for fixing. Major work stress and negative perception can fall on an analytics team when expectations are not set with supporting teams and stakeholders for work that is the responsibility of other teams and is necessary to support analytics. Ideally, the result of an investigation should be fixed and clean data executed by technology teams in a timely manner, but in some cases, the analytics team simply needs to identify the problem and who can fix it, how, using what resources (from where), and under what priority against other already committed work.

By now, you can understand that when building a digital analytics organization, a report may look like numbers and lines on a paper or a screen. The process for creating reporting from conception to roll-out is cross-functional and must be error-free for the reporting to be valid. The importance of working within a process with known roles and responsibilities—the who, how, what, where, and why of your reporting—is critical for succeeding with reporting.

The Five Elements of Excellent Reporting: RASTA

Reports are easy to create if you are one person with a small set of data in one database. As described in the previous section, reports get exponentially harder to create when more than one team and one system is involved.

The following five principles when applied to reporting initiatives help to yield successful outcomes. In assembling this list of five elements—RASTA reporting—I present another way of thinking about SMART reporting (Simple, Measured, Actionable, Relevant, and Timely); what I've done here is make SMART smarter by expanding and refining the SMART concepts into RASTA. I call this approach to reporting, RASTA reporting:

- **Relevant to the audience:** Reporting must clearly indicate quickly to the reader what it is and why it is important. The name of the report or the data in the report must match the informational need and intent of the person or team who requested it—at first glance and when reviewed in detail.

- **Accurate actionable answering:** Although this phrase sounds like new poetry, the idea behind it is that all reporting must be accurate. The data has to be checked until it aligns with data in previous periods. The data in it should lead to actionability in the sense that by understanding the report, business users should qualify and enhance their decisions and begin to have, or at best have, the answer to their question from data analysis.

- **Simply structured specific to the goal:** In a world gone mad with infographics that combine images, text, data, and other visual cues to the world of sleek and professional-looking data visualizations coming out of simple software, it is easier than ever to come up with a format for reporting that amply illustrates data. But just because the data is in a table or is presented in a streamgraph does not mean the reporting is structured as simply as possible or is specific to the goal. Reports should avoid what Edward Tufte calls "infoglut" while trying to combine multiple data points to illustrate complex subjects and multidimensional information.

- **Timely in the decision-making process:** Reports that come 3 weeks after a product launch are often disdained because they weren't available at launch or shortly thereafter. When reports come late to the table, after they are requested or needed, the reporting team providing them is generally not considered valuable. Analysts must get reports (and analysis) in people's hands as soon as possible.

- **Annotated and commented:** Although analysis is discussed in detail in other chapters, it is delivered in writing or verbally. Words communicate the meaning behind the data. By adding a section for an executive summary or key takeaways to the data, the value of your reporting can go up. In the same sense, adding text annotations to charts and graphs is an excellent way to call out data and is helpful for communicating to the business.

The Difference Between Reporting and Dashboarding

Reporting is not dashboarding, and dashboarding is not reporting. Following are the differences between reporting and dashboarding:

- **You will have fewer dashboards than reports.** Dashboards are created from details contained in reports. Having too many reports is often one of the main reasons for wanting to create dashboards.

- **Dashboards bring together key data from multiple reports in one representation.** Data existing in multiple systems or across multiple reports are brought together in dashboards.

- **Dashboards are high-level overviews of what's contained within reporting.** By distilling the most important data in reports, dashboards simplify data for easy comprehension.

- **Dashboards contain visual representations of data with fewer data tables.** Reports contain tables and perhaps a graph. Dashboards are largely visually driven with different iconography to help speed the understanding of the data and information communicated.

- **Dashboards often link to the raw data within reports.** Linking or enabling drill-down in dashboards to the detailed data is common.

- **Staffs create reports. Managers and leaders identify dashboards.** Reports are often identified as part of projects or programs by various middle managers, analysts, or business owners. The need for corporate dashboard(s) are more often catalyzed and propelled by senior management.

As you can determine from the preceding list, without a doubt, dashboarding is different than reporting, but, of course, there is overlap. After all, you can't have a dashboard without existing reports. (Well, you can, but it will be rejected when you can't explore the data in it via reporting or tools.) And without dashboards, it is hard to encapsulate, synthesize, and communicate the key data and interpretations from multiple reports. In a real way, dashboards serve as constructs for reducing the amount of data to only the few items and visualizations necessary to run the business. It is then no wonder why companies constantly invent and reinvent dashboards as the goals, staff, and marketing, product, and strategic mix change over time.

What Is Dashboarding and How Does It Happen?

Dashboarding happens as a top-down initiative—as opposed to reporting that happens as a bottom-up initiative. When running analytics teams in companies from 6,000 to more than 100,000 people, reports are expected by line managers and lines of business-people; dashboards are often suggested by those same managers or requested by senior management. Consider that the outcome of the implementation of a Web analytics tool is a set of reports and some dashboards that may be customizable, which can be used as input to data analysis. As previously mentioned, dashboards are suggested to teams by management. Now that isn't to say that analysts and other staff do not suggest or create dashboards, but because dashboards reduce information to salient key points and visualizations, thus, executives are big on dashboards. After all, the more senior the managers, the less time they have to read reports and dig for the details that complement the analytics team's analysis. Thus, to answer the question at the heading of the subsection:

- Dashboards happen as a result of management wanting to distill data into simplified metrics and KPIs that identify the critical few measurements to track, trend, and monitor over time for business planning and performance.

Dashboards become core artifacts which teams use for planning and tracking performance to goals. A typical dashboard creation scenario may look like this:

1. A senior leader asks the marketing team, sales team, and IT team for data about the performance of a digital channel, such as the website.

2. The senior leader gets more than one different answer with more than one conflicting and different data points, which confuses the executive.

3. The executive notices that each different team has provided the same data, but it's different, and each team's performance is shown in a positive light. The data further confuses the executive because not only are there at least two numbers for the same metric, but it also seems every team is performing excellently, which the executive knows is not the case.

4. After trying to get to the bottom of the issue by meeting individually, the executive realizes that the company needs to centralize or at least better control data.

5. The executive decides that the executives should collaborate on creating one "dashboard" like he read about in *Harvard Business Review* and "kind of wants a balanced scorecard" approach, but more specific to the business and trended over time.

6. The three executives from marketing, sales, and IT create a plan to deliver the dashboard by taking an IT engineer, a marketing associate, and a sales manager as a custom team. The marketing associate works on the format, the sales manager determines the requirements, and the IT engineer finds Pentaho for free on the Web and creates a dashboard.

7. Everyone is happy in the first week. When the data changes in the second week, the executives ask the three people to explain why the data changed, which takes about a week's worth of work and effort to answer. In the meantime, the dashboard goes down, and one type of data disappears by week three due to technical issues.

8. The marketing, sales, and IT executives are on the hook for fixing the problem. Collectively, they pool their budgets to hire an analyst.

9. The analyst applies best practices and improves the dashboard to ensure its accuracy and maintainability.

10. The executives are happy and now want three more dashboards for a total of four: executive dashboard, IT dashboard, sales dashboard, and marketing dashboard.

11. The finance team sees the dashboard and wants to get involved, so does customer service and the call center.

12. The company determines that it should extend the dashboard to sales, marketing, IT, customer service, and the call center, and to do so, the company should hire more analysts.

13. At this point, the company needs to staff a team responsible for building dashboards from the company's reports and data.

14. The executives then determine the cost for staffing and maintaining dashboards requires more than reports and needs human analysts to run it all. The executive team then (sometimes painfully) allocates a leader for dashboarding, usually in marketing or finance.

15. The company then allocates the analyst to run the team as it tries to hire staff and extend technology....

And thus a culture of dashboarding is berthed.

In reality, the oversimplified sequence of events illustrated in this list is what happens at a macro level. But I think it illustrates a reasonable scenario under which dashboards come to exist in corporations. Again, dashboards are important as reducers of reports and function as distillers of the critical few KPIs discussed in the section "Understanding Key Performance Indicators (KPIs)."

The Five Elements of Excellent Dashboarding: LIVES

Dashboarding is a type of reporting; however, it is different enough from traditional reporting to outline it as its own analytics activity. Although there is no rule of thumb, you may have 100 reports but only one dashboard. Or you may have 10 reports and only one dashboard. The relationship is always that you have fewer dashboards than reports. RASTA-reporting principles can also be applied to dashboards. Dashboarding requires special handling and treatment so that the most relevant, useful KPIs and data are presented in such a way that the data can be explored. The high-level KPIs can be drilled into and explored. The concept of LIVES dashboarding presents an easy-to-remember mnemonic for creating useful dashboards:

- **Linked:** Dashboards may be delivered in hard copy, but it is more common to view dashboards via a browser or application. Hyperlinking then becomes key to dashboarding because linking can be used to link to other relevant artifacts, such as detail reports and written analysis about the business condition expressed in the dashboard. It is becoming more frequent to see mobile dashboards and even apps for reporting data analysis and dashboarding.

- **Interactive:** Although it is common to see dashboards that do not enable the exploration of the data within them, the best and most useful dashboards enable drilling down and filtering into the data from the charts and graphs. Often these drill-downs are into detailed data or secondary KPIs.

- **Visually driven:** Whereas reports are mainly composed of columns and rows of data, dashboards communicate data through charts and graphs. A strong visual narrative using data visualization best practices and clear information design and user experience is always helpful for dashboarding.

- **Echeloned:** Organize information and data presented in dashboards by relevance and priority to the audience. Put KPIs and other visualizations on your dashboard in the best position for the culture. For example, English speakers look up to the top left on a page, but Hebrew speakers look up and to the right.

- **Strategic:** Dashboards are not supposed to simply include total counts of this or that metric or data point. Instead, they are supposed to quickly communicate important numbers, KPIs, trends, and data visualizations to the business. These KPIs and data visualizations must be tied to business strategy. The tactics of the business, thus, influence the movement of the data on dashboards. And the movement of data in one direction or another should indicate tactical success or failure to help pinpoint the outcomes of current strategy.

Understanding Key Performance Indicators (KPIs)

KPIs are the Kaushikian "critical few" metrics that identify the most important business data absolutely necessary to monitor over time to understand the health and success of your business.

KPIs are numeric in nature and show trending across time and against goals and benchmarks. The actual numbers in KPI dashboards are never raw numbers alone (that is, "no lonely metrics" says Avinash Kaushik) but can contain other numerical representations of data derived from doing math on raw numbers:

- **Averages:** The arithmetical mean either geometric or not. See the discussion in Chapter 5, "Methods and Techniques for Digital Analysis."

- **Percentages:** A number that is a fraction of a basis of 100, such as 23 percent or 23 observations in 100.

- **Rates:** Think of a conversion rate. According to Google: "A measure, quantity, or frequency, typically one measured against some other quantity or measure: 'the unemployment rate.'"

- **Ratios:** Google has a good definition of ratio: "The quantitative relation between two amounts showing the number of times one value contains or is contained within the other. For example, 'there is a three to one ratio' of people visiting the site from organic search than paid search."

- **"Per X":** Common to the advertising and online media industry, there are several "per" metrics, such as Cost per Thousand, Revenue per Thousand, Effective Cost per Thousand, Pages Viewed per Visit, and so on.

- **Derivatives:** Created or transformed from something else, like raw data. A derivative is the result of a calculation, transformation, or data analysis, like an R2 value or probability estimate derived from a predictive model. Return on Advertising Spend (ROAS) is a derivative as are other similar "return"-based measures.

KPIs can grow rapidly, and it is not uncommon for each business unit, or group at all levels to have their own specific KPIs for their function. KPIs can then quickly become numerous. As a guideline, you should consider identifying five KPIs "plus or minus two." That means between three–seven KPIs are a manageable number to track for the highest level of reporting—though a business, of course, may have many sets of three–seven KPIs for each line of business, such as marketing and sales. From the set of three–seven primary KPIs, the dashboarding may allow for drilling into another three–seven secondary KPIs, then a deeper, tertiary set of more KPIs. Take the example in the previous section where there was an executive dashboard, sales dashboard, marketing dashboard, customer service dashboard, finance dashboard, and call center dashboard for a total of six dashboards. Given there will be some redundancy in KPIs (for example, the executive dashboard may have the same KPIs as other groups' dashboards), you can imagine a situation in which the analytics team can manage the processes supporting the downstream data collection, quality assurance (QA) testing, reporting, and data governance of somewhere between 18–42 different, function-specific KPIs.

The greater number and more metrics and KPIs you produce, the larger the risk something can go wrong. The more reports and KPIs managed, the more staff needed to do the work managing, monitoring, alerting, and following-through with analysis and extension of the dashboards. Take, for example, Table 7-1 which lists KPIs and the different sources systems, staff needed, and time needed to verify and analyze the data, which is more complex than it seems on the surface.

Table 7-1 Examples of Challenges with Reporting KPIs

KPI	Where KPI Data Lives	Barriers to Integration
Cost per New Customer Acquired	Financial Systems, Customer Relationship Management Systems, and Business Intelligence Tools	Data between systems is not integrated because keys do not exist nor does a unified data model. Teams have other projects on the roadmap.
Repeat Visitor Rate	Varies from log files to site analytics systems to audience measurement estimates	Cookie deletion. Different teams own various views of this data; thus, different definitions and systems.
Conversion Rate	Spreadsheets, data marts, and site analytics tools	No standard definition exists across the company. Different conversion rates are measured. The site analytics tool can't track visitor conversion.

KPIs are meant to compel action when they change. Although data is not actionable alone, people can act on the data. Another way to understand the myth of actionability is that nothing happens without people, so data is not actionable. Data can't really do anything but be data from which people draw insights, conclusions, observations, and recommendations from analysis. KPIs help to make data actionable by helping businesspeople concentrate on the signals in the data and disregard the noise. That's another way of saying that when KPIs change, it should matter to the business to learn why they are changing, what is influencing the changing, and if the business should action off the data. If a KPI changes and the business does not care to determine whether people should take an action, then the KPI likely should not be a KPI at all.

Many books exist about creating reports and dashboards; however, in part of the digital analytics industry concentrating on Web analytics, there has long been the idea of using KPIs to understand and improve business performance. Web analytics KPIs tended to focus on site and browser-based digital marketing and e-commerce. Digital analytics, of course, requires newer and evolved thinking about KPIs. Many approaches to creating KPIs have been defined by vendors and consultants—but there are a few fundamental reference models for KPIs:

- **Peterson KPI Model:** Eric Peterson authored a useful text that brought together various good ideas, *The Big Book of KPIs*. You can read the book to see what the industry was thinking several years ago because it is still relevant. Although some of the KPIs Peterson lists have evolved, there's a lot of rich information in the book you should read (and it's free).

- **Kermorgant/Manninen KPI Model:** In 2006, Nokia's Vince Kermorgant and Illake Manninen published publicly to the greater analytics community the model they created at Nokia. Their method was different than Peterson's in the sense that Peterson explained what KPIs are and provided examples of specific KPIs and how to communicate them, whereas they took a different approach based on goals and actors on the site both direct and indirect. Given the number of stakeholders and simultaneous digital activities at Nokia, Kermorgant and Manninen were less concerned about explaining KPIs. Instead, they and Nokia created a document that explained how different "actors" need different KPIs and provided a framework for defining those KPIs and then actually executing KPIs in a globally distributed multinational company.

- **Phillips KPI Model:** Digital analytics requires new ways of thinking about KPI creation, and I've documented an approach I find helpful for creating and extending KPIs. This model brings together the best thinking in KPI creation in order to support the Analytics Value Chain discussed in Chapter 2.

Peterson KPI Model

Focused on Web analytics, Peterson's book, as would make sense when written, does a fantastic job of capturing the difficulty, challenges, and complexities of using Web analytics tools to report KPIs about websites.

Fundamental concepts are covered about understanding about web data and how cookies, browsers, and externalities that are uncontrollable by companies and employees (such as cookie blocking or deletion) can impact KPIs. He discusses many important concepts around the way KPIs can be communicated. Peterson's KPI framework has four sections, which remain highly applicable in 2013:

- **Definition:** A substantial amount of space in this book is dedicated to discussing data definitions. Peterson suggests that raw numbers are not KPIs and he's right in most circumstances; however, it is common to see one or more raw numbers on KPI reports (adjacent to a percentage change or visual indicator). For more information about definitions for digital analytics, see Chapter 6, "Defining, Planning, Collecting, and Governing Data in Digital Analytics."

- **Presentation:** Peterson alludes to the importance of presentation for enabling an easier understanding of KPIs. For more information about best practices for presenting KPIs, review the professional work by Jennifer Vesseymeyer (currently at Merkle). When presenting KPIs, Peterson speaks correctly about how KPIs should be trended on a timeline; have color coding, informational cues, and directional data movements (like arrows); use visualizations (like speedometers); use percentages as values; and has targets and thresholds identified.

- **Expectation:** Simply put, Peterson's idea of expectation is that the business already knows the results it wants to achieve and documents them in writing for each KPI.

- **Actions:** The decision made and work performed as a result of data analysis completed when done when a KPI changes are considered "actions." The analytics team's job when the KPI changes is then to evaluate the KPI against expectations in order to take actions.

Kermorgant/Manninen KPI Model

Kermorgant and Manninen published a document in 2006 titled "Implementing Web Analytics the Nokia Way." The document focuses on actually enabling a culture focused on KPI analysis using their work as employees of Nokia as a reference. Kermorgant and Manninen identify three main concepts, two of which by now in this chapter you understand:

- **Actors** are the people, the humans, who make decisions about the digital experience. You may not have heard of actors in the context of KPIs before. They further subcategorize actors that either work "directly" or "indirectly" on the site. Equally as important to focus on are "direct site actors" or people who actually make tactical changes to the site (like marketers or agencies) as well as "indirect site actors" who influence strategy (like managers) but do not perform tactical work on the site.
- **KPIs:** Which we are discussing now.
- **Dashboards:** Discussed previously in the chapter.

Kermorgant and Manninen claim, "The end result of the (Nokia) process is that you should have enough information/data about a site and relevant other factors affecting it so that you can derive a comprehensive set of Key Performance Indicators, and present those to various Actors inside specific Dashboards."

The inclusion of the concept of "actors" is an extremely valuable entity to identify. Actors, of course, are humans. And even if you have the most appropriate KPIs with excellent definitions, solid presentation, agreed-upon expectations, and known actions, the human side of delivering analysis and managing based on KPI dashboards within the Analytics Value Chain is where the most challenge exists. Actors help reduce the challenge of delivering analysis based on KPIs by incorporating whether or not the actor makes changes to the site and, if so, how those changes are made.

Kermorgant and Manninen define two types of actors: decisional and nondecisional. The idea is to disregard nondecisional actors (like people who upload content) and instead focus on both identifying the types of decisional actors and the KPIs needed for direct or indirect work.

A counterintuitive and perhaps unexpected conclusion a reader could take from Kermorgant and Manninen's excellent work is that dashboarding—when making tactical changes to a digital experience—is of the same importance for people who actually do the tactical work, than for the people who manage the people who do the work and the strategy that informs and gives context to the work.

You've heard Avinash Kaushik's idea of the HiPPO and how analysts should be ensuring the HiPPO "gets it" about data and analytics by communicating analysis from reports and dashboards to help run the digital business. Kermorgant and Manninen appear to turn that notion on its head (or at least partially) in the sense that tactical workers (that is, decisional direct actors) are just as important as managers (that is, decisional indirect actors). The LiPPO (lowest paid person's opinion) may get the same level of analytical attention (and maybe more) than the HiPPO. The idea here being autonomy and empowerment of tactical workers who are expected to actively interpret and make decisions based on the data in the dashboards to do their jobs—and not depend only on the interpretation of the KPIs by managers in their dashboards.

The method espoused by Kermorgant and Manninen has a great deal of detail about the types of artifacts (card decks, user maps, and functional maps) that help the KPI creating, reporting, analysis, and communication process. For example, the following types of KPI dashboards are discussed:

- **Actor-based:** Each direct, decisional actor gets his own KPI dashboard.
- **Macro Goal-based:** Because all digital experiences have goals—from earning profit to conversion to mission-driven—dashboards can be given context by having all KPIs in them associated with a macro goal.
- **Role-based:** In the fictional narrative in the previous section, the various dashboards created for each team are role-based. That is, the marketing team gets a dashboard, the sales team gets a dashboard, the executive team gets a dashboard, and so on.

Phillips KPI Model

I've used the approach outlined in the following list to create new KPIs and dashboards and to extend, manage, and optimize existing dashboards. The approach is explained below and overlaps with some of the concepts presented by both the Peterson model and the Kermorgant/Manninen model; however, it attempts to reduce and simplify the complexity of KPI creation based off digital data from multiple digital sources. The model also incorporates the need for individual people, teams, and larger organizational entities to have access to KPIs and dashboards that tie together data in clearly-defined relationships that help visualize and communicate business analytical data that impacts multiple teams:

- **Data Definitions:** Data definitions for KPIs are often business definitions that explain clearly the meaning of a KPI in business terms. However, it is important to include both technical definitions and operational definitions. For a deeper discussion on data definitions and governance and examples, see Chapter 6.

- **Business Goal:** The end state you plan to achieve by successfully executing your business strategy. Goals should be focused on outcomes that are measurable based on the KPI.

- **Audience:** Similar to Kermorgant and Manninen's concept of decisional and nondecisional, direct and indirect, actors. The audience is the person or group of people for whom the dashboard was created.

- **Systems:** Although the ideal state would be to have one system for collecting data, building, reporting, and publishing dashboards, unless you work in a start-up or are leading a new initiative that is independent of other groups and processes, it is likely that more than one system will be used for a KPI dashboard.

- **Dashboards and KPIs:** Although it is optimal for all dashboards to cascade and fit into a larger dashboarding framework—where the primary KPIs are tied to secondary and tertiary KPIs—not all dashboarding will be unified. As such, it is important to list the dashboards, who owns/maintains them, and the KPIs in them.

- **Communication:** Central to success of any analytics team is communicating analysis to stakeholders. Although the timing, method, and frequency can vary by company, do not underestimate the importance of solid analytics communications.

- **Expected Actions and Outcomes:** As a result of monitoring a KPI, you should define what are the expected actions stakeholders may take and the possible outcomes that could result from the movement of the KPI.

Where Does Reporting and Dashboarding Fit in the Analytics Value Chain?

Reporting and dashboarding is something that is often performed after data collection. In this case, the requirements for reports and dashboards may have been specified in advance. Sometimes, though, the dashboards and required reports are considered or reviewed only after the data model and data collection has been specified. The digital analytics teams can suffer from the inability to fully deliver against reporting and KPI dashboarding requirements when the process for creating KPIs does not begin early in the project and program planning process. Ideally, when a new digital experience is created, the digital analytics team should be involved immediately to begin asking the right questions to define potential scope, constraints, and boundaries of the project based on the KPI models presented in this chapter.

Although the Analytics Value Chain discussed in Chapter 2 shows that reporting and dashboarding are done, tactically, after data is collected, the strategic work must begin as soon as possible (at phase zero in engineering parlance). When asking for business requirements yet being given data, ask, "How should the report look? What are the columns and the rows?" In the early days of creating a new product or planning a new release, the analytics team needs to consider the systems involved, the data required, the state of how well defined the data could be, the audience for the reports and dashboards, and how the information can be communicated. Thus, although the work to create and analyze reports and dashboards occurs later in the Analytics Value Chain, make sure the strategic work for informing, contextualizing, communicating, and modeling KPIs and the related reporting occurs as early as possible—and often as soon as the business questions are identified.

Example KPIs: Averages, Percentages, Rates/Ratios, "Per X," and Derivatives

This section discusses a few of the more common and more useful KPIs of a variety of types. The goal here is by no means to indicate you should use these KPIs. These KPIs are examples only; however, in most cases, the KPIs discussed here can be modified to fit your business goals. Also, here's a comparison of how Peterson, Kermorgant/ Manninen, and I would begin to document the KPIs. All our models have useful commonalities in each approach that can be adapted and tailored for your business case. After all, one particular approach or methodology may not be sufficient or applicable to your business; thus, combining elements of each approach might be helpful.

The following puts the KPIs discussed here in the context of the three models—all of which are useful—as discussed earlier in the chapter:

- **The Peterson Model** would require a KPI definition, the method and manner for presenting the KPI, the expectation the business would have for the KPI, and finally the action the team and business should take as a response to KPI movements.

- **The Kermorgant/Manninen KPI Model** would require the identification of the people (actors), their goals, and whether they directly or indirectly make changes to the digital experience. In that context, dashboards with KPIs would be created to cater to different audiences based on roles, macro goals, and the requirements of different actors.

- **The Phillips KPI Model** requires the creation of KPI data definitions that address three audiences: technical, operational, and business. Business goals need to be identified from each business stakeholder. Dashboards should be created for the stakeholders where each KPI is tied to a specific business goal(s). Each dashboard should have a communication plan for communicating KPI analysis to the audience. The expected actions people may take when the KPI changes and the potential outcomes expected from movements up or down are identified. Finally, this model involves mapping out the systems and integrations necessary to successfully stage and phase the creation of a comprehensive, business-focused KPI model according to the processes established to support the Analytics Value Chain (as discussed in Chapter 2).

KPI Rate Example: Conversion Rate

The concept of *conversion* and the associated derivative, *conversion rate*, is one of the most enlightening KPIs in digital analytics.

In many ways, the idea of conversion is the centroid around which digital measurement developed from the late 1990s forward. Conversion is simply the idea that a person (or visitor or cookie) on your site will complete a value-generating activity with a digital experience. For example, in an e-commerce digital experience, conversion may be defined as "ordering a product," whereas on a content and information site, a conversion could be "signing up for an email" or "registering for a white paper download." Conversions occur in the context of an unknown visitor becoming a customer who may or may not be known, while in other cases conversion may be less focused on the customer and more on areas of the site or specific products or product categories.

The key takeaway when understanding the digital concept of conversion is that it occurs when a person does something that the creator of the digital experience thinks is valuable—and thus creates business value in some way. In that context, there are several different mathematical definitions for conversion.

For example, conversion can be measured based on a visitor, visit, customer, or audience basis. Various camps exist about the usefulness of each denominator. Visitor measurement has inherent challenges with accuracy due to cookie deletion and externalities of the Internet (like cookie blockers), social media, and mobile. Some analysts argue that using "visits" is a better denominator for conversion than visitors because a visit represents a unique opportunity to convert, whereas the visitor metric could include more than one visit. The best metrics will, of course, be based on your business case and fit of the data to your business goals.

Regardless of your preference for the denominator in a conversion calculation, the larger point is that conversion occurs when a person does something that is considered valuable. And as such, conversion and the movements in conversion rates can be tied to financial measures, such as revenue and profitability. Conversion rate is one of the most common and most critical metrics to track and optimize. In fact, conversion optimization is data science and analytical discipline in and of itself.

KPI Rate Example: Step Completion Rate

Step completion rate, sometimes called *micro conversion* or even *waypathing*, is similar to conversion in that a step is a transitional point in a digital experience that is part of a conversion flow. The idea of moving across a digital experience from one page to another is a *step*. In the process of conversion, as a person moves across a step to complete a goal, step (micro) conversion does happen on the way to the final conversion point.

Step completion can best be understood as an example. Say, an e-commerce site's goal is to sell products. Products are sold via orders. To get to the order page, a person must access a landing page (like the homepage), search for a product, view the product page, and complete an order. The conversion steps would be as follows:

1. View a landing page.
2. Search for a product.
3. View a product page.
4. Order the product.

CONVERSION = View the order thank-you page.

In the previous example, steps 1 through 4 begin with arriving on the landing page and taking the next logical steps to complete the product purchase. As those of you who have worked in digital analytics may notice, the steps leading to conversion look a lot like a clickstream or path, and you would be correct. In this case, the path is known prior to the behavior in which each step in the path is required to complete a task or goal. By tracking where people enter and abandon steps in the conversion process, friction that prevents conversion (and thus improvements in conversion rate) can be identified.

KPI Average Example: Average Order Value (AOV)

One of the standard metrics in e-commerce experiences where a purchase occurs is AOV. Simply constructed, AOV is the sum total cost of the items purchased divided by the number of items. It's the average cost of all the items purchased—easy and informative. Even small sites that sell only one product benefit from tracking AOV. After all, AOV helps to identify inventory and purchasing trends as well as influence marketing, advertising, and promotions. Related is MOV, which is less common, and stands for Median Order Value. MOV is useful where e-commerce transactions create data with a large range in cost where the outliers skew the average.

KPI Average Example: Average Visits per Visitor

By tracking how many visits a visitor has in a certain time period (most commonly monthly), you can use this KPI to indicate site depth. It has even be used, perhaps suspiciously, as a proxy for "engagement." This metric is not always the most useful metric in all contexts; however, it can be insightful when trended and segmented for sites that are content-, mission-, or advertising-driven. The number of visits can be understood in the context of page views to serve as a proxy for calculating potential demand for advertising inventory. The main reason this KPI is in this chapter is that it is a good example of a derivative KPI created from two of the most common metrics: visits and visitors. In that context, you could easily swap out visits for another metric such as revenue or profit. Keep in mind that any visitor-based metric dependent on using a deletable object (such as a cookie) to identify uniqueness in visitors may overestimate the number of visitors.

KPI Derivative Example: Loyalty—Time Since Last Visit (Recency)

Customer loyalty is what businesses with short, repeat purchasing cycles (toothpaste) strive to create. Even businesses with longer usage cycles (appliances such as washing machines and home windows) between new purchases benefit from loyal customers. One way to measure loyalty is with a concept derived from traditional marketing named *recency*.

The concept of recency is simple to understand. It is the time since the last visit or purchase by a customer. As a time-based metric and one tied to individual customers, it is a metric most easily measured in experiences and transactions in which the visitor is known via login, registration, unique ID, full name, or some other identifier.

In environments with more anonymity, recency is identified on a segment level for identifiable customer segments—and at an object- or event-level, for example, time since the last download in a mobile application for a smaller developer who can't associate a known person with a transaction.

Recency can be a helpful metric for tracking how loyal your customers are to your brand, products, or services.

KPI Derivative Example: Retention—Time Between Visits (Frequency)

Retention is another common concept in traditional marketing that is reused in digital analytics. *Frequency* refers to how often a known person or an anonymous or mostly anonymous person comes back to a digital experience she has visited previously.

Frequency, like recency (previously discussed) is also a time-based measure. As such in digital experiences in which people are identified by some mechanism, the ability to timestamp when that person last came and then recently came to a site can be straightforward. Frequency in anonymous or mostly anonymous environments, such as those dependent on browser cookies, is harder to pinpoint. Cookie deletion and the inability to persist an association between one cookie and another over time impact the accurate calculation of frequency.

Frequency is important to track in businesses where repeat visits are important. For example (news sites or social media sites), a decrease in frequency could indicate an issue with content relevancy. On e-commerce sites, the cause of an increase in frequency around a particular product or by a particular customer is something to investigate.

KPI Percentage Example: % of X from Source N

In the above heading, X is meant to be some measure from a source named N, for example, the percentage of customers from paid search. Or the percentage of revenue generated from marketing campaigns. As such, the abstraction of the percentage of something

X from some source N is helpful to apply to the concepts in digital analytics. Distributions of the sources where people come from when they enter a digital experience are one of the most frequently encountered analyses requested to a digital analytics team. For websites, the sources of traffic (as discussed in Chapter 2) can be other sites or advertising campaigns. In mobile applications, users can click links to visit other mobile applications (most commonly for payments) or from within "store experiences" like the App store.

The many different ways in which a person enters a digital experience can be tracked in percentage terms and against the key metrics you want to segment by source. As a result, you can derive KPIs such as percentage of visitors from online advertising, or percentage of profit by marketing campaign. This KPI can be segmented and widely applied to digital data.

KPI Percentage Example: % New Customers (or N Metric)

Percentage of new customers is a helpful KPI for sites that want to measure customer growth rate or market share. The idea of the percentage of new X is highly used in digital analytics, for example, the percentage of new customers from search or the percentage of repeat customers from display advertising. Site owners want to know the percentage of new customers, new visitors, or repeat visitors. Taken to the next derivative, the percentage of new customers in the last 30 months or year over year.

In this example, and others that use percentages, it is important to determine what percentage of the segment or segments you are tracking are part of the total audience, total reach, total monthly unique visitors, and so on. And then compare those percentages across time to other periods while also contextualizing the KPI with other data, such as the actual integers that make up the percentage changes over the time period analyzed.

KPI per Example: Cost per Visitor

At this point in the chapter, you can likely see where this is going with KPIs. The highest value of a KPI is when it can be tied directly to a financial metric. In the case of advertising, the "cost per" metrics are numerous and their usage widespread and well understood. The most common advertising-based "cost per" is the Cost per Mille (CPM) or the cost per thousand (in the context of display advertisements). Digital analytics uses "cost per" metrics in similar ways. The cost can be any object in the digital analytics data model, such as cost per visitor, cost per conversion, cost per action, cost per lead, cost per engagement, cost per Facebook Like, or cost per user-generated tweet. These metrics may be too vague, so again segmentation or further derivation can be helpful as are time-series comparisons of the cost metrics.

KPI per Example: Revenue per Customer

The counterpoint to the cost metrics reviewed in the previous section are revenue-based metrics. The ultimate link to the business is when KPIs are joined with financial data. Helpful insights can be found when the digital analytics team focuses on bringing together financial data related to the "revenue per" of events, behaviors, transactions, or customers in the digital experience with the "cost data." That way profitability can be calculated. Thus, a useful KPI to track for measuring business performances are "revenue per" metrics. As the counterpoint metric for "cost per" metrics, the "revenue per" metric indicates how much money was generated. The most common usage of a "revenue per" metric is the revenue per customer KPI or revenue per product category. Also related are the "revenue per customer segment X or Y" and derivatives "revenue per new customer" or "revenue per repeat customer," and so on. Again, by associating "revenue per" metrics with "cost per" metrics you can get "profitability per" metrics—of which C-level executives take notice.

If your KPI strategy can execute to the level where "cost per X" and "revenue per X" KPIs are known, such as the "cost per paid search campaign" and the "revenue per paid search campaign," then you can calculate the "profit per paid search campaign." Taking this to a deeper level, the analytics team could tell you "profit per keyword in search campaign X" and related comparative and time-series views of the KPI. As you conclude, the power of such insights in transforming the profitability of a business using digital data and derivative

KPI analysis cannot be underestimated—and will not be digital data ignored by business leaders.

Real-Time Versus Timely Data: A Practitioner Perspective

During the past few years, many analytics practitioners, consultants, and vendors referenced varying opinions about real-time data. Some people believe real-time data is a revolutionary innovation in data collection, while others remain skeptical of the utility of real-time data in many business contexts. Real-time data for human analysis is not useful unless automation based on the data is involved and leveraged. Real-time data can be crucial for providing the fuel for automated activities such as targeting, detecting, interacting, or some other form of automating an experience. But real-time data isn't needed very frequently in non-automated, human approaches to data analysis where timely data makes more sense than real-time data.

Few business decisions are made or site optimization activities made in real time, so it is not necessary to have real-time data in those cases—timely data will suffice. Actually, analysis and the resulting business-focused insights and actionable recommendations can sometimes take months to execute—whether on a site (within a controlled release schedule, Agile, or more ad-hoc), as part of an inventory fulfillment process, or within a mathematical model that results in some downstream business change (such as a promotional mix or offer modification across time zones). That said, of course, there is a value of information and insights in real time but not much utility of real-time data for *human* (that is, *manual*) analysis.

People have mentioned rare cases in which real-time data was acted upon in real time by people, not by systems or by automation, immediately after it was collected. One case is online marketing campaigns or CRM emails, where looking at real-time data about whether the campaign is driving traffic back to a site might be useful for making sure the campaign worked immediately. However, acting on that data won't be done in real time. Thus, what business impact would occur if the data came in 3 hours later or even with a 15-minute delay? Again, where data fuels automated outputs that are based on algorithmic response to data movements, or within artificial intelligence and other advanced data-processing systems, real-time data can be helpful and even critically necessary. For example, real-time data is absolutely necessary for the innovations in the buying and selling of online advertisements in ad exchanges and networks, which are often based on real-time bidding (RTB). The same can be said for data used for targeting people as they move across digital experiences and devices.

Timely data, which may be in real time but likely is not in real time, is what is most often required by the business when doing analysis to answer business questions that are communicated back to people. After all, it's going to take time to do anything after the data is collected. It's going to take time to fix whatever problem occurred and retraffic the campaign or re-email the list. And with today's campaign management technologies, if you mess up a campaign, it's likely a process or people problem, not only data. Thus real-time data may indicate a problem but not provide the insight on where it has occurred. It also takes time to analyze data, create analytics deliverables, and find suitable scheduling with stakeholders to present it.

The same can be said for real-time site data where people claim you can see if the site works by watching the data move across time. Sure, it looks cool to see the data tally in real time—impressive eye candy and infrastructure in the back end. But any resulting recommendation based on "watching the data" can take time to implement. Development teams don't generally make real-time changes based on what people see change in real time. Cases can exist where digital data changes in a very peculiar, dramatic manner where investigation identified a problem that must be hot-fixed immediately on the site. For example, a problem with campaign response from a recently sent email campaign may be noticed and reacted to from real-time data reporting. But even hotfixes take the time to implement.

Timely data is necessary and required for creating analysis and insights that help guide decisions generating revenue or reducing cost. But the timing that defines "timely" depends on the business and business situation. Timely data is data that you can use to make a business-critical decision delivered when you need it. Thus, timely data can come in 5 milliseconds, 5 seconds, 5 minutes, 5 hours, 5 days, 5 weeks, 5 months, or 5 years depending on your business needs and goals and event horizon. And timely data can suffice because the action that results from any decision is rarely executed in real time. Think of operations management and inventory replenishment. It's not "just in real time." It's "just in time" because the process is timely to business needs and goals.

Where real-time data is useful, without a doubt, is for automated systems. Consider a highly advanced behavioral detection system where the data input is used to render some immediate result or experience. Read more about the future of analytics in Chapter 13, "Future of Digital Analytics."

Take a simple case from the financial services industry. A bank knows the average account balance for each customer. When an outlier deposit is made, say one million dollars, the bank detects that deposit, and, when the customer next logs into his online bank account, the real-time detection of that login—in the context of the outlier deposit—could be used to automate the delivery of a promotional offer for a mutual fund or other financial instrument. Then, if the customer does not act upon the offer, a discount on the product could be automatically sent, in real time, to the customer's email address, texted to his cell phone, tweeted to the customer's Twitter account, or commented on Tumblr. Another example is ad targeting, similar to ad exchanges and RTB approaches to advertising, where cookies are evaluated in real time and a targeted ad is served in real time.

In these cases, real-time data enabled a competitive advantage, reduced cost, and maybe even increased profitable revenue. In these examples, real-time data is only useful to the business because of automation. But at the end of the day, real-time data is not often useful outside of automation, and business leaders should express the need for timely data and analytics, not only real-time data.

8

Optimization and Testing with Digital Analytics: Test, Don't Guess

Multiple maturity models, such as those created by Bill Gassman at Gartner and Stephane Hamel at Cardinal Path, suggest a mature digital analytics program will perform work focused on the nebulous and abstract concept "optimization." This word will inevitably and always enter conversations about digital analytics. The work of the analytics team may be referred to as "optimization." A digital analyst may have a conversation like this, "What will the data be used for?" says the analyst. "Optimization of the site" claims the businessperson. "Optimization" as a general concept makes sense at first glance. The word simply means "improvement." Using the data to improve the business is a much more complex concept to apply to digital experiences. The concept of *optimization* is something that every analyst must understand. But what is digital optimization?

Before defining digital optimization, you must understand what people mean by optimization because it is thrown around in front of every phrase you might ever hear in the digital world. Optimize ads. Optimize spend. Optimize site. Optimize conversion. Optimize landing pages. Optimize search. Optimize our apps. Optimize this. Optimize that. Optimize Seussian with persona hats. Analytics executives have a real issue when people speak about optimization without defining it and the context in which the improvement will occur. Optimization in the context of digital could be defined as:

Optimization is when the user experience (UX)—such as the text on the page, the images, the offers, the promotions, the creative, the calls to action, the buttons, and other elements—is rendered differently for segments of users, and the performance of those different segments is measured against

223

predefined goals in real time. As a result, the best possible combination of the elements of UX—the best "recipe"—can be identified for maximizing performance of the experience against pre-defined business goals.

The act of optimizing is much more than improving—though improvement is at the heart of optimization—and, as you may have concluded, optimization involves testing and controlled experimentation. For example, you might test whether people convert better when forms have fewer fields, even just one field (email address). Or if people are more likely to spend more time, view more pages, or get more engaged with your site when various colors or features are used.

Digital optimization's roots share aspects of traditional marketing and acquisition in print media for paid or controlled circulation. When print was king, it was not uncommon to send variations of subscription cards or other types of outbound marketing materials via direct mail or catalogs to determine which mailings were most effective. These types of tests were called champion/challenger tests—from whence derived the contemporary AB email test. Later, modern cable networks like the Home Shopping Channel (HSC) and Quality Value Convenience (QVC) brought real-time testing to another level. HSC and QVC have control rooms, in near real time, which feed data about the audience and sales directly to the production staff where the broadcast can be tailored to maximize sales. In other sectors, such as operations management, reducing cycle times and error rates within manufacturing is important and is done by testing different types of assembly lines and methods for manufacturing. Most car enthusiasts who have studied car manufacturing are familiar with the Japanese ideas of *kanban* and *kaizen*.

In many ways, it is useful for the digital analyst to understand that digital optimization is a nexus between the Japanese concept *kaizen*, which means continuous improvement, and the evolution of direct mail models of champion/challenger. The idea of *kanban*, which is a rope used by line workers to halt the assembly line when a problem is noticed to fix it and not let it impact downstream production, is similar to what today's digital optimization software does for the business. It provides output that can be used to alert for inefficiencies in a digital experience and recommend the best possible way to fulfill goals.

Although the trade secrets and intellectual property of digital optimization companies, like SiteSpect, IBM, Adobe, and Monetate, provide a value proposition through their products and services well beyond the fundamental theories of optimization, you need to understand the following:

- **Taguchi methods:** Genichi Taguchi was an engineer and statistician who developed revolutionary concepts related to improving the quality of manufacturing processes. His methods have been employed and influenced many digital optimization engineers and innovators. Taguchi looks at the concept of loss—in multiple dimensions—to improve a process by understanding parameters and tolerances. Using complex math to fine-tune the parameters and understand the influence of multiple factors, Taguchi demonstrated that his mathematical and statistical methods could effectively reduce or maximize the output of one or more variables in the manufacturing process. His work is widely employed in multiple scientific disciplines.

- **Choice modeling (or choice design):** A method by which the optimization is considered a function that can be maximized by choice. The notion of choice as something that can be modeled using math was a theory derived from modern psychology where it is considered that choice must have a behavioral basis. As such, the theory is that these behaviors can be identified and applied to estimate the likelihood of a particular person, or customer segment, making a certain decision. One way to understand choice modeling is that concepts like brand affinity and known demographics and behaviors of customer segments can be modeled against previous purchasing patterns to estimate what type of advertising stimuli may elicit the wanted response.

- **Multivariate testing:** According to Wikipedia, this type of testing is also called "multivariable testing." This more descriptive name communicates excellently that two or more variables are tested to determine the impact of one against another. For example, the size of a discount in the promotional offer tested alongside the color of buttons and different types of images.

- **Univariate testing:** Occurs when only one variable is tested. For example, the color of a button may change, and the impact of that change against the original color (that is, the control) is measured. For example, the color of a download button (red versus blue) can be tested to determine which button color results in more orders.

- **Fractional (or partial) factorial testing:** A way to describe the type of testing that will be done. *Partial* means that only a certain set (or fraction) of the possible combinations of all the factors will be tested. In other words, if you have 10 elements to test, you have 10 to the 10th power possible combinations. Testing 10 to the 10th takes a lot of time and a large audience/sample to test, and many of the possible combinations of elements likely make no sense (for example, testing a white button on a white background); thus, partial factorial testing is to accommodate for this fact. The number of combinations is reduced to the most critical set of combinations (which still can be a large number) and then tested for however long it takes to reach statistical significance.

- **Full factorial testing:** When all possible combinations are tested against the control to identify every possible outcome to determine the best possible optimization, full factorial testing has occurred. It is more common to find full factorial testing used in applications where the customer doesn't directly interact with the test; however, that restriction is not always necessary. Full factorial testing is often used in machine learning processes and statistical data mining/controlled experimentation.

- **Optimal design:** A pattern in optimization that involves rapidly cycling through sets of iterations of tests to identify as quickly as possible the combination of test elements that "wins" against defined parameters for the testing is named Optimal Design. This approach takes into account the relationships between the elements being tested, so as not to spend time testing odd combinations (such as white buttons on white backgrounds, which full factorial would test).

Tim Ash, CEO of Site Tuners, and author of *Landing Page Optimization*, cited the following about fractional factorial testing in the context of Taguchi, where he claimed that his experience applying this testing construct to landing pages across sites in multiple industries was problematic. Ash cites the following concerns:

- **Very small test sizes:** Testing has to be performed to a statistical significance level. The sample size depends on the population types of testing, so don't risk your reputation by putting forward analysis based on invalid samples of small sample sets.

- **Restrictive and inflexible test designs:** The underlying digital technologies that render the UXs across websites and other Internet-connected devices, in many cases, can have restrictions and limitations. Some optimization technologies have boundaries and constraints tracking multiple recipes across different sets of features, flows, creative, offers, and experiences.

- **Less accurate estimation of individual variable contributions:** Statistical rigor is necessary when analyzing the results of testing. Manual processes are as good as the people doing the math, and vendor products have nuances and limitations on the types of testing and reporting that can be done. Measures like covariance and various statistical matrices that express the relationships between variables need to be accounted for in testing.

- **Drawing the wrong conclusions:** Optimization and testing may prove that a specific variation outperforms another variation or even the control, but the result does not necessarily mean that performance is guaranteed to continue over a long term to the entire customer audience as it changes.

- **Inability to consider context and variable interactions:** It is often said in analytics that you know what you know, and you don't know what you don't know. In the same sense, the tests are only as smart and applicable as you program them to be. It is difficult to collect every possible interaction on a digital experience, and that fact is exasperated when testing complex sets of different digital experiences. The risk, however, of not doing so is that in testing you may miss other contexts and the interactions between other variables that are important to consider.

The inner workings of the AB and multivariate tools and professional services are likely going to be less important to stakeholders and the team as long as they produce the expected and appropriate business results. Some people may question how statistical models developed for scientific fields, like operations management, or for use within factories and supply chains are relevant to the behavior of digital users. Although in some cases these criticisms could be accurate, the available options for controlled experimentation and optimization testing enable this science to be widely used across all types of digital experiences.

Reviewing the AB Test: Start Here

An AB test used to be called, in traditional marketing, a champion/challenger test. The concept is simple to understand: Two different variations of the same entity are tested to a random sample of an audience. The two variations are compared and assessed against one or more measures to calculate the variation providing the best performance for a given goal. The "A" portion of the test can be considered the control, whereas the "B" version of the test could be considered the test. In this sense, an AB test is a controlled experiment. In some cases, companies actually do ABC testing and call it AB testing. The A is the current digital experience (the control); the B and C are two different tests.

The business case for AB testing (as well as multivariate testing) is simple to understand. By spending overhead and investment on deploying alternative versions of the test, the company can improve performance. At the end of the day, the results of AB (and multivariate testing) are increased revenue (perhaps via improved conversion), reduced costs (perhaps by eliminating wasteful effort on features), and improved effectiveness (perhaps by reducing the amount of maintenance).

Traditionally, AB testing was done digitally in the context of email; however, it can be applied to all digital channels in different ways:

- **User Experience (UX):** When a person engages with your experience, a number of behavioral interactions occur. A visit starts, time is counted, clicks are made, and events occur. In a browser on the phone, people see colors, images, text, offers, links, fields, toggles, buttons, designs, layouts, formats, style sheets, and so on. These elements can all be tested. In addition, underlying functionality to which the user may not be exposed—such as site speed—may also be tested. The best testing programs are not explicit and are deployed in ways where it is unlikely that the user ever knows he's entered a test, unless he explicitly opts-in to the test.

- **Email:** AB testing has its roots and foundations in the history of offline marketing using direct mail. AB testing can be email-based where it's still highly useful. Just like UX, there is a lot to test in email. Subject lines are commonly tested. The calls to action, fonts, colors, offers, prices, and other elements of UX within an email can be optimized and tested.

- **Mobile:** The importance of today's mobile landscape has never been clearer and more ubiquitously mainstream. Billions of people worldwide use mobile phones and many of them are Internet-enabled through mobile browsers. Smart devices have a set of applications available for download. Companies that create the actual handheld devices test the UX of the mobile operating system. Developers who create mobile apps also test their applications, using approaches similar to Web analytics testing.

- **Online advertising:** A profitable area that can benefit greatly is the testing of content, creative, size, and rich-media functionality in online ads. Multiple sets of ad creative, persuasive copy, and promotional offers can be tested against different customer segments to understand performance against goals.

- **Social features:** With the abundant number of social options available to the creators of digital experiences, each can be tested to determine whether the social feature is used by the audience, and if so, what is the impact on the business? For example, it might make a lot of sense to put a set of outgoing links to other sites in a prime area of your media site. The traffic arbitrage might be worth it. But then again, will the people use the feature or will it cannibalize existing page views? These hypotheses and impacts can be adequately tested.

- **Content:** Whatever your company's use for digital content can be alternated out and tested with other content. Pictures, text, phone, video content, and so on as well as the features and functions that enable users to interact with content can be tested using multivariate testing.

- **Promotions:** Although some may consider promotional testing to be advertising testing, it is worth calling it out on its own. Promotions are offers, coupons, discounts, and other incentives that can be altered based on audience profiles, events, and behaviors to provide different prices and options to identifiable customer segments.

- **Flows:** The screens, sequences, workflows, and persuasive architectures that create the experience and narrative within a digital experience are the flows. You may have heard of conversion flows. In this sense, each page or screen within a sequence of steps to complete an action can be rotated and tested.

Expanding to Multivariate Testing

Multivariate tests (sometimes called *multivariable tests*) are optimization methods where a combination of elements (that is, more than one) within a digital experience are tested in real-time against a control and pre-identified goals to determine the combination of elements that perform optimally.

Different from an AB test, where one entire version competes against another entire version, the multivariate test can include any number of elements you want to test. Of course, the more elements selected to test, the exponential numbers of variations that need to be tested increase and so does the size of the population sample needed to complete the test. Thus, multivariate testing usually takes more time than AB testing because in theory you have an almost limitless number of options you could test were you to use full factorial testing as opposed to partial factorial.

Other than the difference in the number of elements tested, the process and handling of multivariate tests has many similarities with AB testing. One major difference is that multivariate testing, given the number of elements available to test, can be complex in the sense of how to effectively create the tests to reduce nonsense combinations from being tested (that is, same color button on the same color background) while providing for the mathematical and statistical rigor needed to calculate valid results. In that sense, stand-alone multivariate and optimization testing software and Software as a Service (SaaS) platforms exist, and many enterprise-level statistical processing tools have techniques and methods that can be applied to multivariate testing, optimization, and analysis.

Creating a Testing and Optimization Plan

Planning is important in all analytics activities because it helps to frame the work to be done and sets expectations and deliverables against an agreed-upon timeline. For testing programs to succeed, they need to be deliberate and controlled by ample and adequate planning. The details of the plan must be captured in writing, reviewed by the stakeholding and supporting teams, and finally "signed off" by the company performing the testing.

Although all analytics projects involve some level of cross-functional team coordination, the act of testing is one of the more elaborate cross-functional activities in which a digital analytics team can engage. By being careful and considerate of the many players and complexity of testing variations of things against a mostly anonymous Internet audience, the likelihood for your testing to yield statistically valid and useful results will be enhanced.

Recommended next are some useful elements of a testing plan to incorporate into a sustainable artifact that represents the testing plan:

- **Plan name:** All plans should have a name that is self-identifying and makes sense in reporting. The name needs to be understood. Something so basic, like naming, in human understandable, business meaningful terms should not be overlooked as being too simplistic.

- **Test type:** Identify the type of test you are performing, such as AB or multivariate test, and any information you know about the underlying algorithms and mathematics used to validate the test.

- **Channel/experience:** Define the campaign, site, application, flow, content, and so on that you will test.

- **Business driver for the test:** When indicating the business drivers for the test, concentrate on defining the business situation, question, or problem area that the test can help to improve. Try to tie the test to business values using financial metrics or a proxy.

- **Test goal:** Because all tests operate to improve a goal, it is important in the test plan to list exactly the goal of the test. For example, your goal may be to increase product purchases, reduce shopping cart abandonment, increase click depth, and so on.

- **Metrics for analysis:** The set of data and definitions (see Chapter 5, "Methods and Techniques for Digital Analysis") must be identified in advance of testing. Pre-identification of metrics for analysis ensures that the data will be collected during the test to evaluate the results.

- **Success criteria:** Related to your goals, what are the indicators of success that you can measure against the results of the test? In some cases, the criteria used to evaluate the test is as simple as seeing a positive change in the value of the goal. For example, an increasing conversion rate as a result of a test can be used to support the business case for modifying the digital experience, where the test must achieve a certain numerical threshold for conversion to be considered successful. For example, a conversion increase of two entire percentage points may be a threshold set.

- **Expectation:** Any testing program or project has an expectation about it whether right or wrong. The expectation is often that one particular test or recipe will outperform others. Testing will prove validity of business assumptions about user behavior in digital experiences. There may even be an expectation that the testing program will be useless and show no results, which is easy to prove to be an inaccurate belief. Regardless, it's helpful to document expectations of the testing in advance so that the expectations and assumptions brought to bear in the inception of the test can be compared to their actual results.

- **Action:** The results of a test are going to be a) keep the current version, b) modify the current version, or c) deploy more tests. Additional testing deployment occurs to not only validate results over time but also to further improve the testing results. Make sure you set the expectation that more tests may be necessary to further determine and sustain the appropriate optimizations.

The Process of AB and Multivariate Testing

Central to any analytics related function, such as AB and multivariate testing, the creation of a process for doing the work is important. Because AB and multivariate testing involve cross-functional teamwork and the support from different functional resources and teams, such as UX and marketing teams, it is necessary that the testing process accommodate for ways supporting teams do their work. As such, a process must be created for digital optimization and testing.

Throughout this book, in every chapter, you probably notice a repeat theme: the importance of process within the operations of analytics focused around the need to establish goals identifying available metrics to be trended for benchmarks; and then ensuring that you track the necessary elements across the digital ecosystem while remaining focused on business value. The same rules and principles apply to the creation of process for testing and optimization. Remember that optimization processes must accommodate for the needs of how other teams execute their work who support the testing process.

The following set of tasks—at a general level—are executed as part of the testing process. You can follow this set of steps, in whatever sequence works for you, when setting up your AB and multivariate testing process:

1. **Brainstorm the metrics or measures you want to increase or improve using testing.** At this point in your ideation for a testing approach, one of the early activities you want to perform is determining the data you want to impact to drive the financial results you want to achieve. Because digital is the medium with many measures, you have a lot of options to work with, so whittle them down to what is really important and what drives the business. Focus on business value as an outcome, such as the ways your business reduces cost and increases conversion, revenue, or profitability. You may even decide to test key landing pages for marketing campaigns.

2. **Determine what and how you will collect, measure, and report results, including the format and mockups for reports and analysis.** A critical step early in the process when planning an optimization and testing program is how you want to report results. In a real sense, back of the napkin mockups and other ways to communicate results can be brainstormed in the early days of the project. After all, it's easy to say what you want to see for data, but it's entirely another story to present it in a way that communicates. The goal should be to ensure that stakeholders have participated in and approved the way the results of optimization and testing will be reported back to them.

3. **Validate the historic performance of the measurement goal by looking at historical data and benchmarks.** After the data is gathered, it should be calculated into trends and benchmarks for evaluating the testing performance: Benchmarks and goals can be derived from past data on averages and other statistical measurements of the data.

4. **Set the goal or threshold that the AB test must pass to be considered successful.** Testing just to see improvement in something may be worthwhile, but generally that's not enough. Because of the overhead involved in testing programs, and the allocation of resources across multiple teams, there might be a threshold or value in terms of performance the test must succeed to be considered successful. You can calculate this threshold from the benchmarking you did previously. Or the threshold might be a more detailed calculation involving the cost of capital and other financial measures, such as hurdle rate/Internal Rate of Return (IRR).

5. **Create a testing plan.** A testing plan identifies what you hope to accomplish when creating a test. Incorporate the perspectives and workflows of the various teams that must contribute work to the AB testing, such as creative, ad ops, agencies, marketing, IT, engineering, and so on. See the previous section in this chapter for more detail, "Creating a Testing and Optimization Plan."

6. **Deploy the test and collect data according to the plan.** Now is the time to execute. It is likely that you have coordinated the creation, verification, and trafficking/deployment of your test through whatever technical development and release process is used at your company. Because you have socialized and gained approval for your test plan, the steps involved for the multiple teams to execute work should be as simple as telling them that the test is beginning. If you've planned adequately and successfully, the teams should know what to do. If, however, you have not aligned with other teams, then it will be difficult in most cases to deploy a test and begin collecting results to analyze.

7. **Evaluate and analyze the reporting and performance of the testing.** You are finally at a point in which all your hard work identifying metrics, figuring out how to handle reporting, preparing, and planning for the test all comes to fruition. Use analytical techniques and methods, if you have to do it manually, to evaluate the results of your testing. Less mathematical calculations by humans are necessary when using automated

home-grown solutions. The best AB and multivariate software will do the hard math for the users and provide statistically sound and valid results in an easy-to-understand format.

8. **Communicate business results.** Given the number of inputs, teams, and stakeholders involved in testing, everyone will want to know how the test is performing as soon as it launches. In some cases, people want to know a couple hours later, the next day, and even at other durations. Although you can evaluate the performance of a test based on partial data collection, remember what Tim Ash mentioned was a challenge: sample sizes and ultimately the statistical rigor and the team's ability to analyze the results. Like releases and software, testing ultimately needs time to produce statistically significant and predictive results. You should push back, sometimes aggressively, when stakeholders want to see the results of testing and optimization too early after the test goes live. Make sure that the results of the test hold up and appear to be valid over time before communicating or deploying them.

9. **Go live with the successful version of the test.** Congratulations! It's time to employ the successful version of the test and enhance the performance of the goal you intended to, and now have successfully, optimized. Work with your technology partners to release the new version live in the digital experience.

Technologies and Methods for Measuring, Analyzing, and Reporting Results of AB and Multivariate Testing

A number of techniques exist for gathering, reporting, analyzing, and making decisions from the results of AB testing:

- **Use homegrown tools.** As discussed in Chapter 5, some companies choose to build their own solutions to their own business problems and desire for business functionality. Internal solutions created to provide for testing are not that uncommon. Typically these tests are simple, low volume tests with simple success measurements. In these cases, the company may choose to use its own tool set or create a specific point solution for simple AB testing and optimization.

- **Leverage digital analytics tools.** Many digital analytics vendors also offer some level of support for AB, multivariate, and optimization testing software. By using campaign codes and advanced configurations within analytics tools and within the data collection layer, it is possible to record the results of AB and multivariate tests in digital analytics tools.

- **Collect data and present reporting in business intelligence (BI) tools.** A more elaborate approach to testing is to customize a BI tool to collect and store the test data. The options for writing digital events directly to databases or to log files that are indexed into data models in a BI tool are extensive. Since BI tools often have rich extract, transform, and load (ETL) and reporting capabilities, the data from the test can be reported in the BI tool alongside other BI data.

- **Load data into statistical processing tools.** Test data may be collected by writing or logging in to a database or using other digital analytics data collection methods (like application programming interfaces [API] calls, JavaScript, or server-to-server connections), and then loading it into a statistical processing tool like R or SAS. The benefit of this approach is that advanced applied analysis can be done on the optimization data—from predictive modeling to other types of statistical approaches to data analysis and analyzing controlled experiments.

- **Infer from spreadsheets based on time-series changes.** A worst-case scenario is when people are trying to manually assemble the results of a test. While the analysis of optimization and testing will be done using many analytics tools, including spreadsheets, the complex math involved in calculating the results of tests is hard to do manually. That said, some companies choose to take this approach, however unsustainable, for many reasons—from budgets to resource needed.

- **Deploy AB and multivariate software or SaaS.** Companies allocating budget and resources to purchase testing and optimization software accelerate success in their testing programs. Software deployed in your data center or in a cloud developed specifically for testing and optimization provides useful reporting, the correct application of the underlying statistical algorithms, and might even plug into your existing digital infrastructure without requiring any client-side changes or direct changes to your website. Testing and optimization software will also provide helpful reports and visualizations that communicate the results of the tests without much manual intervention necessary.

Types of Optimization Enabled Through Testing

The phrase optimization as described at the beginning of this chapter is an often-cited, potentially less than meaningful or descriptive word often used without sufficient context. Although AB and multivariate testing are without a doubt both helpful and proven methods for optimization, you must define the macro areas within the digital ecosystem where optimization via a testing program can occur. Following are several areas within digital analytics where testing can have an impact:

- **Site or app optimization** refers to testing the UX, the surface, functionality, features, flows, and content as part of an overall website or mobile application experience.

- **Landing page optimization** is an activity that occurs on the page or screen on which a person "lands" after clicking or transitioning from one experience to another. There's a whole science dedicated to landing page optimization. Like sites, many elements of a landing page can be tested: text, buttons, images, calls to action, and so on.

- **Conversion optimization:** The act of conversion optimization refers to a value generating click, interaction, event, or transition. Conversion clicks, events, and behaviors are financially meaningful to the business. A whole set of test programs exists around conversion optimization. Testing for conversion often involves modifying the elements you see in the sequence of pages and screens that you move through before you convert. For example, in an e-commerce flow, the number of pages you have to click through, the number of form fields you have to fill out, or the different ways the information can be rendered on the screen are all appropriate to test.

- **Mobile optimization** relates to devices that move around geographic environments while remaining connected to the Internet or at a minimum interacted with the UX. Testing and optimization within mobile is different than testing sites or email. There are different languages, constraints, and interfaces to test. Mobile has browsing environments, mobile applications, and e-commerce sites, integrated to the settings and function of the phone. All these can be tested. In other words, the UX underlying the phone as developed by Apple or Android can be tested. Developers can test the apps they create. Publishers and advertisers can test the content and ads they create both with the mobile browser and mobile application.

- **Inbound referrer, visitor, or marketing optimization:** In companies that commit investment to marketing via inbound channels like search, affiliate, and other forms, the incremental impact those programs have on a particular financial goal can be tested. Paid search can go dark for a month. Display advertising can deploy across different networks one month compared to another month. The mix of affiliates in the affiliate marketing programs can change.

- **Outbound marketing optimization:** Communication sent directly to customers and prospects via email, social networking, Short Message Service (SMS)/text messages, and other digital methods can be tested as described in this chapter to understand which outbound marketing programs are most effective. And which of those programs, campaigns, creative, and other aspects provide the best business benefit for a given goal.

- **In-store optimization:** Mobile couponing, checking-in, and other mobile applications present retailers with ways to identify shoppers and stitch together their physical presence with their online identities while in the store. Offers, coupons, product information, comparative shopping information, and even mobile applications meant to be used in-store can be tested against controls and tests.

- **Shopper optimization:** Companies monitor inventory levels and in-store and online shopping behaviors to identify cues and motivators that lead to a purchase. When the hypothesis has been determined about the shopper experience, you can test persuasion, perception, and motivation using online and mobile methods directly to customers to determine which would compel the next purchase.

- **Customer optimization** means segmenting into customers, who may or may not be anonymous people or cookies, and then serving test variations to promote cross-sell and up-sell opportunities and to test direct response. Optimization can be used to decrease churn rates, increase customer satisfaction, rate, and volume of repeat customers, and so on.

- **Prospect optimization** means segmenting your audience into prospects and providing test variations of digital content that is different than prospects. The goal, of course, is to convert the prospect to a satisfied, repeat customer and brand advocate.

- **Advertising optimization** occurs frequently by testing campaign, creative, narrative, and response in the many different types of formats for digital advertising across all sizes and screens, and the underlying ways the advertising was bought, sold, exchanged, or traded—often tied into landing page testing.

- **Search optimization** refers to both off-site search and on-site search. External search on search engines, whether paid or organic search, can be tested. The relevancy, features, and UX of on-site search can be tested—as can the resulting landing pages referred by both external and internal search.

Setting Up a Digital Optimization Program

In 2013, it is still relatively uncommon to find large teams solely dedicated to testing and optimization, but increasingly companies are investing capital into the testing function; in fact, the digital experiences currently being tested via AB and multivariate testing are performed millions of times daily by millions of people across the Internet. Large, global, multinational corporations whose primary business is digital e-commerce, such as Dell, invest significant resources in testing and optimization functions. Other companies may dedicate part-time resources, or maybe one-full time resource, managing the testing and optimization function. The largest optimization teams in brands have less than 20 team members (and that's a huge number), and the smallest teams are teams of one or part-time when they exist at all.

What works for one company doesn't necessarily work for another, so it's not possible to identify exactly how you should go about setting up a digital optimization and testing team, but guidance can be provided. The following list identifies themes and areas that a manager should consider when building organizational competency in testing and optimization:

- The **team** for testing requires a similar mix of skill sets as the digital analyst; however, given the cross-functional nature of testing, a team with solid project management, coordination, design skills, and social skills is important.

- The **technology** is the underlying infrastructure behind creating, deploying, tracking, and measuring testing and optimizing programs and needs to be solid and scalable enough to accommodate your ambitions. It must also must be used by business and marketing people.

- The **process** for initiating, planning, executing, closing, communicating, going live with test results, and the future next steps after testing must be considered in detail and merged with the ways of working with supporting teams.

- The **resources** for testing require many people to perform the same activity over and over again. Instead of designing one landing page, three may be created by the UX team. The flows and content that varies in each test must be programmed by engineering resources. Content that needs to be rotated across tests needs to be written differently. All in all, these facts mean that testing is actual work that needs to be effectively resourced to be successful. And those proposing investment into optimization and testing need a plan to counter objections that testing is too expensive because of the overhead it produces. Use financial modeling to communicate the potential business impact of the testing program.

- The **overhead** is when astute businesspeople realize that there is overhead when testing, as mentioned previously. To get permission to use the overhead for testing, instead of new projects, you need to show success in dollars or at least in perceived business impact. After you show success (often by starting small using AB testing, not multivariate testing), then you can gain internal support. If testing success can be tied to revenue or profitability, the corporate wallet can open up to fund the initiative. Again, the best way to overcome issues people raise to cost of testing or the overheard inherent in it is to model the potential financial impact of a successfully sustained optimization program. You may even want to identify the impact of a small set of (easier) optimizations to prove that quick wins that have financial impact are entirely possible in the short term.

Developing Controlled Experiments and Digital Data Science

Controlled experimentation is a label that essentially means that scientific method, statistical rigor, and valid mathematics are used to understand aspects and elements of events within a digital ecosystem and the relationships between those events on one another. See Chapter 5 for more information about controlled experimentation. Data science, reviewed in Chapter 2, "Analytics Value Chain and the P's of Digital Analytics," is a new label for the activity of working with often large amounts (big) of data.

Data sciences or the singular "data science" is a newer phrase that describes the set of work activities within the Analytics Value Chain that is more focused on the details of the database and data integration, and on the application of statistical methods and data mining machine learning to data analysis. Data science is often cited in the same breath as "big data" and "predictive analytics." Data scientists is the title applied to professionals who combine solid knowledge and expertise in not only the technical computer science of data, but also the statistical and mathematical application of data. The best data scientists tie their work back to business value. In essence, data science and data scientists are new vocabulary for describing the business activities for collecting, processing, and analyzing new types of technical data and the capabilities for statistical modeling and analytical prowess necessary to optimize, predict, and automate with digital data.

Controlled experiments are often created, executed, and managed by data scientists using the academically, statistically rigorous, and valid models and algorithms from machine learning and experimental design. Data scientists create optimization software and can also be employed within brands to execute optimization and prediction programs. Listed here are some ways that controlled experiments using data science can be applied to digital optimization and that can benefit from testing the results to maximize performance:

- **Recommendations engines** are technologies that take input from past preferences, behaviors, and attributes, and with that information predict the opinion, rating, or preference for something never before considered by that group, for example, the recommendation that you may like a certain movie on Netflix.

- **Collaborative filtering** are systems that consider multiple sources of data, often "big data," and filter it to present some sort of recommendation. The applications for collaborative filters, from book recommendations and so on, are numerous on the Internet, for example, the recommendation that you may like a certain book on Amazon.com.

- **Alerting and detecting** is based on sensing and responding technologies that integrate and process input from multiple systems to detect and alert when an event occurs or is triggered. Detection systems take inputs of all types of quantitative and qualitative data and identify when change occurs in material and meaningful ways based on business rules that can result in automation. For example, you make a large cash deposit and receive an email for a discounted financial product for investing that new money.

- **Messaging and interacting** is when automated messaging and rules-based interaction within a cohesive narrative catalyzes action for attempting to compel a behavioral choice within a digital experience. For example, a bank offers a financial product based on an outlier deposit when a person logs in to a digital experience or directly with an in-app message.

- **Optimizing across omnichannels and multiple channels for testing** the impact of activities, like advertising, across different channels to understand the impact and covariance of those tests on the overall mix of advertising, or against a customer segment or even a single customer, which can be done with testing tools and statistical analysis. For more information, see Chapter 12, "Converging Omnichannels and Integrating Data for Understanding Customers, Audiences, and Media."

Tips for Testing and Optimizing Digital Experiences

Testing can be nuanced, but there are lessons that can be learned through trial and error via direct practitioner experience. Following are a few tips for testing and optimization:

- **Calculate samples sizes** because you want your testing to be statistically significant, valid, rigorous, and to withstand scrutiny. Using basic statistics to your approach to testing is appropriate and valid. Sample sizes are discussed in more detail in Chapter 5. Most testing tools will calculate this for you, but it is nevertheless something to ask about when evaluating vendors.

- **Start with AB testing** so huge gains can be achieved often by changing simple things like the creative, photos, button colors, and other proverbial low-hanging fruit. AB testing is a good way to start with testing and doesn't generally require as much investment as multivariate. You don't need to start with a multivariate approach to start testing. Start small and simple.

- **Understand what you are doing and the software you are using.** Although this may sound obvious, the digital analytics team should understand the testing program, initiatives, plans, and technology. What's deployed within a digital experience will leave its traces in the data. Wondering why one-half of the traffic dropped off on a certain entry page? Ask the testing team. Analytical managers and leaders should encourage their teams to learn and educate themselves on the importance of testing and how to do it.

- **Don't test too many things.** Similar to the previous point about how AB testing is a good starting point, you want to make sure that the test plans aren't too ambitious. Partial factorial versus full factorial testing can dramatically alter the amount of time necessary to return valid results. The fewer people that visit the test, the longer it will take to get results; thus, the more factors and variations you will have to test, the larger the sample size, the more people needed, and the longer it will take.

- **Have a strategy.** Beyond having a plan, the business should have a strategy that ties into the mission and vision of the company. Although this may sound lofty and idealistic, it is not.

Aligning your testing and optimization programs to business strategy makes it easier to gain traction and support—and also easier to tie back to financial performance resulting from the business executing the strategy.

- **Allocate resources and create process to support them.** Like all activities in digital analytics, testing and optimization will be cross functional—from UX to marketing to technology. As a result, it is necessary to ensure that the appropriate teams not only dedicate resources, but all design the right workflows and processes to support testing and optimization within the life-cycle design process—whatever your business uses.

- **Don't overoptimize.** Running a constant series of ever-changing tests is awesome but hard to pull off. Those who do it successfully have a specific set of goals, measures, metrics, methods, processes, and ways of working that are deliberate and focused. The tests may be randomly created by factoring, but the impact on the goals, performance, and data is not random. It's the result of the outcome of the test. In that sense, after you hit your goals, don't overoptimize. Consider where you started, and then plan the next steps, which may be to run more tests or to consider the optimization successful and something to maintain.

- **Consider the impact of all tests on themselves.** Understanding covariance across tests can be useful. In the sense of seeing the forest through the trees, when testing and optimizing, it is important to make sure that the next tests don't impact the results of past and simultaneous tests. Don't cannibalize your previous tests and impact their success with new tests inconsiderate of past optimizations.

- **Follow the advice of experts like the Eisenberg brothers, Tim Ash, and other proven and experienced experts.** These people have deep practical expertise from helping many companies succeed in creating and enhancing their testing and optimization programs.

Digital analytics teams that apply their skills and expertise to establishing, assisting, and helping their companies succeed in testing and optimization not only create new skill sets and advance their careers but also have the potential for dramatically increasing bottom-line financial performance. As such, optimization is a good activity for more easily identifying the return on investment (ROI) from the digital analytics team. The financial impact from successful testing, even simple AB testing, can be huge and fiscally rewarding. Testing and optimization tie in nicely to the recommendations and ideas provided to the business by the analytics team as a result of applying data analysis methods and techniques. By owning or working within or in support of the testing and optimization function, the digital analytics team can be empowered to prove further and in new ways that their work, recommendations, insights, and actions do create business value. As the saying goes, "Test! Don't guess!"

9

Qualitative and Voice of Customer Data and Digital Analytics

A commonly heard mantra in digital analytics is that the behavioral data collected by the analytics tool *du jour*—whether the most advanced site analytics tool to the newest social media listening tool, and from the most basic free analytics tool to the most expensive paid analytics tool—is that data can tell you the "what" about the themes in your data. But the same behavioral, digital data can't tell you "why" the themes in your data are "what" you've identified them to be. You've heard it before, "analytics can't tell you 'why!'" In other words, there is a somewhat accurate belief that you can't determine why data changed from looking at data. That idea is not entirely accurate because often by filtering and drilling down into distributions using segmentation you can identify the detailed data that changed in aggregate key performance indicators (KPIs). The "why" that is hard to measure with analytical tools are the human emotions, concepts, mindset, and mentalities underlying the decision and judgment behind human behavior to identify the origins of why people behaved in a certain way on the site as reflected in the data. Technology and tools collect, measure, and report the quantitative data that reflects a customer experience, but those same numbers do not tell the analyst or business leader much about the people, their motives, their cognitive state as a customer, nor how the sum culmination of the feelings and perceptions of the digital person impact the data and the brand.

The same analytics chorus that sings, "You can't find why in quantitative data" would advocate the way to get to the "why" is by speaking and engaging directly with customers. Qualitative data resulting from asking the customer questions and having them respond in full, thoughtfully (or at least partially decipherable) written or recorded language to explain why they behaved in a certain way is important. Joining the qualitative data derived directly from the voice of the customer (VoC) is something that advanced analytics teams regularly do by comparing responses and the sentiment of responses to behavioral data. Bringing together the qualitative data from market research and other VoC data is an important set of data that must be considered as a business requirement and organizational concern when building a digital analytics organization.

Before getting too deep into the subject of this chapter, it is important to define what is meant by this idea, "voice of the customer." The voice is a simple concept: It is the expression of a person's opinion about a business subject that is either written down, recorded in audio or video, or captured in hard or soft copy in documentation. What's important is that the voice is from a real person who has either purchased or is planning to purchase a product or service from the company. In other words, the person must obviously be a customer (or prospect) in order to provide their voice. Customers are not just people who have bought then or are buying now; they are also the people who will buy in the future—hopefully from your company and not your competitor's.

One of the higher goals of a digital analytics organization should be to provide rich analysis that answers business questions in a way that helps business leaders act on the data. By combining the data in digital analytics (the "what") with the qualitative data (the "why") using market research and VoC data, new insights and opportunities for innovation and profit can be realized from this new combinatorial data set.

Take for example, the KPI discussed in Chapter 7, "Reporting Data and Using Key Performance Indicators": task completion rate. Task completion rate can be measured quantitatively by using a specific behavioral activity captured in your Web analytics. Or you can simply pop up a survey on your website and ask a person to respond to your question, "Have you found what you are looking for?" Or "Have you completed your task?" The yes or no response can be measured as your task completion rate. Taking the example a step further, with qualitative data you can determine, in the words of customers, what exactly is preventing people from completing their task. Looking at this example another way, the Web analytics tool can tell you a conversion rate and let you know when people are leaving the site, on what page, and after how much time, whereas the market research can tell you what specifically or even generally occurred that caused the behavior tracked in the analytics tool. By joining the two data sets, you can tell what happened on the site from clickstream data and why it happened as described directly by the customer as to why they behaved the way they did.

This chapter provides a business leader with an understanding of what qualitative data is and how it can be used alongside and integrated with digital analytics data in a transformative way. To that end, this chapter explains why listening and speaking to your customers is important and how the qualitative research method can help:

- Review the common market research and VoC qualitative techniques that get the data for analysis and integration with digital analytics.

- Describe the work activities done by the qualitative data and market research team(s).

- Identify the possible ways, at a high level, a business leader can think about bringing together qualitative and quantitative data.

- Provide a strategy for the types of digital qualitative data that should be collected and how to analyze it against market research.

- List ways of working with a qualitative analysis team that help lead to success.

Listening to Your Customer Is More Important Today Than Ever Before

When I first started working in technology, it was for a venture-funded, startup software company in the mid-nineties. The company had been created by carving out technology originally created at world-class research centers of two prominent American schools. The type of work we were doing at the time was called "information retrieval," and this company was created to productize a toolkit for searching text. Sounds familiar, correct? We were creating what would come to be known in a few years as a search engine, not only for searching the Web but for searching data in all sorts of databases.

At the time I was working for this company, there was no Google. That may be hard to imagine for many people with less than 12 years' technology experience; however, the field wasn't called Search. It was called information retrieval. This company simply had a way to index text and provide an interface for entering a query. The result was a list of links to the documents most relevant to your query. In short, the technology was an early search engine for content residing in databases, file formats, and even on the World Wide Web (WWW). At the time, not many companies had offerings around searching corporate repositories. The Web from a business perspective was in its infancy. The first initial public offering (IPO) had occurred only a few months before. eBay didn't exist. It was very early in the online world. There was only data, not big data; there was only science, not data science yet.

I recall a decision being made that the company would concentrate not on the Web, but on the data residing in corporate databases. The company chose not to concentrate on indexing websites. The employees were told that "Web search was done." There wasn't a business or identifiable business model in retrieving information from the Web, according to the executive team, but there was a huge opportunity making sense of the data in corporate databases to turn it into knowledge. Thus, the company became a knowledge management (KM) company instead of trying to play the game in what would become, in 15 years' time, the search industry. Google proved that not only could a business sustain an economic model on Web search, it could also be hugely profitable. The rest is history. The startup got acquired, and Google is sailing the smooth and golden seas.

At the time, the decision was made to not focus on Web search; I recall asking the marketing team why? The answer was simply that X person (the proverbial HiPPO [the highest paid person's opinion]) had made strategic decisions by reading analysts' reports and speaking with professionals in the industry. It sounded good to me at the time, for I was fresh out of college. I had not been exposed to market research and VoC data, which if it existed would have likely told a different story to support perhaps a different strategy.

Looking back on that time period in my professional career, a huge opportunity was missed by this startup. At the time, the information retrieval (that is, search) technology that we were working on was based in academia and was state of the art. It is likely Larry and Sergei hadn't even ideated the idea of PageRank. Actually, the technology with which I was working could automatically extract the top noun phrases, people names, and job titles and provide the best passage and all the accouterment we have come to expect in 2013 of both Internet and corporate search. But this was 1997, and Google was not in the market. What was missing from the calculus in determining the future strategic direction of the company was VoC data. Certainly, we had "market research" sold to the United States by researchers, but the customers (especially future customers) were never contacted and interrogated.

If VoC data had been listened to, it would have been learned that customers were quickly moving documents online and wanted not only a browser-based search, but also the ability to search the Web in a relevant way. Remember, there was no Google—Web search was not as easy and helpful as it is today. Paid search did not exist, but "black hat" search engine ranking did, and search engines had not determined how to accommodate for things such as keywords stuffing and link farming. Search Engine Optimization (SEO) and its rules had not yet been invented.

Interestingly, back then we had Weblogs and while we parsed them to look at where traffic came from, we never "tagged" for site search. A 101, no-brainer today. If we had, I wonder if we would have seen searches for the Web search capability we never developed. In addition, if we had simply looked at product usage and what types of data sources were being indexed and searched most frequently, we may have found out that Web search was a main reason for product usage. However, I was just cutting my teeth in the Internet and software technology startup world, so I will always simply wonder if the digital behavioral data and VoC data that existed then—if the tools today were available then—would have helped inform the strategic direction of the business and created the potential for a different level of success out of my first startup company.

Today's business leaders in 2013 have access to the tools, resources, staff, and methods to fully bring together behavioral data with quantitative data. But few do, though the number of companies that are doing or aspire to do data integration across quantitative and qualitative is increasing. Although it certainly is complex activity, the rewards can be significant, such as

- Decreasing customer churn
- Limiting customer attrition
- Gaining customer loyalty
- Enabling customer retention
- Decreasing product and service development costs
- Increasing the speed at which products and services are innovated
- Enhancing customer satisfaction
- Understanding the drivers and motivations behind why customers purchase (or do not purchase) products or services

The net result of actualizing even one of the activities listed in the previous set of bullets is the reduction of cost and increasing of revenue, which ties directly to profitability. Thus, it is reasonable to conclude that a highly functioning qualitative data and research team delivers business value, and that value can be increased and grown significantly by aligning with the work of the digital analytics team.

Tools of the Trade: Market Research and Qualitative Data Collection Methods and Techniques

A market research team that creates qualitative data has more options for reaching and speaking with customers than ever before in human history. The ubiquity of the Internet has sped up the capability of market research teams to find people to speak with. Websites and other channels for digital experiences, such as social and mobile, enable a company and brand to be instantly accessible. All customers need to do is open up their iPhone, Android device, or other smart device, download the company's app, provide feedback within the app, submit feedback on the website, send an email, speak with a live chat agent, or even contact the company through social media.

As a result, market researchers today have many more options for eliciting VoC data than ever before. But not all businesses have all available methods at their disposal, and budgets can be limiting. Companies with legacy research programs may not understand the digital methods for reaching customers so they default to traditional techniques of "what has worked in the past." So what are the contemporary and historic techniques used by market researchers and how have they evolved online? Following are several methods used to collect qualitative data from customers:

- Surveying via online, telephone, mail, or on the street
- Creating communities: online and offline
- Conducting customer in-person interviews
- Building and using focus groups
- Creating customer feedback systems such as call centers and online feedback forms
- Using social media data and crowdsourcing
- Collecting and capturing word of mouth programs that can be tracked for customer verbatims
- Building ethnographies and other artifacts specific to predetermined customer segments
- Keeping diaries, journals, logs, and other types of note taking

Surveying via Online, Telephone, or Mail

The most common form of VoC data results from surveying people. In this context, a series of questions that may be open-ended or constrained in multiple choice formats can be posed about the digital experience. While the discussion of what makes for a good survey is outside the scope of this book, make sure that you distribute it to a large-enough sample so that the results are statistically significant and suffer from no bias or error. For more information about sampling, see Chapter 5, "Methods and Techniques for Digital Analysis." The assumption is that you know or will learn what is meant by a "well-designed" survey. From surveying, people's feedback is gathered on a particular topic area, such as the available product inventory on an e-commerce website. Feedback is collected in a database and analyzed using techniques to bring together the qualitative data in meaningful ways that provide business insight.

With the mainstreaming of the Internet, online surveying is more popular than ever. Online surveys can be configured to pop up (or pop under) based on many different inputs. New visitors who don't have a cookie could be instantly surveyed online, whereas repeat visitors with a cookie are not. Surveys can be programmed to render when a person does something on the site, like abandoning a shopping cart or clicking off a search results page. The options for when to invoke and render an online survey are numerous; however, all the experts agree on one thing: No matter where you pop up an online survey, make sure the person can easily close the pop up or exit the survey. The last thing a digital business wants is a VoC survey compromising negatively the user experience. Mail surveys—think U.S. Census Bureau—are still fairly common. You may receive a survey in the mail after you purchase a product, such as a new appliance. Mail surveys are useful for helping to reach a statistically significant sample of the target population, but the return rates can be low. Thus, companies that employ mail surveys often provide some type of incentive for the recipient to complete the survey. And they may follow up their selected sample with multiple letters that escalate to phone calls that end with on-site visits when appropriate for that type of research.

Telephone surveys still exist despite do-not-call lists and the mobile phone revolution. Actually, audience measurement firms still use random digit dialing (RDD) as a method for reaching out to the population. In political campaigning, it is not uncommon for pollsters to call people and ask questions about electoral issues or candidates. In that context, telephone surveys are often accomplished by trained staff who have been educated in the best methods to reduce friction from the respondent and to guide the call through to a successful outcome; thus, phone surveys can work. And the better trained survey-givers on the phone, the more likely to create quality data more quickly.

Regardless of the technical method and process for getting the survey answered, the larger point you should take away is that today a business leader has more choices than ever before for getting in touch with and soliciting feedback from customers. What can work best for your business is up to you to determine; however, online—especially in the context of social media—can be cost-effective.

Creating Communities – Online and Offline

Local professionals in various cities and regions get together to discuss their professions. Professional social networks exist to bring people together outside of work who do the same work or even just to get local businesspeople together. Many readers use LinkedIn.com or have tried Plaxo as online social networks. Business Networking Institute (BNI) in the United States is an offline group, where local people meet once a week locally and create relationships that help to drive commerce. Whether you refer to trade guilds, mercantile exchanges, industry associations, or other entities that require membership, people like to come together to "talk shop," network with like-minded professional colleagues, and attempt to create business relationships and commerce. The discussion and feedback captured in these communities can be valuable to a company. The challenge is that it is hard for a business to participate in real-world offline events and still look genuine. If Walmart sends a representative to a meeting of the Local Retailers Association, the participation of the world's largest retailer would likely be met with skepticism. Thus, the online world has created entire teams of social media experts and community managers that attempt to bring order, regulations, and guidelines to online communities to promote their adoption.

The world of digital has turned the idea of a community upside down. No longer are communities limited by geography, culture, location, distance, and time. The always-on Internet connects communities according to new parameters such as lifestyles, hobbies, interests, and professions. More than ever before, the largest companies and most well-known brands can actively build communities online in ways that only 10 years ago did not exist or were entirely impossible. Software vendors create communities around their products serviced by entire websites (non-Facebook!) where members can interact. While more and more brands are choosing to move to Facebook, online, brand-based social networks do exist. Private online communities accessible by invitation-only exist within certain professions, such as digital analytics and the online industry. Social networks (discussed more in a later bullet) offer companies and the agencies that work for them the ability to invite people into highly specific online communities based on the matching of social networking profile data to a given demographic. For example, an online community for females above the age of 34 who drive Porsches can be identified over social media. This community, wherever it exists, can be built into a unified online community from people across one or more social networks—whereas the work to create such a community offline might not be possible.

Conducting Customer In-Person Interviews

When products and services are created or enhanced, the information collected in market research may need to be further qualified and investigated in detail. A primary method for digging deeper into the survey answers and content is a detailed, in-depth interview. The idea of an interview is that the person can be asked specific questions, and more details can be elicited to qualify the research. The idea here is that the interview can gauge the response of an individual and further qualify it against the business goal. Interviewing is not something to be taken lightly. It can be time-consuming and expensive. Professionals who are trained in the best practices of interviewing can be contacted to help ensure that the investment in interviewing is best executed and managed to closure.

Building and Using Focus Groups

Focus groups is the term used to describe a set of people who are congregated together—typically offline in a common physical location on-site—and asked a series of questions where an open conversation occurs. A moderator leads the focus group while the entire focus session is recorded for evaluation and analysis later. Focus groups are liked by businesses because the moderator can be from the business (or a hired expert) and other businesspeople can observe the focus group (typically through a two-way mirror or video camera).

Online methods for creating and executing focus groups are becoming more common. Traditional research is transformed by the ability to use social networking profile data to select focus groups.

Actually, a digital analytics team can use methods to segment customer data to help identify candidates for focus grouping.

Although focus groups can be cost-effective and relatively simple to pull off, be aware that this method is not perfect. Because the participants in focus groups are often compensated in some way, bias in selection can impact the quality of the data. Because people have to be physically brought together for traditional focus groups, they may not offer advantages to companies that operate and sell products and services across multiple countries and cultures. Globalizing focus groups can be expensive. In addition, the self-selecting set of focus group participants isn't necessarily a random sample. The participants can bias the group by being overly combative and derailing the moderator or not allowing the group to complete the discussion in a meaningful way. In other focus groups, charismatic and eloquent people can sway other's opinions. The challenges in managing focus groups cause researchers to use them at the beginning of a product to help articulate innovation and also after a product release to help the company understand sentiment and satisfaction. For example, when a new product is developed, a focus group could be convened to help guide product managers, whereas after a product has been launched, a new focus group could be convened to learn what features customers want to see in a future release of the next product version.

Creating Customer Feedback Systems Such as Call Centers and Online Feedback Forms

One helpful way to collect qualitative data is by setting up customer feedback systems, which may involve aspects of surveying or interviewing. For example, having a service desk in retail environments provides a place where people can go to provide feedback while in-store. But do online retailers have service desk employees that capture and record this information?

Front-line employees on the sales floor or in the call center have a special role to play in qualitative data collection. They often enter information about the customer into call center Customer

Relationship Management (CRM) systems. Customer service employees who respond directly in writing to customers represent an often hugely untapped opportunity to listen, understand, and learn from them. Thus, companies need to staff and train the employees who interact with customers accordingly so that the information captured as a result of these customer calls and other touchpoints are captured in sufficient detail and made available for research and analytics.

Using Social Media Data and Crowdsourcing

Within the last 10 years, the advent of social networking has redefined and is constantly redefining how businesses learn from their customers. Whether in a blog, on Facebook, over Twitter, via YouTube, or pinned on Pinterest, the most sophisticated and successful global brands have invested in listening and engaging with customers over social media. Businesses commonly create Twitter feeds, Pinterest pages, Tumblr blogs, Polyvore pages, manage and update Facebook pages, and launch both branding and direct response campaigns across video through YouTube, Vine, Instagram, and other social digital channels.

All these social campaigns generate consumer behavior as important qualitative data both within social media and outside of it in the form of human-to-human conversation, word-of mouth, and interaction. All this qualitative data can be analyzed. The future of market research involves using social media in new ways that help research—from the targeting of products and services based on audience attributes to the easier selection of samples for use in surveying and focus groups. Without a doubt, social media is already and will continue to elevate the importance of understanding what people are saying about your company, brand, product, and services. As social network data continues to be used to select focus group participants—or to simply converse and build the brand with socially active customers and influencers, the digital analytics team must incorporate social data into analysis. Analytics leaders must ensure that the social dialogue is listened to, captured, analyzed, and communicated back to the business, and joined with behavioral quantitative data.

Collecting and Capturing Word of Mouth

Word of Mouth (WoM) is the conversational activity that occurs offline in locations, such as the dinner table, the office water cooler, at the bar, in restaurants, or in various human social interactions. When you talk about a new movie and how you liked it (or hated it) or tell your friend about the new car you brought, you are engaging in WoM conversation. Customers, of course, talk to other people about brands, and it is important to capture that information in a structured way so that it can be used for analysis.

Keeping Diaries, Journals, Logs, and Ethnographies

Back in the days when there was only TV and radio, advertisers wanted to know how and when people watched TV and listened to the radio. Advertisers evaluated the success of content via Reach and Frequency metrics or Gross Rating Points (GRP). It wasn't possible, like it is now, to collect digital TV data or understand what shows and commercials people were watching because the research discipline, such as Arbitron, did not exist, and it was even more difficult to determine the profile of the audience for a particular TV show. Thus, the idea of diary keeping began to be practiced—and the results of this methodology were used as the data inputs to models that estimated total audience reach and frequency.

A diary is just as it sounds and as you might imagine it to be. It's a written log created by people about their activities, such as the shows they watched, the Internet sites and social networks to which they read/listened, the cars they drive, foods eaten, or the different multiscreen devices used to access the Internet. *Ethnographies* are a type of diary. Such written diaries can be parsed by technology and turned into meaningful customer insights. Modern Web technology has improved and enhanced the ways diaries and journals can be created, extended, and maintained.

The Types of Qualitative Data That Are Helpful for Digital Analytics

Qualitative data is a general catch-all phrase for data and information collected from written or recorded materials, such as the written responses or video recording to a set of questions. Qualitative data need not only come from customers. It can come from internal employees, the customers of your competitors who never bought anything from you, or people who aren't even aware that your brand or company exists. However, VoC data can come only from customers—either past, existing now, or future. Although the scope of digital analytics data was covered in Chapter 2, "Analytics Value Chain and the P's of Digital Analytics," you may wonder what are the main categories of qualitative data that are useful for associating with digital analytics and what impact can understanding the insights derived from the data in these sources have on the business.

Qualitative and VoC data commonly unified with digital analytics includes customer experience, satisfaction, sentiment, and loyalty research. By tracking the customer experience, it is hoped that the attitudes, beliefs, feelings, and motivations for customers can be identified.

Measuring Customer Loyalty and Retention

A primary activity of a research team is creating, managing, monitoring, analyzing, and communicating research about whether existing customers remain customers, and if so, how long, how much do they spend, on what, where, why, and when? The goal for measuring these metrics should be to understand if your customers are loyal, how loyal they are, and how those insights can be brought to the business to help retain and grow customers. Correlating all these concepts to financial performance is helpful and useful. As a result of measuring customer loyalty and retention, you can be in a better position to up-sell and cross-sell customer segments and then understand the results performance and impact on sales and thus on the core finances of the business. In addition, metrics such as churn and percentage of customer attrition can help you understand customer loyalty. Ultimately, measuring retention, churn, and loyalty can help provide data for comparing different experiences, products, and services across segments from which insights can be gleaned.

Tracking Customer Satisfaction

One of the main goals of any VoC program is to measure and track customer satisfaction, which is often called CSAT (Customer SATisfaction). Many companies use Net Promoter Score (NPS) to evaluate if their customers are happy. NPS provides a 0–10-point scale. Rankings above 8 are considered positive and are considered to be net promoters, which means the percentage of people with a positive NPS would recommend and promote the brand via some channel, such as WoM. A scale of 4–7 means the person is neutral, whereas a score of 0–4 means the person is a detractor. The NPS score is segmented as a percentage of 100 percent across promoters, neutral, and detractors.

NPS also factors in the ability to leave verbatim and free-text responses to qualify the NPS score. Verbatims are not always required. A numeric score is deemed sufficient to support only NPS analysis. While NPS is traditionally a measurement initiated by customers or users of a product when they decide, for whatever reason, to provide feedback. Some companies, however, prompt customers to enter NPS data. Unhappy customers who are prompted by communications from companies from which they are not satisfied likely ignore such outreach, whereas satisfied customers often respond. Thus, a true NPS measurement should never be prompted. By alerting or prompting users to complete NPS, the data typically skews toward containing mostly net promoters. Keep a careful eye on NPS data to ensure that true NPS is being reported, not a totally invalid and spun number created by asking people to fill out an NPS measurement. For example, if your company prompts for NPS from repeat visitors after a given number of visits, say four–six, and you notice improvement or very positive NPS, chances are your data is skewed from a perverted NPS methodology.

Beyond NPS, tracking CSAT can be done with a number of techniques and methods, such as surveying and focus groups. The way you collect CSAT data is less important than considering the totality of all the customer touchpoints where you can elicit customer response.

The CSAT data should be modeled using statistical methods, reported and visualized in business intelligence (BI) tools, and then communicated with additional information integrated from other sources, such as site analytics, social media, mobile application, or financial data. That way, the CSAT data can be understood in the larger context of other behaviors, interactions, clicks, events, channels, campaigns, and transactional data in the context of overall business strategy and operations. Incorporating other market research about customer loyalty and retention can help to inform CSAT.

Establishing a successful measurement program for CSAT is required to categorize customers into satisfaction levels. An ongoing program measuring CSAT can help the business improve products and product innovation, speed innovation that meets customer requirements, help identify strengths and weaknesses within digital experiences, inform the evaluation of marketing programs both past and current, and can help a corporation make the highest and best use of social data.

Identifying the Attitudes, Beliefs, and Motivations for Customers

When speaking directly with the customers and asking the customer to provide feedback, answer questions, or complete a survey, you can learn the attitudes, beliefs, and motivations of your customers if you ask the right questions or sample an open and honest set of customers. Higher order and often mental or mindset constructs related to why people identify (or not) with your brand and buy (or not) your products can be helpful to understand. These mindsets, mentalities, and motivation-driven propensities can be measured by using research derived from social science, like experimental psychology. The cultural and conceptual beliefs and value systems in which your products and services are sold and delivered can be diagnosed with qualitative data. Dimensions of cultural difference in the perception of brands, motivations, and reasons for using products that differ across cultures can be identified and mined for insights. Motivations can be assessed and compared across different customer segments to gain new comparative data points for decision making.

By working with market research and qualitative data to identify, understand, compare, and reconcile the different attitudes, beliefs, and motivations of people in a way that both integrates and extends cultural and social beliefs and attitudes, you can help the analytics team create research that informs and guides business strategy by communicating analysis about customer trends. The data can be used for creating sales and marketing programs, to guide the marketing process, and to be used as input into other business and sales strategies.

Understanding Customer Requirements and Needs

A comprehensive VoC program provides research about what the customer wants, needs, and requires from the products and services sold by your brand or company. Requirements can be provided in lists suitable for analytical approaches like conjoint analysis. Requirements communicated directly by customers can be evaluated by product management and prioritized into the product roadmap.

When customers express what they want and how they want it, it behooves the company to listen generously and incorporate the customer's voice into product innovations. The way to become customer-centric is, of course, to listen to the customers. When a leader doesn't learn the customer's wants and needs, the business can get off track. By making sure to use qualitative research methods to understand customers, you can set new product development strategies that help match digital experiences to customer's needs and expectations. Customer behavior can help inform pricing and the budget for acquisition programs. Customer centricity demands listening to VoC and analyzing that voice separately and in relationship with other digital data.

Tracking the Customer Experience

Customer Experience Measurement and the related discipline of Customer Experience Management (CEM) are industry vocabulary phrases used for discussing and taking action from analysis related to the improvement of the flows, features, and functionality of the digital experience engaged by the customer or prospect. When I say "tracking the customer experience," I am referring to thinking critically about how people arrive at, use, return, and become repeat users of a brand's digital experiences.

In the online world, it is common to be given the opportunity to participate (opt-in) to a Web survey, and it may be even more common to ignore those surveys that are sent by mail, rendering, or spawned by a browser or mobile application. When customer experience is tracked, the business can find new opportunities to improve the flow and design of the digital experience and determine problem areas and breakpoints in the user flow in need of correction. Comparing the customer experience to competitors can provide input to product development, marketing, sales, CRM, and customer service. CEM technology also may have the unique ability to replay the visitor behavior that occurs such that an analyst could watch a replay of the mouse movements, keystrokes, form field completion, and other user-generated clicks—just as if you were watching the visitor work on her digital device from over her shoulder.

What Does a Qualitative Data Team Do and How Does It Work with Digital Analytics?

The configuration and setup of your organization needs to be identified by the digital analytics team. The qualitative data team may be called the market research team, the research team, the Insights team, the NPS team, the VoC team, and a number of other derivatives if the team is centralized. Otherwise, without centralization, the qualitative data team may exist in stovepipes in silos across the organization. Experts in qualitative research often reside in marketing or in other business areas related to research and advertising. In a matrixed, highly complex, and elaborate organization, qualitative data may exist in pieces here and there all over the organization. Or multiple teams whose work slightly overlaps may have the qualitative data. A review of analytics team structure that is also applicable to the structure for qualitative data teams is covered in Chapter 3, "Building an Analytics Organization."

The qualitative data team has processes that are similar to the Analytical Value Chain discussed in Chapter 2. Digital analysts must understand the following ways of working with digital qualitative data and the resulting analytics:

- **Collect and gather qualitative data.** Researchers employ the various techniques discussed earlier in this chapter—from focus groups to crowdsourcing through social media. The data related to the answers, selections, and verbatims will be captured in either internal or external databases or, in other cases, some type of structured, delimited file format. However, to get any data to report, the method used for data collection must be specified, implemented, and deployed into production. It can take several weeks to go live in production with an elaborate survey—because the survey must be designed in a rigorous enough way that the questions are valid and produce answers that are useful and appropriately detailed. Online, low-cost methods, such as SurveyMonkey, also exist and offer options for potentially reduced-cost and simplified deployment into prestructured formats for qualitative research (which may or may not meet your demands).

- **Synthesize and interpret qualitative data.** After the data has been collected and verified wherever it exists in whatever format, the next step for the qualitative data team is to make sense of the responses and put the data into business context. The first step is producing a report with satisfaction scores or containing the verbatims so that the data can be studied, observed, and potentially interesting patterns and relationships in responses can be investigated. It is common for a qualitative data expert to slice and dice responses to research questions using segmentation based on audience attributes, such as name, gender, household size, household income, marital status, race, lifestyle propensities, personas, and so on. For example, do women have different levels of satisfaction than men? Or do people who live in X area or make Y income think differently about the brand? These types of questions are typically thought out before the synthesis and interpretation phase and can also come to mind when examining the available data and respondent demographics. Researchers dive into the data, start reading the verbatim responses, and create distributions of answers and visualization using sliding scales, histograms, and other charting and graphing techniques to communicate the findings within the qualitative data.

- **Report and communicate results and recommendations.** The final and most important step is the communication of results. Because qualitative data contains the verbal thoughts and feelings of customers, the transparency created from understanding sentiment and satisfaction can be illuminating for the business. On the other hand, the data may contain subject matter, opinions, and results that may not necessarily be positive. Thus, the way qualitative research data is communicated from the analytics team is essential (see Chapter 7).

If the company has centralized the research function, the leaders and analysts on the team have likely identified the stakeholders to whom the information should be communicated. In decentralized organizations, "who needs to know" may be harder to pinpoint. Although the most appropriate groups for receiving customer feedback are numerous, research can be extremely helpful to people in product management, marketing, customer service, and sales. Results are typically communicated in standard business formats, such as PowerPoint or in research papers, which are then followed up with in-person meetings to review the data and ensure mutual comprehensive understanding of the analysis and next steps.

Integrating Digital Behavioral Data with Qualitative Data

As we reviewed at the beginning of this chapter, one of the "Holy Grails" of digital analysis is joining the "what" identified in the measures of behavioral data with the "why" cited in the responses of qualitative data. The theory and value of doing so is fairly easy to communicate and comprehend, and the value proposition is even easier to reconcile financially. Knowing "what" happened is important, but knowing "why" it happened can be even more valuable in certain contexts, such as download or installation errors or product purchases where revenue and potential profits are at risk. It's good to know issues exist with CSAT; the behaviors and quantities of behaviors that create (or do not create) satisfaction. Learning why enables the analytics team to get to the root of the drivers and barriers to satisfaction such that the analytics team's recommendation can focus on increasing CSAT though quantitative and qualitative data integration, reporting, and analysis.

Getting to the highly mature state of combined and integrated behavioral and qualitative data is less difficult than it was several years ago. Recent technologies have been developed that enable using technologies such as Web analytics JavaScript and other technologies to log survey behavior and responses. Companies offering digital analytics tools also provide products for collecting customer feedback. Thus, it is entirely possible to unify an online VoC tool with digital analytics tools. The following options exist for integrating behavioral and qualitative data:

- **Send key behavioral data to the qualitative data tool.** Extracting metrics from a digital analytics tool is simpler than it was several years ago. Many tools offer application programming interfaces (APIs) for extraction and even inserting data (see the next bullet) using technologies such as Representational State Transfer (REST), JavaScript, or deeper programming languages. Other tools allow for server-to-server integrations that, with some configuration, allow easier extract, transform, load (ETL) and combined reporting than traditional BI tools. When measuring CSAT, you may want to send conversion rate, campaign, or marketing landing page data to merge with the verbatims and sentiment.

- **Load qualitative data into the behavioral analytics tool.** In hosted Software as a Service (SaaS) or internally-managed qualitative tools, you can extract key data using different technologies that meet your technology needs. By taking the data from the cloud and moving it to another cloud or your own internally hosted analytics data mart, new insights may be generated from the new relationships created by unifying and joining data models. In the case in which a team wants to reduce customer churn or abandonment, the verbatim and other research data could be pivoted alongside page exit and visit abandonment data as well as duration and site-speed data to explore new segmentations and relationships. Many other types of combinatorial and integrated analysis on qualitative and quantitative data enhance the value of each type of data beyond the value the data has as a stand-alone source.

- **Integrate both behavioral and qualitative data in a data warehouse or BI tool.** Sometimes, vendor technology can't deliver against complex business requirements or the cost of doing so may be prohibitive and outside the budget. When such situations occur, likely in large enterprises or those companies with complex large data sets, key data from both types of tools, wherever they exist—inside or outside the corporation—can be ETLed into existing, business-specific data models. In this case, qualitative data, behavioral data, financial data, customer data, demographic data, syndicated data, and other internal data could be modeled into a unified data set for rich analysis.

- **Add key behavioral data manually to qualitative data reports or analysis.** Sometimes, you don't have the time, money, resources, understanding, or ability to move data from one place to another whether within a company-owned data center or in the cloud-based SaaS. Because some level of reporting is usually prebuilt and customized with tools, manual work can be done to bring the data together in analytical deliverables. When qualitative data is delivered by vendors, consultants, or paid staff, it might make sense to simply expand their existing reporting or other formats for analytical reporting, such as to the PowerPoint decks, to incorporate behavioral data. That way you don't have to reinvent the wheel, and when possible, can extend existing vendor reports with new data.

- **Add key qualitative data manually to behavioral data reports and analysis.** When companies already have comprehensive reporting and analytical deliverables that are scheduled periodically and consistently, qualitative data is usually new data to the business. Perhaps a business has never worked with it directly before and isn't exactly sure how to get it into reports. As such, companies may not want to invest in costly and time-consuming integration projects when the value is risky or uncertain. Putting annotations in existing reporting and analytical deliverables is an easier way to accomplish the goal of considering the "what" and the "why" when managing a business. In other words, carefully assess existing, sustaining automated and self-service reporting to determine if the behavioral reporting can be extended with qualitative data.

- **Manually create new reports that combine key behavioral and quantitative data.** Whether the appetite exists to do integration or if analytic deliverables and reporting structures already exist, the team may not want to touch the existing reports out of fear of breaking or negatively impacting them. Other times, it may make sense not to risk confusing stakeholders with revised or more complex reporting. Other times, the existing reporting is absolutely perfect for the business need. As a result, teams may choose to create new reporting manually. For example, when tracking the customer experience, an analyst may want to use data points from multiple sources without involving engineers or complex technology so that the analyst goes into two or more tools that each contain either qualitative data versus quantitative data and then manually combines them together in a spreadsheet. This type of ad-hoc, manual work is not sustainable over time. If you find yourself or your team manually extracting data from reports out of multiple sources, you should quickly figure out a way to automate the combined work to reduce the constraint on team resources.

Regardless of the way you choose to bring the data together and create new meaningful analysis, the most important thing is that you combine qualitative and quantitative data in the best possible method that supports your team best for business needs as defined by collaborating with key stakeholders that the analytics team supports.

Working Successfully Together and with the Business: Qualitative and Quantitative Data, Research, and Analytics Teams

The digital analytics team doesn't and likely should not report into the same management as qualitative data teams, but it is not uncommon for digital analytics to be on the same team as market research—especially when analytics or research teams are centralized. When organizational alignment and analytics team centralization happens, the integration work discussed in the previous section—however accomplished, technically or manually—can be much easier because the analytics team leader can become the advocate with senior management to make the business impact of the work known and supported by the leadership of other teams. Centralization of analytics teams and supporting resources enables a single analytical leader to be at the same level as other business leaders: marketing, sales, engineering, and IT. This alignment in positional power can help the analytics team leader influence business leadership to dedicate investment to deliver data integrations that lead to new analyses and insights.

The more common reality is sadly not as fortunate. Quantitative data and qualitative data teams can often sit in entirely different organizations and not even speak to one another. Consider when analytics is nested in finance, while research is in marketing. Or analytics may be in marketing, and the survey team may be in public relations (PR). Or analytics may be placed on a BI team, and the qualitative data team may be part of the customer service team. In another case, analytics might be done by one agency, and quantitative research done by a different agency.

Whatever your situation, some key things can help teams be successful when starting to walk or if already running down the path of qualitative and quantitative integration:

1. Find business partners who "get it" and care about data; then focus deliverables and gain feedback, business requirements, and more from those who work well and advocate for the importance of integrated data analysis.

2. Make data-driven recommendations that can be evaluated for their impact if implemented. In this case, it is possible to create "pro forma" models and forecasts that show the impact on the business in the future if the investment is made today.

3. Focus on a business problem where revenue is at risk and people's bonuses or jobs are at risk. By helping people succeed, thrive, and earn more money, you will quickly gain alignment, support, investment, and resources for your analytics projects.

4. Don't be too esoteric. Make sure that you communicate at the appropriate level for the audience. Focus on business vocabulary and financial impact, not on the details of data and tools. Keep it simple and business-focused.

5. Interpret the data; don't just repeat back verbatim responses, simple metrics, and KPIs. Never just regurgitate data. Data must be analyzed before it is communicated (see Chapter 5).

6. Don't bury facts deep in analysis. Highlight the key conclusions, takeaways, recommendations, and next steps. Don't overwhelm with data. Illuminate the data by focusing on the most critical data and ensuring that it is brought to light and fully understood by stakeholders.

7. Identify existing processes for collecting data and map to them. In all but new companies, there will be existing processes for collecting, storing, and integrating data. The analytics team should do their best to support existing processes when they work, and help to enhance and evolve them when they need to be improved. Never create a redundant analytics process, and make sure to gain cross-functional alignment on any new or changed processes.

The rewards of an analytics team working with a research team can be compelling. Not only do the digital analysts learn about the tactics and techniques used for qualitative data collection from real-life customers and prospects, but also the research team gets to learn all about digital analytics. The final result is a team of experts who can work across both types of data sets to deliver greater and more rapid and specific analysis that can be used to better understand the customer, thereby creating the potential for realizing economic value from analytics. As a result, the integration of digital quantitative and qualitative data increases business value as the company focuses on the customer, and as a result evolves the company overall into a more customer-centric and data-driven organization.

10

Competitive Intelligence and Digital Analytics

Competitive intelligence is the process of identifying, collecting, synthesizing, analyzing, and communicating relevant insights and information about the competition, however it is defined, from every available external information source across the entire business landscape and operating environment, including customer, consumer, prospect, sales, financial, and other research sources. The goal of competitive intelligence is to legally create insights that help managers and business owners make key decisions in consideration of what competitors are doing. By doing so the company learns what's going on outside the four (virtual) walls of the (home) office. Essentially, by gathering and disseminating competitive data legally, competitive intelligence is not industrial espionage and does not violate any laws. Those digital analysts who have been following the global analytics industry might see parallels between the legal challenges related to notions of how visitors are tracked, however anonymously, within and across sites, and the fuzzy notions of how competitive intelligence is done.

Competitive intelligence is an externally focused activity. Digital analytics is primarily an internally focused activity. At the intersection and with the union of these two disciplines exists significant value-generating synergies. Similar to how digital analytics tracks the inbound activity of people that visit an experience from another digital source, the competitive intelligence (CI) team monitors and collects data about what happens before or after a customer interacts with a brand's digital experiences and the comparative behavior of key customer segments. Thus, competitive intelligence becomes more than understanding not only the competitor, but also how the past, present, and future customer interacts, thinks about, frames, and considers the competitor's products. When focusing on competition and the insights that can be derived, it is helpful to concentrate on the competitor's' entire business environment and its stakeholders, including aspects of its entire value chain, such as shared or exclusive past/present/future customers, distributors/supply chain, the macro- and microeconomic business climate, and market externalities.

The CI team, by function, is often nested in the strategy, marketing, or product group. It is also not uncommon to see a CI team as part of a larger research organization—and even within the sales organization. As companies mature and remove silos around the open and free sharing of data, information, and insights, it is worth considering whether business value can be created by integrating the CI and digital analytics functions. I would encourage you to consider unifying these two functions or, at the very least, aligning them for shared synergies. After all, digital analytics tools and sources of digital data, such as audience measurement and media planning and buying tools, contain data relevant to competitive intelligence.

Too often, digital analytics is not considered as a data source for competitive intelligence because it is an internal activity performed by analytics teams of varying sizes, shapes, team structures, and locations within an enterprise. Given the relative "newness" of digital analytics, the idea of bringing together the world of competitive intelligence with related digital data may seem, on one hand, an obvious business activity to pursue and, on the other, a complicated endeavor. At the heart of competitive intelligence is a process similar to the Analytical Value Chain discussed in Chapter 2, "Analytics Value Chain and the P's of Digital Analytics."

At the end of the day, the CI team shares the same goals of increasing shareholder value and succeeding at their jobs as the digital analytics team. The CI team's processes are also similar to those of the digital analytics team. Thus, to merge the two disciplines, team leaders on both sides must unify their research on shared goals to create synergy and break down functional and organizational barriers that inhibit the competitive intelligence and digital analytics teams working together. Take, for example, the similar work that can be brought together to help align programs, projects, activities, and deliverables, such as these core activities:

- Determining key business questions can be aligned across CI and digital analytics teams. Each data source can potentially augment and inform the other.
- Gathering information about the competitor's public key performance indicators (KPIs), metrics, and other data so that it can be used for comparative analysis.
- Synthesizing and analyzing information to create research and guidance is similar to analyzing data and creating reporting.
- Coordinating and distributing combined data and analysis to provide fuller context to the research and analysis from each team versus the same data is siloed and only considered in a single context.

Digital analytics can help inform competitive intelligence and help to extract greater meaning, relevancy, insights, and value from it. But combining digital analytics and competitive intelligence can be complex due to the differences in data collection and the structure and location of source data.

When integrating digital data with competitive data, make sure to carefully consider the ethical implications and ethical perceptions of the work you are doing. After all, the roots of competitive intelligence go far back and include rather dubious tactics more akin to espionage than to the collecting of information. Take the example from Tuck School of Business's case, "The Ethics of Competitive Intelligence," which discusses the once uncommonly common practice of businesspeople at Proctor & Gamble going through the trash at Unilever to find information that could unlock the secrets of the company's success or at least help competitors gain an unfair edge by bringing to light knowledge only known to Unilever. Although the act of dumpster diving did not violate criminal law, it raised serious questions about the values and principals under which large corporations, such as P&G, operate.

As a result of more serious cases of questionably ethical or outright outrageously unethical methods for finding out what competitors are doing, the United States passed the Economic Espionage Act of 1996. This act made it illegal to steal or misappropriate trade secrets and other intellectual property from a corporation. In the analytical economy, trade secrets are not only tacit in the minds of the business analytics experts but are also explicit in many forms from database schemas to published analysis. Thus, the same safeguards that the CI industry would be expected to adhere to in the offline world apply to the online world and to digital analytics. The Society for Competitive Intelligence understands that information and data may be used in unethical and possibly illegal ways, and have gone on record as early as 1999 stating that the Economic Espionage Act of 1996 would have no impact on legitimate competitive research.

A gray zone exists around CI information and how far professionals can go when gathering information. Digital data collection and ubiquity of tools for understanding what your competitors are doing across the digital landscape bring new questions about what is ethical (at any given company) and what is illegal (at a given time in a given country). A practice once common on the Internet at times judged to be unethical, if not illegal, is creating a false account on a digital site for the explicit purpose of using the site to gain competitive advantage. Although this type of questionable activity is still done all the time across the Internet, many CI professionals will not do it. Instead, companies that provide competitive intelligence are hired to do so, which is considered ethical. In other words, Twitter CI professionals should not create fake accounts on Facebook and should instead hire a company that audits the user experience and product functionality of social networks to buy similar data and create those accounts.

Although it might seem absurd that an agency can function as the proxy for a CI team and do work that the team is not enabled to do, this type of working relationship does reduce the risk and potential for both unintentional and intentional violations of the law. While it is unlikely a fake account from a competitor would ever be discovered (unless the analytics team was monitoring competitor Internet Protocol [IP] addresses), ethics are only ethics when they are practiced and not preached. In many countries it is now illegal and in almost all countries it is considered a "bad hat" to wear to monitor people's digital behavior. At a personally identifiable information (PII) level, you can buy individual people's data, with opt-in, from various sources and mostly anonymous data, without explicit opt-in, from many data aggregation sources (see Chapter 11, "Targeting and Automation with Digital Analytics").

At this point in the chapter, you may be asking yourself what all this history and information about competitive intelligence has to do with digital analytics? The historic emphasis on the ethical issues related to competitive intelligence are similar to the ethical challenges encountered by the digital analytics team when collecting or working with potentially PII digital data. Yet synergies between combining competitive intelligence are similar to those benefits often cited from combining voice of customer (VoC) data and market research with digital analytics. The behaviors, interactions, and events of key customer segments important to both the CI team and market research team are tracked by digital analytics. Thus, digital customer data can sometimes be used to join together (as the join key) data from competitive intelligence with market research—for example, surveying customer segments, analyzing their site behaviors, and understanding how the same segments engage with the competitor's products and services. The rest of this chapter:

- Explains, compares, and contrasts competitive intelligence and digital intelligence
- Provides real-world examples of digital competitive intelligence
- Reviews, at a high-level, the types of digital CI tools and information sources
- Discusses how to integrate digital analysis with competitive intelligence via process and team alignment

Competitive Intelligence Versus Digital Intelligence

Competitive intelligence is the gathering of data and information about competitors using established processes against available competitive data sources. Like digital analysis, the process for competitive intelligence starts with understanding business drivers and the requirements for competitive data by business stakeholders. Next, the CI process involves gathering, synthesizing, and then communicating back information in a way that is helpful to the stakeholders and can be used to create business value. Digital analytics, fundamentally, aims for the same outcome as competitive intelligence with a process that is reminiscent of the Analytics Value Chain presented in Chapter 2. The major difference between these disciplines is location of the type of data.

Competitive intelligence, as previously mentioned, deals with external information sources, whereas digital analysis makes use of both internal and external data sources. Although you might argue that digital analytics is part of a larger digital intelligence framework, the emphasis is that digital intelligence is broad. Digital intelligence attempts to describe a set of the technology and methods that can be performed by the digital analytics team; however, the orientation of the team and analytical deliverables can be different. Digital intelligence is oriented on both external and internal sources to assist and help the CI team. Whereas the work of the CI team can be used to enhance and add value to the deliverables of the analytics team.

Bringing these ideas out of the hypothetical world, the CI team can use tools to understand the activity and behavior of customers on competitor sites and in competitor experiences. For example, the online recruiting industry uses the data provider named Wanted to understand job posting trends across different job sites, such as Monster, Indeed, and CareerBuilder. Mobile companies use data from a company named Strategy Analytics to identify device and application data and research. In all these cases, the data from these external sources and vendors does not include any data or information held within the internal systems at the company employing the CI team. The digital analytics team, however, has a lot of data to help prove the accuracy and veracity of external data to comparative internal data.

In this way, the digital analytics analyst may take on a new analytical role, named the digital intelligence analyst. The focus of this role is to bridge the external work of the CI team with work done by the analytics teams and other professionals on which the analytics team may rely (such as business intelligence [BI]). The digital analytics team can provide input and help create a competitive advantage.

Types of Digital Competitive Intelligence: Real-World Examples

Competitive intelligence can offer real-world strategic advantages to business owners. You must understand what your competitors are doing and how they are attempting to win and gain market share. Some business owners think they understand their competition because they may look at financial reporting and other quantitative data about their competitors. Those sources alone do not tell the entire story. Competitive intelligence includes mostly qualitative data derived from many sources but it can also include data the market research team obtained. Thus, it is not uncommon to see the CI team make use of data created and maintained by other teams external to the company. One way to think of the difference between competitive intelligence and digital analytics is that competitive intelligence can help qualify and make meaningful the metrics, KPIs, and related analytical trends and data reported by the analytics—within the competitive context:

- **Technology comparisons:** From the technology used for rendering the digital experience, to the databases for storing the data, to the programming languages used to control it all, the CI team can consult various visual data sources to compare a set of technologies used by competitors.

- **Digital audience-reach assessments:** Many metrics and digital analytics such as frequency, recency, and time-based measures are part of audience behavior. These dimensions of the audience are different across competing products, services, and companies. Marketing and sales use audience-reach assessments provided by the CI team as tools that help to market and sell.

- **Audience profile comparisons:** The characteristics of an audience vary across digital experiences. They vary based on how they use the site, the levels of interaction and social media, the frequency of their visits and Internet usage, as well as how demographic and lifestyle habits differ. The CI team may be called in to paint a portrait of the competitor's audience and compare its characteristics, attributes, and value against the company's own audience.

- **Digital product and feature evaluations:** Competitors are competitors because they offer similar products and services yet differentiate them in ways that create a brand. Take for example an airline ticketing site: User experiences are similar across each brand. United Airlines isn't that different than American Airlines when it comes to the functions and objectives of their websites. What's different is the physical experience and the brand. Thus, CI teams are often called upon to determine whether the core value drivers within a similar product or set of features is better in their company versus the competitor's.

- **User experience audits:** The relationship between computing interfaces and systems and their impact on human emotion, experience, and cognition are studied in the discipline of user experience. Because no two digital experiences are identical, user experiences will inevitably differ, as will the perception and judgment of the efficacy of the user experience in fulfilling business goals. Competitive intelligence teams can audit the user experience across competing digital systems to answer business questions like, "Does the difference in site functionality and design versus my competitor create more or less repeat business?"

- **Competitive analysis based on defined business goals:** Companies differentiate their brands using marketing, design, feature, and other aspects of the products and services. Business stakeholders can work with the CI team to provide specific insights around the defined business goals when innovating or improving products and services.

- **Quarterly competitive analysis:** By working with the digital analytics team to understand how internal data is impacted by the external behavior of competitors, the CI team may choose to create a quarterly competitive analysis that stitches together the behavior customer segments across competing digital experiences. The scheduling of quarters can be matched to the calendar or fiscal year.

- **Competitor threat analysis:** The rapid pace of today's global economy means businesses must rapidly respond and adapt to consumer demand or risk extinction. Digital analytics provides insight into how your business performs against goals you've established for your customers and visitors. Unfortunately, that information doesn't tell you much about how your competitors are doing. However, you can infer that if your sales are down, and your competitor's are growing, something is fundamentally wrong with the way you do business. The CI team can work with the digital analytics team to understand your KPIs in the context of competitive performance—and you may be able to determine the KPIs your competitor uses. A comparative threat analysis based on KPI comparisons can help identify issues and any potential threats before they become deadly.

Following are some examples of digital competitive intelligence that made the news in 2012 and 2013:

- A major logistics and transportation company gained significant competitive advantage by understanding the competitor's supply chain and then developing and considering new telematics systems and services that could be adopted in their large fleets. In this way, the CI data helped the company predict and identify advance opportunities to decrease cycle time.

- A major telecommunications and mobile smart device provider used CI information to find its market entry strategy around its developer community strategy was differentiated and catered to different aspects of the developer community to establish a center of gravity to grow an ecosystem.

- A global provider of job search and career-related information used CI data to audit features of its job application flow compared to that of competitors to reduce friction within the flow. Then the conclusions could be tested (see Chapter 8, "Optimization and Testing with Digital Analytics: Test, Don't Guess").

- A Software as a Service (SaaS) vendor used CI information to assess its pricing model and to create new multitiered pricing methodology for future products. As a result, the company realized new ways to create incremental value from their existing software toolkit and adjusted prices downward to remain competitive.

- An international airline corporation used an automated technology to crawl various travel sites to determine the sentiment communicated in social media to improve its customer service. The same international airline used CI data derived from automatically crawling ticketing sites to offer competitive prices and promotions against competitors.

Digital Competitive Intelligence Tools and Methods

No standard toolkit exists for the digital CI analyst, which is another similarity with digital analytics. The arsenal of tools, data sources, and connectedness for enabling digital competitive intelligence has no standards, just like digital analytics. Competitive intelligence analysts define what they need to do the job, and then use or advocate for the usage of those tools (or for the investment necessary to begin using those tools). Thus, it is impossible to say that one tool or set of tools and technologies represents everything needed by a customer intelligence professional to do the job required. The following list, however, presents a high-level set of digital CI tools and methods that are useful:

- **Audience measurement tools:** Use sampling techniques to select a potentially statistically significant sample of users, visitors, and customers—and sometimes combine the audience sample with census data collected directly from digital experiences. The data is then run through a proprietary statistical model, which estimates the total size of an additional audience as derived from applied analysis on the sample. Audience measurement companies sell this data for use in different types of research and analysis. Because the data provided by audience measurement vendors is categorized into industries and other business-understandable dimensions, the data is often used by CI teams.

- **Surveys and focus groups:** Traditional methods and techniques used by market researchers are also used by digital CI teams. Online surveys and focus groups derived from offline and social networking methods can be leveraged to understand competitor's customers, products, and services.

- **Primary research:** Medium and large companies engage in primary research. Simply put, primary research is a collection of a set of research activities, such as surveying and focus groups, which the company performs to investigate and understand the business. Primary research is performed to gain some insight into an ongoing business issue, market, or customer concern. Although primary research includes surveys and focus groups, other options exist, from experimentation and observational analysis to using social networking data.

- **Secondary research assessment:** The CI team from time to time will be called upon to review, validate, confirm, or critique secondary research created within the company, outside the company, and even by competitors themselves. In this sense, the digital analytics team may become the Data Governors. For more information, see Chapter 6, "Defining, Planning, Collecting, and Governing Data in Digital Analytics."

- **Virtual and physical events:** Old-fashioned techniques such as shaking hands, having dinner, attending network events, and normal human socialization are great ways to gain competitive intelligence. Some CI teams journey to industry events and then interview customers, competitor's customers, and even meet and greet with the competitors. Most industries have a set of important conferences and events that are "must attend." Next time you are at a conference, notice how much competitive information is there at your fingertips. Analyze it and determine what it can tell you about your business and its products, services, and customers.

- **Open authentication and persistent objects:** Digital analysts used to talk about browser plug-ins in the context of audience measurement firms. Plug-ins were often used to collect anonymous data about how people used websites and the frequency at which they visited websites. These days, with open methods for authentication on social networking and other sites, it has become possible for the site that you haven't logged out of to keep track of the other sites you visit. For example, some social networking sites have the capability to track users who have not logged out of the main site when they view sites that have code, such as tags, on other sites. It is even possible to retrieve browser history anonymously. These data sources, when put in the competitive context, can be consulted for new strategic business insights.

- **External data sources:** Vendors offer CI tools and data. Typically, this data is sold by subscription or on a per-case or per-use basis for the data wanted, or via a custom researcher professional services project. Even VoC or digital analytics tool vendors often provide industry, geographic, and customer segment-based comparisons for competitive intelligence.

You can see in the previous list that CI tools do not take on any one format. What you need for your team is going to be based on your requirements. The set of tool categories in the bullets previously listed represent the larger categories into which most CI tools fit. All the CI tools and methods presented are useful to consider for your business.

The Process for Digital Competitive Intelligence

Process is as important to digital competitive intelligence as it is to digital analytics. A process is a set of actions that you take in a sequence to accomplish a goal. As with most research-related disciplines, the process under which an analyst executes analytics projects from start to finish has similarities. The digital CI process starts similarly to the digital analytics process with gathering business requirements, and proceeds through a set of activities around data collection, analysis, presentation, and dissemination of the resulting competitive insight:

- **Identify business questions about competitors.** Work with business stakeholders to help them frame business questions that can be answered with competitive analysis. Use insights from competitive intelligence to put competitive context around digital analytics and vice versa.

- **Identify and hunt sources of information.** Given that competitive intelligence is an external activity, the data sources may not be located externally. For primary research created by your company, the barriers to creating competitive research can be lowered or eliminated by working with internal teams and executing the work from within the company.

- **Gather and collect information.** After you identify the sources for competitive intelligence, the team needs to determine what is necessary to gather and collect it. Again, there are many barriers and obstacles to getting at and working with CI data. One of the largest may be cost; another may be available resources; while another may be time. Among the most serious are legal considerations. All information gathered for competitive intelligence must be collected legally and ethically. An impressive number of references to legal and ethical behavior are strewn throughout CI literature. Behaving legally and ethically is important to CI professionals and should be a model to understand and apply for mitigating privacy concerns about the digital analytics industry.

- **Analyze the information and consider it against other information sources.** Competitive intelligence data must be analyzed in similar ways to digital analytics data. When quantitative measures are available, techniques discussed in Chapter 5, "Methods and Techniques for Digital Analysis," are relevant. In other cases, the techniques applied to market research for analyzing and assessing qualitative data are applicable, such as text mining and sentiment analysis. Regardless, the CI analysts' highest and best work is the creation of analysis that draws out insights about the competitive situation that can be told to senior management and used as input to business decisions. Ultimately, CI data must be given context from other data like market research and digital analytics data.

- **Distribute and follow up.** When providing any type of data, research, or analytics service, providing physical evidence that the service has been performed is important; the same fact applies to competitive intelligence. Although much work, conversation, and learning may have occurred as the project was being executed, it is still necessary to summarize the overall findings of the competitive analysis for stakeholders. The CI team should also schedule regular meetings to review standard deliverables for expressing the insights derived from competitive analysis.

The highest performing CI teams create CI processes across the activities listed above. Determining business questions, identifying information, and working on the necessary activities of gathering, collecting, analyzing/correlating, and disseminating the CI information are required in order to succeed with CI. The digital analytics team's processes must accommodate for the CI process listed above and vice-versa for supporting the Analytics Value Chain.

Integrating Digital Behavioral Data with Competitive Intelligence

Your digital analytics team will eventually reach the maturity level where the integration of CI data with other data types will become necessary. Although the traditional definition of integration means bringing together data from multiple systems or sources into one common system and interface, given the nature of the digital ecosystem, deep technical integration with CI data sources isn't always possible because sources, such as conversations, may not or simply do not allow for integration or extraction.

Due to difficulties of integrating CI data with digital analytics data, the approach teams take to doing so varies based on available resources and internal competencies. Digital analytics and CI data doesn't necessarily have to be brought together in one unified data warehouse or reporting and analysis system, but doing so is helpful. A number of options exist for integrating digital behavioral data with CI data:

- **Common systems:** A relatively low-cost method for sharing CI data across the company, and to ensure its use across business teams, is to create common systems that provide universal access to CI data and the data, reporting, and analytics from related research teams. Common systems can be created simply by linking to various repositories of data, or those systems can be more all-encompassing that provide access to data across multiple databases from within a single interface.

- **Data sharing:** Another helpful technique for integrating CI data into the business process is data sharing. Two or more parties agree to share data, for a given incentive or due to shared goals. Shared data can be accomplished in a number of different ways. Feeds can be created and sent on a periodic batch basis to the concerned parties. Usernames and passwords can be provisioned for people to access data that resides in disparate systems.

- **APIs:** Application programming interfaces (APIs) can be provided by both internal teams and external teams to facilitate the transfer of movement of data from one repository to another. APIs are commonplace across today's digital world. Public APIs are available for usage by the general populace (with limited restrictions) while private APIs are not. Because of the flexibility cross-platform APIs provide, it is no surprise that APIs are used more commonly to integrate data across teams, companies, and partners.

- **Manual:** Sometimes it just makes sense to have people sit down and work manually to bring together data. This idea is not to indicate that pencils, erasers, and reams of graph paper are necessary. Instead, it might make sense to convene a task force responsible for quickly bringing together a small set of data manually within a reporting tool and integrate it with CI findings.

- **Data integration:** When a CI team has the ability to work with technology staff, great things can occur. Because CI data exists across multiple sources, as discussed in this chapter, it can be helpful to use BI best practices to integrate data into a central repository with an added-detail level of metadata. When data related to competitive intelligence is housed within BI databases, the data can be more deeply explored and it can be joined with related data. By integrating competitive intelligence at the detailed level into other systems, multiple teams can be exposed to competitive intelligence and help yield increased value for the entire function.

- **Vendors and external staff:** A CI team with a budget can spend it on vendor professional services and external contracting staff. External CI experts not only bring new viewpoints to previously existing business challenges, they also add fresh perspectives and new ideas on integrating CI data throughout the value chain.

Competitive intelligence and digital analytics have synergies with one another from which today's global organizations can create economic value—as long as these teams are enabled to collaborate. While CI data is collected externally, digital analytics data is collected internally. When overlapping data is known to exist in the datasets from these two teams, then shared interactions, events, and behaviors must be analyzed in unison to create insights. Having two views into the data provides an enhanced viewpoint of current business activity and performance—and even more when looking at in analytical totality. There are a number of ways to collect CI data that range from manual, to technical, to professional services solutions, to data integration. The goal for the digital intelligence team should be to integrate digital behavioral data collected from digital experiences with the CI data collected from a variety of extra sources. The rich combinatorial set of unified digital and CI data can be mined and explored by digital analytics organizations to determine business opportunities and create value.

11

Targeting and Automation with Digital Analytics

Targeting your business with input from digital analytical data is possible in 2013. No longer a nascent idea being sold by startups, many digital analytics platforms, such as Webtrends or IBM, have products focused on using digital data to identify an audience with specific attributes and send, often in real time, relevant information and content—where the information and content being sent may be an online ad, content inserted onto a page, an email, an in-application message, and so on.

Many businesses target using data in many ways, often with manual intervention to do so. Take for example the types of targeting that companies like Google and Yahoo do for paid search—targeting within search results, on third-party domains, and within other products like Gmail. Other examples of targeting are as follows:

- Media sites target geographically relevant content to visitors.
- Catalog retailers use traditional data sources, such as consumer research surveys, to target different consumer communications to specific demographics, markets, and geographies.
- Paid or controlled circulation teams may target customer emails or offline mailings to specific subscriber demographics.
- Small businesses may purchase email lists from various emailing-list vendors to send outbound communications to potential customers and use their tools to send different communications to different audiences from the list purchased.
- Point of Sale (POS) data captured in-store at the register of your local Walmart and used to automatically identify and replenish critical inventory items frequently bought, such as those on sale during a given period to ensure stock supply.

- Paid search vendors allow for numerous types of online audience segmentation and then ad targeting in many ways.

Targeting is not without controversy. The Pew Internet & American Life Project between January 20 and February 19, 2012, published research indicating Americans view targeting in online advertising as an invasion of privacy and a nondesirable practice. Sixty-eight percent of those surveyed said they are "not okay" with targeted advertising because they do not like having their online behavior tracked and analyzed. Yet, targeting is not without paradox as the Federal Communications Commission (FCC) recommends: "Also consider the positive benefits of ad targeting for local news and journalism operations." Frequently, the logic I have heard espoused by professionals in the industry who create these targeting systems is that if ads are going to be shown on the Web, those ads might as well be relevant. Yet many consumers are suspicious of exactly what data collected can be used for targeting, how that data is collected, at what level of detail and anonymity, how long the data will be retained, and what it can be used for in the future.

When targeting refers to the process of delivering content or ads to segments or visitors based on their known attributes, the goal is almost certainly to increase engagement in the form of a click, interaction, event, response, or other behavioral event that increases monetization of the digital experience. The goal of targeting is simple to understand: Maximize the business performance of content or an ad by serving it to consumers at a time when they are most open to receiving the message such that those consumers are activated to engage with the targeted item.

For example, you may visit a site and see some type of ad unit calling out at you to "meet singles in <insert_your_city>." When browsing a real estate site, you may see ad units for realtors and mortgage companies. After entering a keyword such as "car insurance" and clicking through the search results, you may land on a site and see an ad for a car insurance company or land on a page that persuades you to begin the process for creating an insurance price quote. After viewing a pair of shoes on Zappos, you may see ads for shoes and discounts for shoes across many sites. That's targeting where one or more customer attributes are identified that will persist over time and can be used across domains and digital experiences for automated targeting based on customizable business rules. The following scenario can help you understand what is meant by targeting:

1. Visitor X has these attributes.

2. A company has content or an ad that it thinks might appeal to Visitor X's attributes.

3. Now show the relevant content or ad. If possible, let's store the visitor attribute and target the visitor on our affiliate or network sites with the same and similar content and ads.

You've probably heard about a specific type of often-discussed targeting in online advertising: behavioral targeting. *Behavioral targeting* refers to the technology and process in which an ad or content is shown to visitors based on their past actions and reactions.

Behavioral targeting involves the following steps:

1. Collect behavioral data about visitors (that is, clickstreams, interactions, events, and metadata).

2. Identify when those visitors for whom you have previously collected behavioral data visit a digital experience.

3. Determine the current context of visitors on the site, such as consumer intent and propensities or even looking at the referrer to give context.

4. Detect the visitor's current behavior, events, and transactions.

5. Serve relevant ads (or content) matched to the behavior in real time.

6. Render the same or similar relevant ads (or) content to the same person as they visit sites within your affiliate, advertising, or partner networks.

The goal is to use past behavioral data to influence the customer buying cycle or marketing life cycle to more effectively and quickly deliver on advertiser and site goals. Targeting can involve prediction based on a dependent variable, but is more likely to involve matching based on known attributes (that is, independent variables).

So where does digital analytics come in? You would think digital analytics data from Web analytics technology would be used to enable targeting. After all, the best digital analytics systems store detailed, visitor-level data about past behavior. Digital analytics data certainly can be used, but in most cases it is not. Instead, targeting is often a function provided by the ad server or network, perhaps the Internet Service Provider (ISP), or another technology called the *behavioral targeting platform*. That said, digital analytics data can be integrated with behavioral platforms.

To make analytics data useful for targeting, you need to use your data to

1. Define segments to a target or identify visitors to a target.
2. Feed past behavioral data about segments or visitors to the targeting technology.
3. Analyze segment and visitor performance against business, site, or advertiser goals after targeting.

Targeting has a proven ability and amazing potential to generate tremendous returns, especially when combined with the rich, detailed behavioral data available in Web analytics. As a method for optimizing site content and advertising, targeting technologies that integrate with Web analytics data will become more important and a necessary "must have" for innovative companies that want to maximize business opportunities on the Internet. Targeting can even be used in testing and optimization (see Chapter 8, "Optimization and Testing with Digital Analytics: Test, Don't Guess").

Types of Targeting

In digital analytics, targeting is associated with paid search campaigning, ad serving, and content optimization based on recognizing and responding to the following attributes:

- **Device targeting:** Where ads or content can run exclusively on different versions of various operating systems, such as Apple iOS, Android, and Windows Phone.

- **Category and subcategory:** Conceptual constructs such as categories of topics on a media website or products on an e-commerce site can be targeted to include certain types of ads or messages. The idea is that if visitors browse your category for "hardware floors," you could offer them an ad or content specific to "flooring installation services." Targeting can also be based on more complicated formal categorization approaches like taxonomies and subject headings.

- **Signal targeting:** Wi-Fi targeted content and ads can be different than 4G targeted content and ads on mobile devices.

- **Geography:** Country, region, city, state, designated marketing area (DMA), and metropolitan statistical area (MSA) are all targetable constructs. You may run a sports site and choose to target people surfing in from 02116 (Boston) with an ad for Red Sox tickets or content about the recent game with the New York Yankees.

- **Browsing environment and Internet Protocol (IP) data:** Such as the connection speed, type of browser, operating system, user software, domain, and ISP. An ISP could target an ad for a new service or premium upgrade. Your IP address can be used to target.

- **Time and temporality:** The idea of showing content only during specific periods of time is called *parting*. Common types include day-parting and season-parting. For example, a business-to-business (B2B) site choosing to show ads for a particular manufacturer's product during business hours—the site's busiest time of day—would be an example of day-parting.

- **Keyword:** There are many different types of keyword targeting. Search engines target ads based on keywords in queries. Content Management Systems target content based on site search keywords or referring keywords. Keywords may be associated as metadata with site sections or pages, similar to zone or category targeting on an ad server. After a page is associated with keyword metadata in an ad tag, you can tell your ad server to target ads to that keyword on whatever page or pages the tag was placed.

- **Language:** When a language can be detected or known in advance, you can target ads to visitors in their language.

- **Demographics:** If the ad server is aware of a segment's demographics, such as age, gender, income, title, purchasing power, and so on, an ad can be targeted on that basis.

- **Context:** Think of AdSense and how it matches text ads based on the semantics of in-site content, your emails, or from summarizing the content on a web page. Another example is when, after adding a product to your cart, a site offers you free shipping if your total purchase exceeds a certain price. This is content targeting based on context.

- **Profile:** Targeting is possible based on conclusions drawn and rules created from attributes about an individual or segment (such as purchasing propensity or job title).

- **Rules:** Rules are formal guidelines that control an activity. Targeting can be done based on business rules developed by the business. For example, serve an interstitial ad only to visitors who don't have a cookie set for the site. Or show only an AB test variation for every 10th new visitor.

- **Behavioral:** Data collected by ad serving, digital analytics, and other tools about the customers who visit websites, mobile applications, and other digital experiences can be used to target consumers through ads and content. Behavioral targeting is the most common form of targeting that consumers see in the digital space.

- **Events:** Events are instances of change in which a shift from one state to another occurs. Events in digital analytics can be as simple as a click to more complex events. For example, an account holder deposits a large sum of money into his bank account, so the online banking site offers him a Certificate of Deposit (CD) product on his next login.

- **Intent:** A newer form of targeting is by intent, which some companies claim to do by inferring it from data available "from the click" (such as the keyword), the content of the page, metadata, partnerships, attributes derived from third parties, and proprietary information.

Where in Digital Does Targeting Occur?

Targeting across the digital ecosystem occurs in two constructs: advertising and content. By far, advertising is where the majority of digital targeting occurs, whereas targeting of content is something seen less frequently but at an increasing rate of presence across the Web. The most common type of targeting you hear about is behavioral targeting.

When the creators of digital experiences collect data about people and then use that data to improve the customer experience and increase the effectiveness of business activities, behavioral targeting has occurred. When a certain sequence of events is performed by a visitor on the website, and then a specialized, custom user experience is presented to the visitor, rules-based targeting has occurred. Were a user of a mobile application to perform a certain action in which a customized advertisement or offer was presented, advertising targeting has occurred. When data is combined from referring URL or IP address and third-party data sources, content-based targeting may have occurred. If the digital experience renders a customized, specialized user experience based on some input, contextual targeting has occurred.

Many of these themes of targeting can be further optimized by applying some of the concepts previously presented, such as geography, time, and language. Rarely would it make sense to target a non-English speaker with an English advertisement. Nor would it make sense in most cases to show content related to advertising a winter sports activity to someone not geographically located in a wintery climate (unless the targeting was based on intent of the person to take a winter vacation). Understanding customers or prospects and targeting by time of day or weekday versus weekend can improve engagement, clickthrough, and performance of ads and content.

The following list identifies the common themes and methods where targeting occurs in a consumer context. A person could encounter these in today's digital world on any number of devices or screen sizes—from interactive billboards to smartphones:

- **Display advertising:** Online advertising "impressions" are containers for content called insertions. Not only can a publisher or advertiser fill online display advertisements with various insertions, it is also possible to control the type of ad and in some cases even the size. One use case for targeting the digital display advertising would be to present an advertisement for a product that the person previously looked at during the recent past visit.

- **Social networking:** Targeting on social network sites is commonplace in 2013. When you log in to your preferred social network, you see sponsored advertisements for products, services, people, and brands within your social graph. Targeting on social networks may include advertisements for products that you have expressed an interest in or preference for. Or targeting may be for content relevant to what you typed into the social network.

- **Content sites:** On the content media sites, you can set up an audience profile or customer profile to allow targeted content to be sent directly to you across any Internet-enabled device. It is likely that the data from your responses to the targeted content on media sites is used to further target you. Retargeting is discussed in the next section, "What Is Retargeting?"

- **In rich media, such as video and chat:** Whenever a person uses free digital content, it is likely that the time and attention from that person is being bought and sold to advertisers by the publisher behind-the-scenes. A good example of this fact is in rich media video where advertisements can be inserted to the various points of the stream based on insights derived from aggregate behaviors within the video stream. That sounds complex; it is, but an easier way to describe it is that video sites know when you play, rewind, fast-forward, stop, and replay their video content. The data is known at micro-increments, by specific frame and timestamp such that online ads can be inserted into peak periods of engagement and interaction when not only watching the video, but also when interacting with the controls.

- **E-commerce sites:** As a visitor engages with an e-commerce experience, various advertisements are presented. The user experience may shift and change based on what the user does, and so can the ads. The advertisements can change based on advertiser control or publisher control, where the content, features, and flows of the site can be adapted and modified based on rules. When the goal is to sell products in the most frictionless way possible, targeting presents a broad set of options for creating individualized user experiences that persuade and cause conversion. In e-commerce use, the types of targeting methods previously described to provide, in real time, visitors, users, and customer segments with relevant content, promotions, offers, and other incentives to complete the purchase immediately—or to compel them to come back and purchase after abandonment.

- **Outbound marketing, like email:** Rules and events on the site can trigger targeting activities that occur immediately or at a point in the future. A good example is when a visitor steps through the conversion flows in an e-commerce site, finally selects a product, and after adding it to the shopping cart flow, abandons it and leaves the site; the site might in a couple hours or a couple days send the visitor a targeted email with an offer or promotion to complete the abandoned transaction. This type of targeting for shopping cart abandonment happens frequently on e-commerce sites.

- **Inbound marketing, like search engine optimization (SEO)/search engine marketing (SEM):** Information taken from the query string, http headers, or other available technical information can be used as an input to render an experience, serve an ad, or target content to a visitor. For example, a business rule can be created for identifying every fifth visitor referred from a particular search keyword; then the site can target relevant context based on the keyword's meaning.

- **Set-top boxes, digital television, and interactive billboards:** A more recent innovation is targeting on television within Digital Video Recorders (DVRs), on-demand video experience, or directly within streaming or broadcast television. In the United States, all cable signals and television signals are digital. DVR set-top boxes are commonplace. Interactive billboards, which are almost a type of gigantic outdoor television, are seen more frequently in cities throughout the world. By understanding viewer behavior and the usage of the DVR, including the shows watched in commercials, the cable company has excellent information for targeting its advertiser's advertisements to subscribers. Depending on the location and the level of user-generated input to an interactive billboard, it is possible to target different content, either macro-level segments of the population or interact on a one-to-one or one-to-many relationship via mobile social input.

What Is Retargeting?

Retargeting is the activity of serving advertisements to visitors and customers based on data previously collected about those visitors from previous visits, clicks, interactions, events, behaviors, or responses to previous attempts at targeting. Because visitor identification is challenging on websites and mobile phones, retargeting is usually anonymous and performed based on cookies and other identifiers that persist for various durations. Susceptible then to the deletion of the unique identifier, such as cookies, retargeting is still one of the more compelling, profitable, and new ways to create additional value through digital advertising. In fact, Facebook Exchange (FBX) is a retargeting network of which Facebook users are largely unaware.

Retargeting can also be called *remessaging* or *remarketing*. The name of the activity—retargeting—is an important construct. Targeting was previously discussed, but we did not discuss the prefix re-. For it is in the "re-" of retargeting that much of the hype, reality, and value potential can be created. The "re-" refers to the fact that the person, customer, prospect, cookie, visitor, browser, or device has previously used the digital experience at some point in the past. During this previous visit, data was collected about the object to target (for example, most commonly, the cookie), which is then used as the basis for retargeting.

To identify a unique person for retargeting, cookies are often used as are other unique identifiers that can be carried across sites by persisting on the user's machine. Because visitor identifiers, like cookies, are often deleted, companies exist that stitch together anonymized cookies and their associated attributes for use in retargeting. To accommodate for the fact that cookies get deleted, the deleted cookies are tracked and linked together to the current cookie. This historical cookie data and metadata is stored and used for retargeting over time, helping to build richer and richer data sets for targeting.

Any available set of data that is related to the visitor being targeted can be used in retargeting. But because the visitor has already visited the brand's digital experience, information can be gathered and aggregated from different sources, if available, that have also touched or captured information about the visitor. Whether internal or external, these sources can be integrated and included for using in the customer's profile that is used for targeting. Attributes from a Customer Relationship Management (CRM) system, previous interactions with salespeople, expressed preferences and research surveys, the clickstream of digital behavior, and other demographic and psychographic attributes can be mashed together into a set of attributes with which to base rules for retargeting.

Retargeting generally occurs outside the original experience first encountered by the visitor that initiated the need. Said differently, when a person comes to an e-commerce site and abandons a product, an offer for a related product or an offer to purchase the abandoned product or shopping cart can be displayed on a different site entirely. For example, you abandon a pair of shoes on Zappos and see a discount coupon for Zappos on Amazon.com. Retargeting can occur on the same site to the same visitor over and over again based on the frequency and inclusion rules set by the advertiser.

Although it is entirely possible to target past visitors and previous customers on the same site or within a network of related sites, it is a less common use-case. However, it is done all the time on ad networks, advertising ecosystems (like Google), and with other advertising-based social networking sites, such as Facebook. Media and content sites can target particular content to display more advertisements in digital experiences with a repeat visitor base that expresses brand preference or interest in a particular product, service, or brand. The potential to profit from retargeting is large.

Types of Retargeting

Retargeting can take on many forms across many different types of digital media. From Internet-enabled devices in public environments to private-, browser-, or device-based experiences, the options are numerous for businesses to retarget from digital analytics data.

Following is a list of the types of targeting found in the digital ecosystem:

- **Mobile retargeting:** A mobile device can be recognized when it visits a site and is associated with a profile that can serve advertisements related to the previous behaviors, events, rules, context, and so on to occur.

- **In-store retargeting:** A newer form of mobile targeting driven by awareness of location, through global positioning system (GPS), Wi-Fi usage in-store, signing in, or via a check-in. Using a location-based service or through geolocation or by alerting, a mobile phone can be sent a promotion or offer based on simply being in a particular location, such as a retail store. Browsing for a product on a mobile phone, scanning your mobile coupon, and receiving an up-sell or cross-sell offer directly can occur in real time on your mobile device.

- **Email retargeting:** Old-fashioned email is as useful as targeting more recent innovations. Retargeting email is based on the behavior and activity performed within an email—potentially aggregated as part of a visitor profile.

- **Contextual retargeting:** When different sites partner with each other to share data about their customers, visitors, and audience as part of the fulfillment of an economic value chain, contextual retargeting has occurred. Take for example the airline site that also provides hotel and rental car reservations. The companies could then collaborate and combine audience profiles to create new, innovative, dynamic digital experiences as a one-stop shopping flow.

- **Off-site search retargeting:** When a visitor visits the site from search, the keyword for that search is known. This keyword can be appended with other data and used to target the visitor as she moves around the Web. For example, her search for "free video" and an offer for a free Netflix trial account may follow her around the Web.

- **On-site search retargeting (SEO/SEM):** Similar to search retargeting, on-site search retargeting uses the information available from SEO and SEM campaigns to inform targeting. Because a visitor may have been exposed to one or more paid search ads, this information can be collected, used, and built into a profile about paid search referred visitors to target them in more intuitive ways as they move across the Internet.

- **Behavioral retargeting:** Similar to its predecessor behavioral targeting, behavioral retargeting means taking behavioral data gathered from any number of inputs across available digital information sources, and then using that behavioral data to target a person to reactivate a previous interest expressed about a product, service, or brand.

How Can the Digital Analytics Team Assist the Process of Targeting and Retargeting?

The digital analytics team has many opportunities to provide input and guidance for both the targeting and retargeting processes. After all, digital analytics data is used to (re)target, and the rules and filters applied to (re)targeting are digital data. The expertise of members of the digital analytics team in collecting, defining, verifying, analyzing, and communicating data can prove helpful when planning and executing targeted and retargeted campaigns.

As a result, the digital analytics team can play a helpful role in projects, programs, and initiatives:

- **Segment customers based on known attributes and behaviors.** An input from the digital analytics team to the marketing, agency, and advertising teams involved in targeting and retargeting can be customer segmentation analysis. The available attributes and common customer behaviors can be analyzed and reported to identify new insights for targeting.

- **Identify successful content and popular products.** One thing the digital analytics team is good at is rank ordering the frequency of particular concepts such as pages, products, visitors, and so on. Ranking the information about customers and the products they buy can be helpful when planning targeting initiatives.

- **Deploy tracking and measuring the success.** All retargeting and targeting campaigns must be tracked and measured to understand performance. Digital analytics tools can be instrumented and customized to function as data collection and reporting tools for understanding the performance of targeted and retargeted advertising campaigns.

- **Provide insights about the sources of visitors and what they do on the site (and don't do).** Visitor-level tracking, whether anonymous, partially anonymous, or not anonymous, is a core feature of the best digital analytics tool. Many out-of-the-box and customized reports are available for communicating how the visitor moves across the site and what aspects of a digital experience resonate for an audience. These inferences, clickstreams, and insights provided by the digital analytics team are relevant to targeting programs.

- **Identify the impact of search on the customer.** Keyword-based targeting and retargeting is a fairly common use-case. Digital analytics systems capture and report information and behavior that indicate how search—both internal and external—is used by customers and prospects. Search analytics data about keywords, zero results search pages, and other search behaviors can be valuable to consider when setting up targeted campaigns.

- **Indicate what marketing campaigns are profitable.** More than almost any other team, besides perhaps finance, the digital analytics team is in a prime position to understand the performance of all marketing campaigns and which of those marketing campaigns is most successful for driving revenue, profitability, and engagement. Combining financial data with marketing campaign performance can help identify the best campaigns to use for targeting and planning purposes.

Suggestions When Targeting and Retargeting: Lessons Learned

There are no magic bullets when executing targeting and retargeting programs and projects. The best practices and lessons learned from this innovation are only learned by doing the work. Some guidance and lessons learned are listed here:

- **Concentrate on the creative, and refresh it; don't leave it as is.** The narrative expressed within a piece of advertising creative is important. Not all creative resonates with all customers or prospects. Some creative just doesn't work at all for some people. Advertisers will be needlessly wasting money if they don't rotate creatives when attempting to retarget.

- **Use multiple attributes.** Leverage the full set of retargeting tools at your disposal by segmenting, ruling, and targeting based on multiple attributes. Target specific segments and analyze the difference in performance. Don't just target past visitors from Boston. Instead, target males under the age of 35 who speak English in Boston and use the site between 12 to 1 p.m. EST.

- **Avoid overexposing and thus fatiguing people.** Control the number of times a particular advertisement is retargeted to a particular visitor. You can use techniques like frequency capping and other forms of filtering to do so. The reason why should be obvious. By overexposing a visitor to the same creative, the advertisement is likely to get lost in the background and be considered noise. Digital analysis will tell you how many times an advertisement has been exposed to a customer before a click and the decay after that point and audience. Consider such input from the analytics team to avoid overexposure and the risk of retargeting fatigue.

- **Stop when you are successful; don't overtarget.** Congratulations! You successfully retargeted a customer segment, and you were able to track and prove to stakeholders that the work led to increased sales. People you work with are excited, especially the customer who finally purchased what it was you and she thought she wanted, and hopefully what she actually needed. At this point, the next step is simple. Stop retargeting. I know it sounds simple, but don't risk overtargeting and messing with your accomplishment. After a retargeted purchase was successfully made, the last thing a customer wants is more advertisements for what they bought, or even worse, advertisements for a product they didn't buy. Not only is overtargeting annoying to your customers, it is also a waste of their and your time and budget. Ensure you track the success of your retargeting campaigns. Use analytics for monitoring post-purchase campaign performance and the resulting transactions to prevent overtargeting.

- **Figure out the right level of targeting.** When targeting and retargeting, you want to create a signal that is recognized as relevant and differentiated by the visitor. That signal has to come above all the other noise competing for the attention, engagement, and clicks on the page or the screen such as other content and all types of ads. To maintain a signal from the noise in targeting retargeting, you want to apply filters and limit the number of impressions you serve the visitors. It's that simple. You want retargeting to be recognized but not overwhelm or annoy or feel wrong or spooky. Based on the data collected from previous retargeting campaigns, the digital analytics team can identify, predict, then optimize for the more successful timing, pattern, or frequency for retargeting.

- **Don't compete against yourself.** Your team may use multiple vendors and systems for targeted retargeting activities, but that can get risky due to competing budgets for the same set or overlapping population sets. You do not want to create a situation in which the target or retargeting budget is being cannibalized by competing vendors, agencies, and technologies that are all working for and being paid for by you. You want to prevent a situation in which this problem could occur. It's never a good day when you find out that you have been bidding against yourself to target wanted customer segments. One option is to work with one team or agency to handle retargeting, while another is to ensure alignment across multiple teams or agencies by analyzing the data and verifying that you aren't playing a game against yourself that you can't win where the only option is to lose your money.

- **Track the results and attribution with digital analytics.** It goes without saying that to measure your success, you must track it. Without campaign codes and the other persistent identifiers necessary for bringing together the data related to behavior, engagement, and performance for targeting and retargeting campaigns, businesses can never measure their success. The digital analytics team should dedicate resources, time, and investment to helping the team's involvement targeting retargeting collect, measure, report, and analyze the data. In the case where an agency or multiple agencies are doing this work, ensure your analytics team gets reporting or analysis from the agency.

Targeting is one of the newer uses for digital analytics data in online marketplaces. Many methods for targeting and retargeting are available. Multiple types of targeting and retargeting exist. Make certain to consider how the digital analytics team can use their expertise and digital data to participate and fuel business processes for creating value from targeting and retargeting.

12

Converging Omnichannels and Integrating Data for Understanding Customers, Audiences, and Media

The title of this chapter sounds buzz-wordy, and it well may be, yet it accurately expresses a goal of many different companies that seek to understand customers and people across more than one digital channel, such as a mobile application and a website. In deconstructing the chapter title:

- **Converging** means bringing together into one. See the idea of "convergence analytics" postulated by Andrew Edwards.

- **Omnichannels** are, as your requirements dictate, the digital channels from which you want to bring together data for business purposes. Omnichannel data is from more than two sources online and offline. For example, you may want to bring together customer-level demographic data with reach data from online advertisements and with syndicated research about purchasing propensities from a third-party data vendor. Omnichannel data integration isn't just internal data integration, it also includes data integration across multiple external sources.

- **Understanding customers, audiences, and media** refers to using available, ethical, and legal customer-level data to comprehend the patterns, behaviors, and performance of digital audiences, customers, or media (such as online advertising) or customer segments across omnichannels. Understanding enables targeting content, advertising, and other digital media directly to identifiable audience and customer segments as well as known and identifiable people. Addressing audiences or specific people, understood from anonymous or mostly anonymous data, or in the case of opt-ins, full customer profiles with

305

detailed attributes that may include Personally Identifiable Information (PII).

Converging omnichannel data may sound a lot like integrating multichannel data. Although there are similarities, there is a key difference. Multichannel refers to looking at the channels and the performance of those channels in silos or against each other in the context of marketing campaigns. Omnichannel convergence, on the other hand, attempts to bring together data from as many channels as necessary, wherever the data resides, into a single pooled data set that is focused on the customer, audience, or media.

Any attempt at converging or integrating refers to the totality of all processes and activities related to defining, extracting, transforming, and loading (ETL) from disparate and multiple data sources, whether internal or external into one location, which is most often a data warehouse or operational data store (ODS).

One of the reasons it is helpful to have integrated data is that it reduces the time it takes to prepare data before beginning data analysis. Because the digital analytics team is often required to locate relevant and specific data for answering business questions, wherever that data might exist, significant time and money can be allocated in each project to bring together data manually or via some limited automation. As the requirement for manual data integration becomes more prevalent in analytics projects, consider the business efficiencies gained. By integrating data into a common location and interface that is relevant to a specific business function, efficiencies can be gained and new insights learned. Schools of thought in computer science around data warehousing, such as those by Kimball and Inmon, express similar ideas in the alignment of business in technology and implementation of data warehousing solutions for business intelligence (BI) and analytics.

The biggest data of the big data results from massive data integration from many different large databases. The reason that analytics teams advocate for giant and complex data integration projects is that requirements for analytics often require seeking out and bringing together data from multiple sources. In addition, a pool of data structured and intended for analysis makes it easier and more effective to apply analytical methods and techniques, often automated with software algorithms, to find relationships, patterns, insights, recommendations, optimizations, and predictions. Although data integration can be an expensive business activity, it is also necessary and a cost of doing business when value can be proven from answering those questions that create economic value, which can only be answered by omnichannel data integration to understand customers, audiences, and media.

Types of Omnichannel Data

Omnichannel analysis integrates and unifies two or more data sources across multiple channels—often focused on the customer or shopper—such that detailed customer-level data sets are more comprehensive and representational of all the elements a business may want to analyze to detect and predict common relationships and insights about customers, segments, behaviors, and transactions. Omnichannel analysis, at a macro-strategic level, would consider all sources as really one giant source (albeit scattered in multiple sources) that must be brought together in new ways to find insights using methods. This business strategy is similar to the related and underlying analytics technical platform strategy of data warehousing. In fact, BI teams build data warehouses to represent, store, and provide access to omnichannel data. Types of omnichannel data include the following:

- **Internal data** is the type of data created by systems within or controlled by your company. Typically, paid and owned media falls into this category.
- **Digital analytics data**, discussed throughout this book, is behavioral, interactional, event, click, and transactional data from websites, owned social networks, email, mobile, and other digital formats. Digital analytics data can be categorized as behavior of customers or audiences across paid, earned, and owned media.
- **Social data** is data collected about people from their inputs, behaviors, clicks, interactions, events, and transactions in social media and on social networks. Social data can also come from aggregators, such as Klout or ShareThis, who collect social data

and use their intellectual property to derive new types of social data, such as the Klout score.

- **Syndicated research data** is often surveyed, sampled, or panel data about the behaviors, propensities, tendencies, preferences, wants/needs/desires, attitudes, and beliefs about an audience. Syndicated data and the market research that supports it is discussed in Chapter 9, "Qualitative and Voice of Customer Data and Digital Analytics."

- **Audience data** is household-level and geographic information about people in a specific population or sample frame, for example, attributes of an audience such as household income, family size, race, religion, geography, purchasing habits, and so on. Audience data is frequently segmented by the constructs of Designated Marketing Area (DMA) and Metropolitan Statistical Area (MSA). Audience data is often consulted for competitive intelligence (see Chapter 10, "Competitive Intelligence and Digital Analytics").

- **Financial data** is information related to the creditworthiness, credit scores, and other household financial, bank-owned, and investment-related information derived from available public and private sources whether transactional or not.

- **Business-to-business (B2B) data** is corporate data, sometimes called firmagraphic data, and is both structured and unstructured data about companies and business across regions, countries, markets, cities, and so on. The information may include profile data, company size, revenue, and other corporate data.

- **Specialized and customized research data** are insights provided by out-of-the box or customized research areas about audiences. Specialized data may be focused on particular products, lifestyles, markets, behaviors, geographies, and other vertical segments of wanted audiences. For a discussion, see Chapter 9.

- **Television and cable data** is specifically tied back to subscription and customer record data that identifies what people were shown what content and advertisements and when they were shown them. Customer data collected by digital televisions and subscriber-based cable services can be used for targeting (see Chapter 11, "Targeting and Automation with Digital Analytics").

As you can see from the previous list, many different and unique data sources exist for omnichannel analysis. Not all of them will be helpful or relevant within every project, but the analytics team should consider these data sources and the providers of these data when formulating analytical plans and analytics strategy for building a digital analytics organization.

Omnichannel Data Metrics

When data is brought together into one database, or assembled together in however you choose to do it, there are metrics and measures that are helpful. You can look at these measures as snapshots, time-series, distributions, and other analytical views (see Chapter 5, "Methods and Techniques for Digital Analysis"). Following are several measurements and descriptions of metrics that can be applied to omnichannel data analysis:

- **Intent to do X, such as a prediction to purchase or convert:** Omnichannel data is useful in marketing mix models that use statistical methods to predict the revenue, profit, and/ or audience/business propensities and intent on spending or investing in business activities.

- **Financial measures:** By understanding the cost and revenue of activities and the resulting audience behaviors, financial metrics can be enhanced and better understood. With omnichannel data integration, the revenue per customer on the digital channel can be unified and compared against the cost data for full understanding of profitability.

- **Audience reach:** A deduplicated number of people in the audience—or the data collected that represents that number as closely as possible. By associating one person with her signature from across channels, you can deduplicate the visitor and refine the count of people in your audience. For example, if the same person logs into a website and uses the same login for the mobile application, it is a known individual person on both channels. In theory, it is possible to bring together the Web and mobile data on a visitor level and determine how many people went to both, instead of counting the same person twice (that is, once on the site and once on the mobile device). The looking up and decoding of big data from omnichannel sources is complex and expensive. In some cases, identifying people across the channels for estimates of audience reach and other uses (such as targeting and retargeting) are propositions that require careful deliberation around privacy and ethics. In fact, in some countries, the identification of people in digital channels can be illegal or considered a potential privacy violation.

- **Recency:** When examining digital data, you must ask, "When was the last time my customers came to my site (or other digital experience)?" This time period is called *recency*. Depending on your goals, recency may vary. Watch critical customer segments for volatility in recency. Jim Novo, the excellent author of *Drilling Down*, calls recency "time since."

- **Frequency:** When examining digital data, you must ask, "How often do my customers come to my site (or other digital experience)?" This time period is called *frequency*. Depending on your goals, frequency may vary. Watch critical customer segments for volatility in frequency. Jim Novo calls frequency "time between."

- **GRP (Gross Rating Points):** Often simplified into the expression "reach times frequency," but that as a definition is oversimplified. GRP is a known and common metric for buying and selling an audience and has been used for decades in transactions and purchases of traditional media audiences by advertisers, such as those who watch TV or listen to the radio. Because GRP was derived from traditional advertising where the market dynamics, populations, lifestyles, channels, technologies, and analog user experiences were different, the use of GRP for measuring digital data and online devices has caused some disdain around the applicability of the metric. Still, GRP has applicability to today's digital medium, but it must be applied in a way that accommodates for the nuances of Internet access, multiscreen usage, shared devices, audience duplication, and for measuring minorities and audiences using digital devices in second or third world countries—and the other attributes mentioned previously.

Defining Customer Analytics: Enabled by Omnichannel Data Integration

Customer analytics requires applying methods for analyzing paid, owned, and earned media from a different perspective than from the marketing campaign, the website, the mobile application, the advertising experience, and the power of the creative content or digital narrative. Customer analytics, of course, focuses on the customer—who, in the age of "freemium" business models, may or may not actually generate *direct* revenue for a company. Thus, the *customer* is defined in digital analytics as

A mostly anonymous person or entity that generates direct or indirect revenue for a business via one or more digital channels. The customer has a known attribute identifiable or persistent across sources that functions as a primary key for joining data from more than one channel for digital data analysis.

In this context, *customer analytics* is defined as the following:

The applied analysis of person-level data from multiple and omnichannels for answering business questions about how to generate new or incremental revenue, reduce cost, or boost profitability of existing, new, or potential customers. Customer analysis requires data collection, governance/management, reporting of customer, unit-level data, which is achieved through cross-functional, analytical operations, and execution across the business, marketing, sales, finance, vendors, and technology.

Profiting with customer analytics is the goal, and in order to do so, the Wharton Customer Analytics Initiative (WCAI) proposes a useful and helpful academic definition, which Table 12-1 deconstructs, evaluates for applicability to the reality of the business world, and reconfigures for digital executives to apply as a management framework.

Table 12-1 WCAI Framework and Business Reality and Goals

WCAI Attribute of Customer Analytics	WCAI Commentary	Business Reality	Business Goal
Inherently granular	Must be individual-level.	Granularity is subjective and based on the size in which data is divided into fields. Customer data has a fine grain and may not be possible to identify at the sufficient granularity you need without aggregation, summarization, or sampling. Significant expense is incurred by storing granular customer data.	A customer dimension must exist at the granularity relevant to answering your business questions now and in the future, which means extensibility for supporting slowly changing dimensions and evolving data models.
Forward-looking	Orientation toward prediction, not just description.	The irony of this statement is that to predict the future, you must analyze the past (based on assumptions and fitting the rigor of models) using descriptive data on past events. Prediction requires description and the usage of past data. Thus, there is significant cost in storing granular data to make forward-looking assessments.	Predictive analytics is different than customer analytics; however, the techniques and methods for predictive analysis can and should be applied to customer data to do analysis, such as churn reduction and lifetime value (LTV) modeling.
Multiplatform	Combining behaviors from multiple measurement systems but with best efforts to do so at the individual level.	The idea of multiplatform is antiquated. Customer analytics is frequently understood using multichannel methods, which means multiscreen across multicampaigns. Businesses don't just combine data from multiple measurement systems, they combine customer data from outside those systems from source databases—and the name for doing this work is omnichannel, which is inherently multiplatform. The physical platform in 2013 is less meaningful than understanding the customer on the platform as being an actively engaged device-agnostic and likely mobile customer.	Establishing the organizational capability (across people, process, and technology) for collecting customer-level data from multiple channels and sources, such as mobile, social, email, Customer Relationship Management (CRM), and, and so on. Businesses must also consider omnichannel data integration where a view and profile of the customer is created by bringing together and unifying data from two or more internal and external data sources.

WCAI Attribute of Customer Analytics	WCAI Commentary	Business Reality	Business Goal
Broadly applicable (and industry-agnostic)	Consumers, donors, physicians, clients, brokers, and so on.	A good call-out academically and professionally is that idea that the techniques, methods, rules, functions, and models that you and your team create should be, at a fundamental level, applicable to other industries. Industries certainly have nuance; however, the fundamentals of a model for predicting customer churn are similar if not identical across industries.	Understanding of how customer analytics has been applied across people, process, and technology in other industries and on other teams. This understanding can provide ideas and confirmations for your customer analytics initiatives. For globally distributed companies, it is absolutely necessary to look within at what already exists. (You may be surprised.)
Multidisciplinary	Marketing, statistics, computer science, information systems, operations research, and so on.	As discussed in Chapter 3, "Building an Analytics Organization," businesses organize analytics teams in different ways. Although an eventual goal may be bringing together multiple disciplines, it is likely that many companies can't allocate or simply don't have multidisciplinary resources to do this work. There is acute insufficiency of qualified staff. Refer to the McKinsey Global Institute (MGI) estimates in Chapter 1, "Using Digital Analytics to Create Business Value."	Audit your organization to determine the skill sets that exist and determine what type of organization would work for your company (see Chapter 3).
Rapidly emerging	Traditionally viewed as just one form of business analytics but starting to take on its own unique identity as a "standalone area of analysis and decision making."	The Internet and the digital industry that supports its evolution are by definition "rapidly emerging." And have been since the beginning. Although this callout may seem like a "no-brainer" to digital professionals, it is important to note that even with the best effort at maintaining currency and fluency, the world moves quickly; thus, it is necessary to determine periodically your "current state." Just keep in mind the digital world moves even quicker.	Maintaining current awareness of a "rapidly emerging" business activity requires ongoing immersion and study of the topic. Fortunately, from the Interactive Advertising Bureau (IAB) to WCAI to the Digital Analytics Association (DAA) to the Analytics Research Organization (ARO), many resources exist for staying up to date and currently aware of new knowledge. Teams should go to at least one relevant industry conference per year and if budget, time, and geography allow, possibly attend more relevant events. The best digital analysts participate in the local analytics community in their geography.

WCAI Attribute of Customer Analytics	WCAI Commentary	Business Reality	Business Goal
Behavioral	Many firms' customer analytics problems incorporate descriptors such as demographics and attitudes, but, the customer analytics' primary focus is on observed behavioral patterns.	Behavioral data about customers is readily available from free and paid technologies; however, customer-level, person-level behavioral data is complex and sometimes unethical or illegal to work with. Systems such as Google Analytics to SAS purport the ability to report and analyze customer data but consider that customer data has various levels of granularity and anonymity that must match business purposes to be useful. Again, significant costs and overhead are necessary for storing and maintaining access to granular digital data about customer behavior.	Scrutinize the definition of "customer behavioral data" as available within your data and analytical systems. Verify that the types of business questions, analytical methods, and granularity of person-data is available and can be joined, in some way, with other customer data (as necessary).
Longitudinal	It's all about how these behaviors manifest over time.	Time-series data trended over time (such as DoD, WoW, MoM, QoQ, and YoY) are important and useful. The completeness and accuracy of customer-level data may be challenged at your business; thus, be careful when setting your expectations about the availability of past, historic, time-series, longitudinal data. Without the data in the business, the business reality is that the older data definitions, the more likely the risk and potential for the previously recorded data to be wrong. In addition, the "rapidly emerging" state of the digital world calls into question the utility of looking far back into the past. Take for example, how social media has impacted business, in some cases very significantly. Three years ago Facebook and Twitter had not entirely mainstreamed, so does it make sense to consider data from four years ago? It may or may not.	Create data governance and processes for defining and sustaining the long-term accuracy of longitudinal data. The ability to trend defined, standardized data and compare across time periods is fundamentally important to success with customer analytics. Develop the capability if it does not already exist by following the principles outlined in Chapter 6, "Defining, Planning, Collecting, and Governing Data in Digital Analytics."

Questioning Customers Using Their Data and Your Analytics

Thinking about customers and their data helps to humanize the analytical process. Instead of dealing with pages, clicks, interactions, events, transactions, and other business data, customer analytics requires the customer at the center and core of the data. The customer may be anonymous, known, many subtle shades of mostly anonymous or mostly known, or the customer may be fully identifiable by PII. Regardless of the given level of anonymity and ambiguity in customer analytics, the goal is still the same overall goal of digital analytics teams: answering business questions that stakeholders have about the impact of their ideas, innovations, program, projects, plans, campaigns, and initiatives on the performance and profitability of the business. These questions can be asked by stakeholders with specificity or with frustrating generality. Actually, one of the signs of a good analyst, as described in Chapter 3, is the ability to help stakeholders— at all levels—ask the best possible business questions about available, relevant, and timely digital data. Questions from stakeholders about customer analytics often refer to the ideas and concepts presented in the following list, but will rarely ever be asked for in such a clear and straightforward way. Thus, the analyst needs to help his stakeholder ask the best questions often by simplifying what is being asked. Here are some examples:

1. What customers are most valuable?
2. When is it best to engage, market, campaign, contact, message, or reach out (that is, touch) to customers?
3. Where (what channel or channels) are most effective for generating profitable customer performance?
4. Why did the customer respond in one way to a business activity (such as an online ad or channel), what have we learned, and what are the next best steps for maintaining the customer relationship?

5. How can you use customer data to improve customer performance, such as reduce customer churn, increase customer retention, and improve customer satisfaction, customer engagement, and conversion?

6. What behaviors did the customer engage in in the past that impact the current business and what decisions should we make based on the data?

7. What customers are most valuable now, in the past, and will be in the future—and how can we maximize customer LTV?

As you can see from the themes in the questions presented previously, the best customer analytics programs can answer what has happened to the customer in the past, what's happening with the customer now, what may happen to the customer in the future, and what are the possible actions and best actions to take for achieving business goals with the customer.

Answering questions about the customer may be as simple as analyzing campaign performance for a snapshot in time to compare across a recent time period (such as Month over Month [MoM]); however, you must consider the entire customer life cycle from the higher order, qualitative research to loyalty and lifetime value modeling as discussed in the next section.

The Unified Customer Life Cycle

Customer analysis centers around segmenting individual-level data (as discussed in the next section, "Work Activities in Customer Analytics via Omnichannel Data Integration") based on one or more shared attributes. As a result, customer response and customer's periodic and LTVs can be calculated using statistical methods. The best-performing acquisition sources for a specific set of customers can be identified, which helps planning future campaigns. Customer behavior and value can be predicted using methods and techniques discussed in Chapter 5, such as regressions, correlations, and data plotting and visualizations.

Digital data like referrers, search (search engine optimization [SEO]/search engine marketing [SEM]), CRM, emails, and other forms of paid, owned, and earned media can be used to build, inform, and enhance customer profiles. Although these applications of customer analytics are all valid and serious business activities, customer behavior and profitability are too frequently analyzed separately by channel. In other words, a single customer may be tracked and analytics done on that customer, but the customer engagement with the brand extends across multiple channels. Thus, an important facet for customer analytics is understanding the performance of customers within each channel (that is, multiple channels) and when combined across all channels (that is, omnichannel). Because it is necessary to deduplicate customers across channels, campaigns, and media, I created the Unified Customer Analytics Life Cycle (UCAL) model to help frame customer behavior.

The UCAL is a concept for understanding and lighting the "dark spots" in your multi- and omnichannel customer analytics. Dark spots exist in your customer analytics because you aren't considering the influence of one channel against another. UCAL identifies several phases for understanding customer behavior in their life cycle. Each phase associates a set of customer data, analytics, and reporting.

You can apply UCAL to both funnel (linear, single-channel) and nonfunnel (recursive, multichannel) customer analytics. Funnel analytics considers the customer to be the result of one channel through which value was created in a linear sequence of steps. Funnels are a metaphor for customer acquisition, value creation may make sense, and it's easy to comprehend. But funnels are linear whereas customer behavior is not. In other words, while funnels may represent the steps a customer takes to convert and create value, the steps are presented in a forward-looking series of phased steps. That's not really how people buy things, but the oversimplification in the linearity of the funnel makes it easy to comprehend. In the funnel, the customer goes through a series of steps that lead to value creation:

1. **Phase 1: Activation:** Although the concept of activation is often considered part of internal marketing execution, customers also activate themselves. Activation is a higher order analytics concept, like the first five UCAL phases, which is measured

qualitatively via surveys and Voice of Customer (VoC) data. Activation in customer analytics refers to the "awakening" of need in the customer. Activation can be acute (occurring suddenly) or realized (a result of long-term influences).

2. **Phase 2: Exposure:** In a state of activation, the customer sees and perceives a brand and its associated physical and psychological properties and qualities through paid, owned, or earned media.

3. **Phase 3: Awareness:** In an activated and exposed state, the customer who is exposed to the brand becomes cognitively aware of the exposure. In a similar way to where your mother told you "You may hear me, but you aren't listening," you can understand how awareness results from exposure, but not all exposures create awareness. Another case in point is the online advertising industry's emphasis on a "viewable impression," which suggests a similar relationship between exposure and awareness.

4. **Phase 4: Differentiation:** The process of evaluating a brand and its product or service qualities against competitors and substitutes. A customer compares attributes one against another to determine how to work through the infoglut of advertising. During this phase, the narrative of the advertising and exposure is either accepted, viewed as aberrant, or resisted by the customer.

5. **Phase 5: Consideration:** A customer considers the brand against competitors and substitutes based on judgment of applicability of the brand's perceived qualities against the customer's perceived needs. Consideration is where the many are slimmed to the few—and where it is mostly likely a customer will seek and be exposed to brand messages from multiple channels.

6. **Phase 6: Acquisition:** Accounting for the many paid, owned, and earned media across which your customers may have been exposed: One of those channels was "last click" just like a channel was "first click." The first click may be the last click or not, and many clicks might have occurred between first and last. In fact, the idea of attribution as a construct to model using

approaches that weigh every customer touchpoint against the other to determine which have the most influence on purchase or conversion to approaches use statistical modeling and machine learning, as well as the attribution methods described in Chapter 5.

7. **Phase 7: Conversion:** Having transitioned from acquisition sources to attributable marketing channels, the customer engages in digital behavior. Clicks, interactions, behaviors, and events create profitable transactions. The series of clicks (clickstream) and resulting digital narrative enable the potential for scenario and micro conversion within macro conversion flows.

8. **Phase 8: Retention:** Tracking customer conversion allows for the calculation of how long it takes and how much money it costs to create a customer. In this case, the "engagement time" can be translated to "revenue dollars." While an impressive achievement, it is even more impressive and profitable when the customer comes back to buy again. Customer retention is the key to increasing customer LTV. Thus, the business activities of nurturing a customer, repeating a visit, and engaging a customer by building a long-term "customer relationship" to reduce customer churn and attrition are crucial to measure. Measures such as LTV and customer satisfaction are necessary (see Chapter 9).

9. **Phase 9: Loyalty from satisfaction:** A customer can be considered loyal after their second purchase. Loyalty analysis involves understanding why the customer purchased again, whether it was a purchase of a new product or one previously purchased, and the source and method for the customer's transactions. Even more critical is how—post-purchase—the customer again became activated and moved through Phases 1–5. In both Retention and Loyalty, customer churn LTV analysis is important to measure and analyze as is customer satisfaction and the impact of time on it (such as lags and decay).

If you are an advocate of the linear funnel, such a theory for linking advertising to behavior to value creation might read something like this:

1. Create awareness through differentiation.

2. Position the product or service so that it evokes favorability.

3. Reach enough people so that the advertising strengthens the brand and supports or maintains brand equity.

4. Inform purchasing behavior via a certain frequency of exposures.

5. Lead to a site visit via clickthrough (direct) or view-through (direct).

6. Compel a direct purchase from which economic value is created.

7. Generate or sustain loyalty and reactivation during the next cycle of realization of the intent to purchase.

In 2013, brands have to, basically, consider UCAL as a constituency of phased parts to understand it. Web analytics can measure items 3, 4, 5, and 6 in the previous list, but what about items 1, 2, and 7?

Items 1 and 2 are the domain of advertising research, brand awareness, and qualitative brand studies. Online, response-based inputs to these studies can be integrated (via cookies or login) with past and future web behavioral data. Some vendors are attempting to do this work today (see Chapter 9).

For item 3, you have media planners using third-party tools that have few standards. Behavioral data from digital analytics adds a dimension of customer performance to those media plans. In other words, digital data can qualify reach with performance and correlate it to exposure on a referring site-by-site basis. The funnel only provides a limited way to express the phases in the UCAL. The funnel, as discussed previously, is attempting to apply a linear progression of steps to a recursive activity with phases that occur over time and not necessarily in a linear order. Thus, companies that concentrate exclusively on funnels are missing the full picture of the actual customer life cycle both before and after conversion. Nevertheless, the funnel metaphor is still commonly used and applied to understanding conversion.

The funnel metaphor and linear customer life cycle, however, is not often suitable for customers with long or complex life cycles. Thus, the UCAL model is extensible in that it not only includes the traditional marketing funnel, it also expands on the top of it with higher order concepts (like awareness and consideration) with post-purchase concepts and customer-level measurements (like churn, attrition, satisfaction, loyalty, and LTV)—all of which are considered in the UCAL but not necessarily in the traditional marketing funnel.

UCAL's multi- and omnichannel emphasis suggests that the customer constantly goes in and out of the phases described in the funnel model. That is a customer who is presupposed to have been exposed to many different impressions of a brand from many different sources at many different times and levels of exposure. For example, a customer may not just view an advertisement on TV and then buy a product on a website immediately upon the television commercial ending. It is more likely the person saw a TV advertisement, used organic or paid search to research the product and price, went to competitors' websites, signed up for a newsletter, researched the brand on social media, clicked a display ad, and then decided not to buy for several months, before finally doing all these customer activities again. The funnel can't capture this up-and-down, non-linear, step jumping. UCAL and the Tumbler can capture this latency and complexity in customer and shopper behaviors. In this sense, the antithesis of the funnel metaphor is the "Tumbler" metaphor:

> The Tumbler considers customers to move up and down the phases in the linear model at will across the phases of Seeking > Shopping > Sharing. The Tumbler accommodates for all phases in the UCAL and also for the nonlinear, periodicity, recursiveness, conditionality, and temporality of the customer life cycles:

- **Seeking:** You determine a need for something, such as a product (or service) in the context of not being aware of what you aren't aware. Then media like TV, radio, word of mouth, billboards, and maybe even the Internet help you gain awareness and identify what is favorable to you, which you may or may not be exposed to via one or more messages that position the product (or service). Sometimes you just stumble upon what you think you may or may not need or want when you are looking for something else. As Joel Rubinson, CEO of Rubinson Partners, says, "Different media amplify that." Seeking is where consideration, awareness, and activation occurs.

- **Shopping:** Simple to understand, but complex in the sense of "shopping around" and jumping back and forth between the "seeking" (via various media) and then from what may or may not come next or came before. Shopping is where acquisition and conversion occurs.

- **Sharing is complex:** Amazingly complex. A person tells you in the terminal of the airport, SMS/texts you, calls you, you read about it in a magazine, on Twitter or Facebook, see it on Pinterest, read about it on Tumblr, see it on a video site, talk about it at dinner, read it in a magazine, hear a stranger talking about it on the subway platform, and so on and so forth. Retention, loyalty, and satisfaction can be identified by sharing—and sharing must be factored and enumerated in customer LTV models.

Customers jump in and out and across the phases in parallel in the Tumbler. The Tumbler construct for understanding customer behavior is new because customers have traditionally been thought of as pathing on a linear flow of acquisition to conversion to loyalty. As I've described, that belief is oversimplified and misses much of the digital path to purchase and new insights about shoppers and customers. Because of the complexity of the digital and nondigital ecosystem, which has a multitude of customer touchpoints that lead to value-generating customer performance, it becomes necessary to use many different sources and analyze the data in an integrated way to answer complex business questions that generate revenue or reduce cost. UCAL and the Tumbler provide a flexible, accommodating framework for doing so.

Telling "data stories" enables the creation of economic value through the detection of new insights that help leaders take action to improve the customer experience. For example, integrate data from the website, television (set-top boxes), mobile apps, social media, and qualitative research (VoC and surveys) into a holistic, full view of the customer at various stages in the life cycle. UCAL and the Tumbler can be applied for framing an approach to analyzing such a use-case.

Taking a step back from the grand vision of the multi- and omnichannel customer experience and how analytics enables understanding it, there are some "off-site" channels that integrate well with digital analytics. Marketing campaigns like email and paid and organic search integrate fairly easily with site behavioral data. But it is more challenging to bring effectively together behavioral analytics with online advertising. I am not talking about simple campaign coding. Instead, larger opportunities for more highly relevant, value-generating linkages exist between off-site (and offline) advertising behavior and on-site customer behavior. Huge opportunities exist in this type of integration for a few reasons:

- Online advertising represents more than 15 percent of the total advertising spend in 2013, a figure approximately $500 billion globally annually—more than magazine and radio advertising "spend" in digital combined, which is predicted to grow at 16 percent per year forward into 2015.

- Most agencies and online advertisers don't have a solid understanding of digital data that results from media buying, placements, and exposures. Nor do they have the staff because there are not enough people around with this understanding. Remember from Chapter 1 that MGI estimates a need for millions more data-savvy professionals into 2020.

- Digital analysts—the people that do the digital data drilling—are well positioned to comprehend the full customer life cycle because they not only understand "digital" but also arguably optimize the most important part: the path to purchase and where the money finally changes hands online. Tens of thousands of new data analytics jobs will be needed, according to MGI, by 2020 (beyond the millions of data-savvy professionals mentioned previously).

The (global) Internet and digital analytics industries require a more integrated methodology, system, and framework that provide a data-driven narrative for proving advertising effectiveness and customer value generation from high-order ideas, such as awareness and favorability, rather than more concrete and infinitely easier (and less expensive to measure) concepts like conversion to loyalty (and all the steps between). The UCAL model and the Tumbler, along with the traditional funnel, help to advance the conversation and allow the United States to view shopper and customer life cycles in new ways.

Beyond what I've presented in this chapter, there are few if any compelling frameworks that bring together shoppers' and purchases' intent and mindset with digital behavior and the resulting value generated over time. The UCAL and Tumbler models presented in this book help digital analysts represent and consider the customer value creation across from digital behavior. The data to support the UCAL and Tumbler frameworks can be put together from the existing internal and external sources by well-resourced analytics teams.

Work Activities in Customer Analytics via Omnichannel Data Integration

The work streams, activities, and business processes that must be considered by digital analytics teams when executing omnichannel integration and customer analysis include the following:

- **Data mining** is an activity in the Analytics Value Chain. Data mining is defined by Wikipedia as:

  "A field at the intersection of computer science and statistics is the process that attempts to discover patterns in large data sets. It utilizes methods at the intersection of artificial intelligence, machine learning, statistics, and database systems. The overall goal of the data mining process is to extract information from a data set and transform it into an understandable structure for further use. Aside from the raw analysis step, it involves database and data management aspects, preprocessing, model and inference considerations, interesting metrics, complexity considerations, post-processing of discovered structures, visualization, and online updating."

  Data mining involves extracting, transforming, and loading (ETL) data based on querying raw data. Data miners may create new data models, implement them in databases, and define data collection. They often work with or are data scientists who create models for recommending, predicting, optimizing, and automating with digital data.

- **Customer segmentation:** Segmentation, as discussed in Chapter 5, is the division of a whole into parts based on attributes. For example, determining all customers who purchased through your mobile site in the last 60 days is an example of a simple segment. Segmentation is easy to understand as pie or, more specifically, slicing the pie into eight segments. Yet, it also is complex enough to require data mining and statistical processing.

Of all techniques for analysis, customer segmentation can be the most profitable because it focuses on a person's known behavior in the context of past, present/current, future, lifetime, behavioral, or event value. Segmentation allows you to cross the dimensions in your data and filter and drill-down to understand the detail behind the numbers and trends. Segmentation and cluster analysis can help to identify new insight about customer behavior that may otherwise stay uncovered.

- **Customer churn and propensity modeling and analytics:** Customer churn refers to the process by which customers "die off" and no longer buy from your company. More seriously, customers move in and out of UCAL and other life-cycle models for a number of reasons:

  - Customers no longer need the product or service.

  - Customers are not satisfied.

  - The purchasing cycle is too long.

  - The brand offers no up-sell or cross-sell.

  - The brand does not understand customer data and no longer is effectively differentiated or positioned in the mind of the consumer.

- **Customer satisfaction:** Customer satisfaction refers to the human condition of fulfillment and contextual happiness. For example, if you always buy a certain car, enjoy it, and recommend it to a friend, you are likely satisfied with that brand. Satisfaction is measurable, and measuring it can be a central focus of customer analytics teams. For more information about measuring customer satisfaction, see Chapter 9.

- **Customer Lifetime Modeling (CLM):** What if you could use math to allocate a value to a customer that accounts for all past, current, and future transactions? What if you could allocate a value of prospects and customers each stage in your customer life cycle? CLM attempts to do just that with statistics. CLM uses methods and techniques discussed in Chapter 5.

Challenges to Customer Analytics

Companies that expand their analytics teams to add responsibilities for understanding customers and bringing together data from multiple channels or omnichannels can encounter roadblocks and obstacles to taking on this data and analytics challenge, which include but are not limited to the following:

- **Unavailability of customer-level data:** The sources of customer data are not always available or possible to access in the way that is wanted. Sometimes the data doesn't exist in the granularity, the history, or with the view needed to solve for a business problem. Significant cost may be associated with storing detailed and granular customer behavioral data generated from online digital systems and experiences.

- **Lack of available financial resources:** The cost of data integration projects can easily enter seven figures and have a material impact on the financial performance of a company.

- **Inexperience applying models:** Due to the newness of data integration for big data and with customer-level data as well as an insufficiency of qualified resources, it can be challenging to find people who have direct, real, professional experience working with omnichannel data integration.

- **No commitment from IT:** Because of the technical nature of data integration, whether on small data or big data, technical resources are needed, which can often require a commitment from IT (but not always) or at the very least alignment with them.

- **Privacy concerns:** The potential for concern when querying across or integrating omnichannel data is real and must be considered, whether or not you think privacy concerns with digital data are overblown.

What's Required for the Digital Analytics Team to Do Customer Analytics via Omnichannel Integration?

Omnichannel data integration is a complex proposition for companies to execute. The following requirements are necessary for omnichannel data integration:

- **Access to the necessary data and the ability to store and process it:** Omnichannel data exists in separate systems, both inside and outside the company, that should be brought together or, at least, queried or accessed in a way that allows for meaningful relationships in the data to be extracted and applied in business context.

- **Infrastructure:** The underlying computing power, including disk space, processors, storage, electricity, and so on required to integrate big, omnichannel data can be significant in scale and cost. Newer database processing infrastructures such as Hadoop can be required.

- **Software:** Omnichannel data unifies data sources containing big data. As a result, omnichannel data is the biggest of the big data. Thus, software that was applicable to large scale data sets just years ago runs too slowly for processing big data. Online Analytical Processing (OLAP) engines may not suffice.

- **People with data integration skills:** It has been anecdotally reported that there are fewer than 100,000 certified BI professionals and technologists. On the digital analytics side, there are fewer than 3,000 members of the DAA. Given the volume of data, the people to work with it are few. That's why MGI estimates a need for tens of thousands of more data analytics professionals and millions more data-savvy managers into 2020.

- **Necessary permissions and opt-in:** Omnichannel data contains the clickstreams, patterns, events, behaviors, clicks, interactions, metadata, attributes, sentiment, and information about where people live, what they buy, what they earn and spend, their families, and maybe even who they are. As a result, data integration of digital data requires adherence to existing rules and forethought about the potential future legal, ethical, and moral implications, ramifications, and potential slippery slopes from bringing data together.

- **Process:** As has been mentioned numerous times in this book, process is absolutely necessary. It is no different with omnichannel integration and becomes even more important due to the number of sources and teams involved to coordinate cross-channel data integration. For more information about analytics process, see Chapter 2, "Analytics Value Chain and the P's of Digital Analytics."

13

Future of Digital Analytics

The future of digital analytics, big data, data science, and applied analysis is certainly a bright one in a vibrant environment full of economic opportunity. Between now and 2016, the business analytics market will grow at a compound annual growth rate of 9.8 percent, reaching $50.7 billion, research firm International Data Corporation (IDC) claims. Meanwhile Indeed.com, a global job aggregator, claims a 4,000+ % increase (and rising) in digital analytics job trends as well as 100% annual increases in the trends for employment with "big data" and "data science." Clearly the future will involve these concepts in the economy, in businesses, and in consumer environments.

Collecting data, applying it to solve business problems, and generating value will continue to evolve and spread in importance across industries. Data and the resulting analytics from it will continue to tendril and pervade into everyday life—from the ubiquity of recommendations for related content already widespread on the Web to the penetration of more powerful applications and devices to wearable devices, such as Google Glass.

I call this evolution in the importance of the usage of analytics in today's business world, *The Analytical Economy:*

> *The Analytical Economy describes how data, research, and analytics are being used in traditional, new, and differentiated ways by unifying insights derived from more than one channel (or sources) about audiences, customers, and media and using those unified insights to create, evolve, and optimize existing and new methods for creating global commerce and culture.*

Take for example that right now, you can monitor your behavioral data about your personal home energy usage and use the data to fine-tune automations to ensure energy use falls within an acceptable cost range and/or environmental impact. The savings in energy costs from not wasting energy and from decreased pollution, when added up across millions of homes, can dramatically impact human society, politics, the environment, and culture. This type of consumer application of data that impacts business, economics, natural resources, and culture is just the beginning of automated and intelligent applications of digital data analytics in consumer products. The next steps of data pervasiveness and the usage of analytics in the home and in public spaces are also just beginning. From customer-profiling via radio-frequency identification (RFID) and in near-field environments, to the hyperlocal usage of global positioning system (GPS) and social networking data, to streaming media automatically in your car via an always on Wi-Fi signal, to creating a custom menu of selections on an iPad at your local restaurant based on dietary preferences, to the intermingling and intermeshing of data collected from sources about your behavior that is used in ways we don't notice to improve lifestyles and eliminate friction and obstacles in daily life will be (and is now) a revolutionary Analytical Economy.

On the other hand, there are serious privacy concerns that digital data collection creates the potential for a surveillance society that would make George Orwell blush or Joe McCarthy happy. The 2013 whistleblowing of the National Security Agency (NSA) digital surveillance network, named PRISM, and the capabilities described have brought privacy, civil liberties, and human rights to the forefront of the conversation about digital data collection, mining, and analytics.

Digital devices, from those that broadcast location via GPS to the emergence of wearable computers (currently limited from enabling facial recognition technology in Google Glass apps and the future competitors to it), have the potential to capture data in public spaces that will have and are having an enormous impact on the evolution of human society and how people communicate, socialize, collaborate, understand, remember, judge, memorialize, and relate to each other across time, space, geography, and culture. Facebook has more than one billion members—and is larger than many countries. Mark Zuckerberg has more money than some countries. You are leaving your clickstreams for free across multiple channels, and companies are selling it to make money off your identity, social connections, pictures, content, and behaviors in ways the general population doesn't understand and might have never considered. It is apparent the U.S. NSA has the capability to freely collect and store your digital metadata, and in some cases, the contents of your digital communications on private and corporate networks. Companies are connecting all of this big data using data science to do data analytics about °you° and automating, targeting, and monetizing digital experiences by marketing to you, your friends, and families.

Safeguarding and managing digital analytics away from the spooky big brotherisms and the perception of surveillance culture, especially in light of the 2013 U.S. NSA PRISM technology, and into the light of transparency, disclosure, and public conversation is necessary for the industry. The future of analytics will involve the application of data in analytical systems that are human-managed and, in many ways, automated based on sensors and actuation with sensors based on digital data inputs and other feedback that automate digital outputs and response in real time when necessary. Our collective global shared analytic future could involve the following topics discussed in the next few sections:

- Predictive personalization
- Closed-loop behavioral feedback systems
- Real-time relevant content and advertising delivered to your eyeglasses and other wearable computers
- Sensing and responding
- Interacting and alerting
- Geo-specific relevance and intent targeting
- Automated services and product delivery
- Data-interactive shopper and customer experience

Predictive Personalization

The growing knowledge and understanding of the power of predictive analytics in corporate settings beyond the traditional sectors and industries, such as biotech, manufacturing, and pharmaceutical industries, will continue to grow in new applications across new industries. You can already see predictive analysis being personalized through routing on mapping applications, identifying the predicted price of car-sharing services delivered on mobile apps, and recommending when to purchase an airline ticket based on industrywide price changes and consumer supply and demand. In the same way, insurance companies' and pharmaceutical companies' staff have formalized prediction and data analysis into their product and marketing life cycles from data collected digitally. New sectors are already seeing an impact from the power of prediction in food and beverage companies and restaurants as well as consumer and Internet brands. Predictive personalization will take account of person-level data whether randomly anonymized or opt-in provided by consumers as additional independent variables into predictive models.

Closed-Loop Behavioral Feedback Systems

In sectors where data is collected to provide input into manual or automated processes that result in something occurring as an end state, digital data will enrich capabilities. Behavioral data about the way humans touch the interface and use their hands (and other input devices) to instruct machines to do something will be applied to "optimize" the user experience and improve efficiency in human computer interactions (see Chapter 8, "Optimization and Testing with Digital Analytics: Test, Don't Guess"). Right now, tablets are used in supply chains; handheld mobile devices are carried by merchandisers in retail environments; and waiters are carrying devices to take orders. Employers are using the data collected from handheld devices, such as the geolocation data and time spent using the device, to understand what their employees are doing (or not doing). These human resource metrics' impact on business value can be modeled using the behavioral inputs collected by users to help companies execute work and manage people in less costly ways. For example, in a warehousing environment, the use case of the device (such as receiving versus shipping freight) requires different interfaces, and how people use the same interface varies widely. A company can collect and analyze the usage data on tablets to create the best possible interfaces for their employees and their business when shipping and receiving freight. Saving even a few minutes per person per day in large supply chains can add up to significant efficiencies and savings.

Real-Time, Addressable, Relevant Content and Advertising Delivered Unified Across Multiscreens

From Google Glass to the wide set of disparate Internet connected devices, whether fixed or mobile, Carat, a leading advertising agency, predicted that 1/5 of all global advertising spend will be on digital advertising. And that number will only grow in the future as more people go online across the world. As only one of many channels for digital analytics, online advertising (from paid search to display) and data collected from other digital experiences will continue to be applied, often in real time, to adapt to advertising that you see on digital screens. Digital content experiences will continue to be delivered across multiscreens wherever you are located based on your pre-identified preferences and topical interests. Content and experiences will adjust in relevancy as a response to your interactions and based on what is known and can be derived in real-time about you by advertisers and publishers. Rand Schulman, one of the founders of the Digital Analytics Association (DAA), speaks about "relevancy bubbles" that envelop your digital signal causing personalized changes and experiences in digital advertising in public spaces, which does a good job of illustrating the concept I am trying to communicate. The idea of putting relevant, targeting advertising in front of a customer already exists—after all, I wrote an entire chapter about it—and in the future, the algorithms and data that fuel targeted relevancy will evolve to include addressable, highly specific ads within one cohesive narrative across every screen you own and even those you don't own and see in public spaces. Taken to the next logical conclusion, the preferences on your mobile device, your consumer profile, and information known by brands about your cookies and other persistent objects on your laptop, will converge to create the biggest of the big, big data to drive global commerce by serving you more relevant and targeted ads. The application of this data to the advertising ecosystem will occur in real time, which will require massive infrastructure investment, in not only the platforms, but also the centers of innovation that support analytics globally both professionally and academically.

Sensing and Responding

RFID, regardless of privacy concerns, has active and passive methods of communicating data about where the tag exists. In supply chain and shipping environments, RFID usage is already widespread to improve transportation and logistics. Sensor actuation that cues a physical or a digital experience based on using sensors to, well, sense a state, profile, persona, or segment, and then respond in some way—whether physically, virtually, or digitally—will grow in application and presence in the consumer world.

Given the vast privacy and regulatory concerns with active field data-passing and sensing of that data in public environments, it will be preferred to sense and respond within explicit opt-in environments. Take for example a futurist situation in which you have a transponder that broadcasts you like "pizza" and a sensor within retail and market environments that lets you know where the nearest pizzeria is, delivers a mobile coupon, and parses social data to recommend the pizzeria you will like best given your expressed preferences, past pizza orders, and social ranking input you and others in your social graph provided on pizzerias already visited and preferred. The same types of automated and relevant customer experiences could also be enabled by GPS in your mobile device. For example, you enter a retail store environment where Wi-Fi is available. The Wi-Fi connection requires your phone's GPS to be turned on (if not already) and the information about your location is detected and recorded, and because you have the retailer's mobile app on your phone, you get an alert that a new coupon is available for a product you previously purchased using a Quick Response (QR) code promotional offer on your mobile device.

Interacting and Alerting

On websites, if a person dwells or hovers too long, she may see a "modal" delivered over the content indicating that a click on the modal will open a chat window with a live human who can help you. This simple, already existing, use case shows how real-time, behavioral data collected from digital experiences creates the potential for virtual human-to-human interaction. Outlier behavior can be detected using digital data to alert when an important event happens. The simple example is an outlier deposit in a bank account, which invokes an alert to call the customer with an offer for a financial planner or investment opportunity.

Geo-Specific Relevance and Intent Targeting

The world knows it is possible to track people using GPS location sent by digital devices over the network. The surveillance and intelligence sectors make use of GPS signals to track people as they move across Earth. Because anyone with a mobile device typically has a GPS signal set to "On" by default, it then becomes possible with data integration to create a map of where addressable people, customer types, and segments are physically located and also who and what else is nearby. Take the example of locally targeted Daily Deal sites, such as Groupon, which delivers via email or mobile device. Given the availability of geolocation, it then becomes possible to recognize the location of nearby merchants, and when in-store, deliver mobile coupons within the shopper experience near the point of purchase. With more and more commercial and retail establishments providing free Wi-Fi, this potential will only grow. (For more information about targeting, see Chapter 11, "Targeting and Automation with Digital Analytics.")

Automated Services and Product Delivery

The innovation, growth, and wider commercial and personal application of consumer and business technologies that are driven off of or that use digital data for predicting, sensing, responding, detecting, interacting, alerting, recommending, and personalizing will continue to reach into our daily lives both personally and professionally. Digital data can help create and deliver the vision of the semantic Web. After all, digital data is commonly used in web services. Said another way, your refrigerator will log your inventory of items, sense when they expire, detect your usage patterns, and order your milk, bread, cheese, vegetables, and meat online delivered to your door.

Or, at least, let you know on your refrigerator's screen what you need and what's expired—and then tell you the nearest route to the closest market with the lowest item cost and average shopping cart value (that is, order value) based on your past food choices and dietary preferences (see Chapter 7, "Reporting Data and Using Key Performance Indicators").

Data-Interactive Shopper and Customer Experiences

Data-interactive shopper and customer experiences are in humanity's future. Big data and data science will be applied to create timely digital experiences that enforce existing customer perceptions and brand narratives with reduced human and manual analysis as needed currently. Today, companies hiring resources to staff analytics teams are responsible for some or all of the following: business requirements gathering, data collection, testing and quality assurance (QA) of data collected, analytics, reporting, and the inherent data governance and analytics management necessary for the perception of success. In other words, humans manage all aspects of the Analytics Value Chain, as discussed in Chapter 2, "Analytics Value Chain and the P's of Digital Analytics."

Analytical data is being collected and/or extracted from various internal and external tools for reporting via matrixed, cross-functional teams that execute data collection, analysis, and analytical delivery to stakeholders. The reporting and delivery of analysis may even be automated or regularly scheduled. Key behavioral events and related Key Performance Indicators (KPIs) are likely tracked, and their directional movements across time-series, and analyzed for causation. In a few cases, data collected in near real time may be modeled or otherwise used automatically for business activities to reduce abandonment or decrease churn. For example, it was commonplace in 2012 for sites to follow up with an identified visitor who abandons a shopping cart by emailing that person and offering to complete the purchase.

Collaborative filtering and recommendation engines on Amazon. com and Netflix are expected by customers despite the complexity of building these complex digital experiences. Targeting based on many attributes—from cookies to geography to past behavior to keyword to referrer to intent—can be enabled. *Showrooming* and the ubiquity of mobile devices in-store enable location-based services from real-time data streams.

The next step for Internet commerce is the evolution of these business activities and their related functions to improve accuracy, usefulness, and ease of execution. The function of media analysis will become larger than using big data and data science for decision support, reporting, business-case justification, performance evaluation, or static or dynamic modeling. The future of analytics becomes based on *data-interactive experiences* consistent across multiple screens and unified digital experiences created dynamically from the application of past, current, and predicted future digital-behavioral data—wherever it exists—as input for increasing revenue, decreasing cost, and delivering on a value proposition.

Enablers of the future state of analytics include the following:

- **Standards:** Although few, consensus-based, widely adhered standards exist in digital measurement, vendors offer flexibility in customizations to accommodate for nuance. Standards applied to digital data, such as those applied to other quantitative fields, like accounting, can be helpful. In that context, the future may hold a set of Generally Accepted Analytics Principles (GAAP) held to the same high regard as the U.S. GAAP.

- **Privacy regulations and opt-in:** Implicit and widespread opt-in must be a known, obvious, and easy-to-use capability in future analytics architectures to comply, define, and transform privacy law in a nonspooky and freedom-focused, non-big-brother way that is ethical and legal across countries.

- **Addressable databases:** Addressing content or ads from rich, detailed, personally identifiable information (PII), and social data is available from few companies and data vendors. For example, Facebook and Google have gigantic stores of person-level data that are used at some level of aggregation and anonymity that they readily monetize via advertising and retargeting on Facebook Exchange (FBX). Beyond social data, other person-level data exists only behind the firewalls of companies with which they have transacted or visited. The analytics ecosystems of the future, which will be dependent on addressable content and advertising to people and their preferences, can only be delivered from large scale, reusable, extensible, cloud-based, addressable consumer databases—which bring together omnichannel data wherever it resides inside and outside of the business (see Chapter 12, "Converging Omnichannels and Integrating Data for Understanding Customers, Audiences, and Media").

- **Scalable infrastructure available anywhere:** The future of analytics might exist within corporations and their databases, but the future analytics environments will require massive computational processing, indexing, and query power. Huge databases for storing the big data in the cloud (Software as a Service [SaaS]) and retrieving it for reporting, targeting, and automating in near time and truly real-time detection and actuation will become more necessary and important than in 2013.

- **Educated and trained people, the human resources, to create it all:** The biggest bottleneck to the analytics future is a dearth, an acute insufficiency, of the data analysts, data scientists, technologists, engineers, managers, leaders, executives, and visionaries who have the skills and talent to build the analytical future and create the Analytical Economy. To fill these gaps, analytics curriculums will grow in number and importance in both undergraduate and graduate programs in the world's colleges and universities. Remember, McKinsey estimates the future analytical economy will require 1,500,000 more "data-savvy" managers (who can understand and use analysis) and 140,000–190,000 new roles for analytical talent.

The Future of Analytics Requires Privacy and Ethics

As business leaders, data analysts, and scientists, it is not only your goal, but it is also your responsibility to protect every person's analytical data from misuse and abuse. Data analysts are largely left to self-regulate their analytical activities in much the same way the analytics tool vendors are left to self-regulate their innovations. That is why you must apply ethical principles to analytics, to ensure privacy and the application of analytics in a way that positively promotes, protects, and safeguards both global commerce and human society. Either the industry self-regulates or many governments will legislatively regulate for you. In light of the 2013 acknowledgement that the U.S. NSA's PRISM application exists, it seems necessary for a global, societal conversation and consensus-driven alignment to set the boundaries of digital data collection, storage, and analysis in a manner that respects human and civil rights, self-reliance, and individualism while sustaining liberty, freedom, privacy, autonomy, and advancing the destinies of people.

Consider several rules when dealing with digital data, whether behavioral, transactional, qualitative, quantitative, mobile, social, video, first or third party, and private or anonymous digital data and metadata:

- **Be absolutely transparent about what data you collect and how you collect it by creating and frequently updating a Privacy and Data Usage policy and prominently displaying it on your site.** Write it in English, not legalese, and keep it simple, comprehendible, and summarized. If needed, link it to a more formal legal document.

- **Understand and provide, on request, a list of the tracking and measurement technologies currently deployed on your site.** Such a simple idea is hard to execute and deliver— especially at globally distributed enterprises—but smart companies should create and maintain a list of all social media (and digital) tracking and measurement technologies deployed on the site and have that list ready for review when requested.

- **Publish a simple metadata document that people both externally and internally can review that describes the digital data being collected and how it will be used.** For every technology deployed, the vendor should be providing a document answering the following questions: 1) What is this technology? 2) What data is being collected? 3) How is the data being used? and 4) How do I view, modify, and prevent my data from being collected? These answers can be used to craft your policy and privacy statements relevant to analytics that support it.

- **Create formalized governance around measurement, tracking, and advertising technologies and involve cross-functional representatives from teams across your company.** Companies that use analytics should have a governance council driven by their business, not the technology side. Teams from research, analytics, legal, marketing, sales, and technology should participate to ensure that best practices for protecting consumer privacy are practiced.

- **Enable easy and logical "opt-out" and, in the best case, only allow tracking and targeting to be "opt-in" for social media—and all digital tracking in general.** Don't create digital experiences that automatically apply new features and changes to everyone without gaining or at least attempting to gain their consent.

- **Eliminate all unnecessary data collection while regularly reviewing the data you have collected and delete unneeded data.** So much data can be collected, but little is actually useful, insightful, and actionable (UIA). Figure out what is UIA generating profitable revenue; then determine what to do with the remaining data (from archiving it to deleting it).

- **Don't exploit new technologies in tricky ways that attempt to circumvent a user's choice or perception of privacy.** In other words, do not use technologies to reset or force the persistence of cookies after the user deletes them. Do not use hacks to store cookies forever—when doing analytics and any other digital activity. Don't try to get around what the customer wants by technical wizardry. Don't violate the perception of privacy or civil rights or create situations in which your work could be considered unlawful, unethical, immoral surveillance.

- **Make your voice heard by writing your government, such as a senator or congressperson.** The heart of a democracy is the citizen's voice—whether you live in a democratic, free society or are reading this text in more creative ways in a country where freedom is limited. Imagine the potential for understanding and alignment that could be achieved if the thousands of readers of this book wrote an email, made a phone call, or advocated in the public domain positively for our industry and what we consider safeguards on and appropriate usage of digital data and analytics. If you do speak up and voice your opinion about the progression and evolution of your livelihood and business, no one is going to do it for you, but many will try to regulate your work as you choose to remain silent.

Digital analytics requires professionals who advocate for the people being tracked worldwide. Many of these people do not live in countries, like I do, in the United States where we (or at least I) have a reasonable expectation of privacy. Although some may consider it beyond the scope of an analyst's role to focus on the ethical, proper, and private use of data, the preservation of privacy and anonymity—especially as we progress into the brave new world of the always connected, pervasive Internet we have today—is not only necessary but also critical for the preservation of freedom, liberty, autonomy, and greater personal power, education, and intelligence.

Sergey Brin, cofounder of Google, once said when referring to the Stop Online Piracy Act (SOPA), "Very powerful forces have lined up against the open Internet on all sides and around the world.... I thought there was no way to put the genie back in the bottle, but now it seems in certain areas the genie has been put back in the bottle. If we could be in some magical jurisdiction that everyone in the world trusted, that would be great. We're doing it as well as can be done." The same can be said for the digital analytics industry and people practicing, consulting, and vending the tools, technologies, and techniques within it.

Digital analytics professionals, when building their organizations, need to keep what Brin said at the top of their minds by creating digital analytics organizations and teams that execute analytics in the future in a more profitable way than we are executing the profession today, but also in a way that protects individual autonomy, liberty, the pursuit of happiness, and safeguards privacy and personal freedom. By applying the learnings and techniques contained in this book in your offices, careers, and work, you can both protect consumer privacy and create significant new and incremental business and economic value for your company, your team, and yourself. You can integrate people, processes, and technology to deliver digital analysis across the Analytical Value Chain in the Analytical Economy. Good luck with your digital analytics organization!

Works Cited

Granville, Vincent. "Data Science Tools." 24 Nov. 2012. *Data Science Central.* www.datasciencecentral.com/profiles/blogs/data-science-tools.

Manyika, James, Michael Chui, Brad Brown, Jacques Bughin, Richard Dobbs, Charles Roxburgh, Angela Hung Byers. "Big Data: The Next Frontier for Innovation, Competition, and Productivity." May 2011. McKinsey & Company. www.mckinsey.com/insights/business_technology/big_data_the_next_frontier_for_innovation.

Arikan, Akin. *Multichannel Marketing: Metrics and Methods for On and Offline Success.* Indianapolis, IN: Wiley, 2008.

Kaushik, Avinash. *Web Analytics 2.0: The Art of Online Accountability & Science of Customer Centricity.* Indianapolis, IN: Wiley, 2010.

Kaushik, Avinash. *Web Analytics: An Hour a Day.* Indianapolis, IN: Sybex, 2007.

Kaushik, Avinash. "Occam's Razor." www.kaushik.net/avinash/. Accessed 29 Dec. 2012.

Grove, Jennifer Van. "Facebook Helps App Makers Hawk to Android, IOS Audiences." *CNET News.* http://news.cnet.com/8301-1023_3-57576630-93/facebook-helps-app-makers-hawk-to-android-ios-audiences/. Accessed 27 Mar. 2013.

Pew Internet. "Pew Research Center's Internet & American Life Project." www.pewinternet.org/. Accessed 22 Apr. 2013.

Kohavi, Ron, Randall M. Henne, Dan Sommerfield. "Practical Guide to Controlled Experiments on the Web: Listen to Your Customers Not to the Hippo." 2007. http://dl.acm.org/citation.cfm?id=1281295. Accessed 26 Mar. 2013.

Institute for Statistics and Mathematics. "The R Project for Statistical Computing." www.r-project.org/. Accessed 3 Apr. 2013

Crook, Thomas, Brian Frasca, Ron Kohavi, Roger Longbotham. "Seven Pitfalls to Avoid When Running Controlled Experiments on the Web." 2009. http://dl.acm.org/citation.cfm?doid=1557019.1557139. Accessed 29 Mar. 2013.

Lacey, Michelle. "Statistical Topics." www.stat.yale.edu/Courses/ 1997-98/101/stat101.htm. Accessed 16 Dec. 2012.

Kohavi, Ron, Alex Deng, Brian Frasca, Roger Longbotham, Toby Walker, Ya Xu. "Trustworthy Online Controlled Experiments: Five Puzzling Outcomes Explained." 2012. http://dl.acm.org/citation.cfm?id=2339653. Accessed 1 Mar. 2013.

Wikimedia Foundation. "Analysis." *Wikipedia.* http://en.wikipedia.org/wiki/Analysis. Accessed 22 Nov. 2012.

Wikimedia Foundation. "Behavioral retargeting." *Wikipedia.* http://en.wikipedia.org/wiki/Behavioral_retargeting. Accessed 19 Mar. 2013.

Mandese, Joe. "Carat Projects Digital at One-Fifth of All Ad Spend, Beginning to Dominate Key Markets." 20 Mar. 2013. *MediaPost News.* www.mediapost.

com/publications/article/196238/carat-projects-digital-at-one-fifth-of-all-ad-spen.html#axzz2UmqsIce4.

Wikimedia Foundation. "Experimentation." *Wikipedia.* http://en.wikipedia.org/wiki/Experimentation. Accessed 5 Feb. 2013.

Wikimedia Foundation. "Multivariate testing." *Wikipedia* http://en.wikipedia.org/wiki/Multivariate_testing. Accessed 1 Feb. 2013.

Wikimedia Foundation. "Nonparametric regression." *Wikipedia.* http://en.wikipedia.org/wiki/Non-parametric_regression. Accessed 1 Feb. 2013.

Wikimedia Foundation. "Regression analysis." *Wikipedia.* http://en.wikipedia.org/wiki/Regression_analysis. Accessed 13 Jan. 2013.

Wikimedia Foundation. "Student's *t*-distribution." *Wikipedia.* http://en.wikipedia.org/wiki/Student%27s_t-distribution. Accessed 30 Dec. 2012.

Wikimedia Foundation. "Student's *t*-test." *Wikipedia.* http://en.wikipedia.org/wiki/Student%27s_t-test. Accessed 22 Feb. 2013.

Wikimedia Foundation. "Ted Nelson." *Wikipedia.* http://en.wikipedia.org/wiki/Ted_Nelson. Accessed 11 Jan. 2013.

Plomion, Ben. "5 Tips to Maximize Your Retargeting Campaigns." 4 Jan. 2013. *Search Engine Watch.* http://searchenginewatch.com/article/ 2233818/ 5-Tips-to-Maximize-Your-Retargeting-Campaigns.

Wikimedia Foundation. "John Tukey." *Wikipedia.* http://en.wikipedia.org/wiki/John_Tukey. Accessed 12 Dec. 2012.

"What Is Retargeting and How Does It Work?" *ReTargeter.* http://retargeter.com/what-is-retargeting-and-how-does-it-work. Accessed 13 Feb. 2013.

Ash, Tim. *Landing Page Optimization.* Indianapolis, IN: Wiley, 2008.

Croarkin, Carrol, Paul Tobias, and Chelli Zey. *Engineering Statistics Handbook.* Gaithersburg, MD: The Institute, 2001.

Davenport, Thomas H., and Jeanne G. Harris. *Competing on Analytics: The New Science of Winning.* Boston, MA: Harvard Business School, 2007.

Davenport, Thomas H., Jeanne G. Harris, and Robert Morison. *Analytics at Work: Smarter Decisions, Better Results.* Boston, MA: Harvard Business, 2010.

Digital Analytics Association. "Standards Committee Deliverables." www.digitalanalyticsassociation.org/?page=standards. Accessed 22 Dec. 2012.

Eisenberg, Bryan, Jeffrey Eisenberg, and Lisa T. Davis. *Waiting for Your Cat to Bark?: Persuading Customers When They Ignore Marketing.* Nashville, TN: Nelson Business, 2006.

Eisenberg, Bryan, John Quarto-von Tivadar, and Lisa T. Davis. *Always Be Testing: The Complete Guide to Google Website Optimizer.* Indianapolis, IN: Wiley, 2008.

"Bringing Big Data to the Enterprise: What Is Big Data?" *IBM.* www-01.ibm.com/software/au/data/bigdata/. Accessed 23 Dec. 2012.

Isson, Jean Paul, and Jesse Harriott. *Win with Advanced Business Analytics: Creating Business Value from Your Data.* Hoboken, NJ: John Wiley & Sons, 2013.

Kotler, Philip. *Marketing Management*. Upper Saddle River, NJ: Prentice Hall, 2000.

NIST/SEMATECH e-Handbook of Statistical Methods, www.itl.nist.gov/div898/ handbook. Accessed 4 Jan. 2013.

Novo, Jim. *Drilling Down: Turning Customer Data into Profits with a Spreadsheet*. Bangor, ME: Booklocker.com, 2004.

Peterson, Eric T. *The Big Book of Key Performance Indicators*. Portland, OR: Scribd Free Version, 2011.

Peterson, Eric T. *Web Analytics Demystified: A Marketer's Guide to Understanding How Your Web Site Affects Your Business*. Portland, OR: Celilo Group Media, 2004.

Ratner, Bruce. *Statistical and Machine-learning Data Mining: Techniques for Better Predictive Modeling and Analysis of Big Data*. Boca Raton, FL: Taylor & Francis, 2012.

Sterne, Jim. *Social Media Metrics: How to Measure and Optimize Your Marketing Investment*. Hoboken, NJ: John Wiley, 2010.

Sterne, Jim. *Web Metrics: Proven Methods for Measuring Web Site Success*. New York: Wiley, 2002.

Tukey, John W. *Exploratory Data Analysis*. Reading, MA: Addison-Wesley, 1977.

Tukey, John W., David R. Brillinger, D. R. Cox, and Henry I. Braun. *The Collected Works of John W. Tukey*. Belmont, CA: Wadsworth Advanced & Software, 1984.

EMC News. "New Digital Universe Study Reveals Big Data Gap: Less Than 1% of World's Data Is Analyzed; Less Than 20% Is Protected." 11 Dec. 2012. www. emc.com/about/news/press/2012/20121211-01.htm.

Taylor, Paul. "Lack of Data Analysis Worrisome." 11 Dec 2012. *Financial Times*. www.ft.com/cms/s/2/67d7de00-43d3-11e2-844c-00144feabdc0.html#axzz2Umu HzMF1.

Everts, Tammy. "The Average Web Page Has Grown 20% in Just Six Months." *Web Performance Today*. 15 Nov. 2012. www.webperformancetoday.com/2012/ 11/15/average-web-page-grows-20-percent/.

Edwards, Andrew. "Convergence Analytics: Digital Measurement in Transition." *Efectyv*. http://efectyv.com/. Accessed Mar. 2013.

Index